ADOLESCENT RELIGION

Charles William Stewart

ADOLESCENT RELIGION
A Developmental Study of the Religion of Youth

ABINGDON PRESS ⨍ Nashville • New York

ADOLESCENT RELIGION

Copyright © 1967 by Abingdon Press

Library of Congress Catalog Card Number: 67-11712

To
Mark
Louise Anne
Peter and
Heather

Gifts of love
Products of nurture
Copers extraordinary

Preface

Adolescent religion is of importance not only to youth themselves but also to the teachers of youth. Since the time of Socrates and before, the older generation has been concerned about what young people think and has feared for the corruption of their souls. Opinions about the radical orientation of the cool crowd, assumptions about the morals of the beat generation have added tinder to the fears of parents and teachers. But facts about what they think and, in particular, unbiased and undistorted expressions of youth themselves are at a premium.

To discover what youth themselves think, feel, believe, and value, I set aside a research year in 1962-63. That year lengthened to three before the data were gathered, analyzed, and put into this written form. I discovered it was important to go to a place where a project was already underway, and I was very fortunate to be asked to become a part of the Normal Development Project, a fourteen-year-old longitudinal study of normal personality, directed by Lois Murphy, child psychologist at the Menninger Foundation. The project became a reality through the funds granted to the Menninger Foundation by the Danforth Foundation. Before the study

7

was completed, other public and private moneys were expended to bring together more of the children's interviews and more data from the children's homes and churches. As with all research, it moved not through great flourish and publicity but through sacrifice and steady, patient effort of many individuals.

I wish to express my gratitude especially to Dr. Murphy, who consulted with me weekly throughout the research year and who gave me untold help in research method, clinical insight, and warm humanity in unfolding her lifetime of experience working with the young. I want also to acknowledge my thanks to Thomas W. Klink, Director of the Program in Religion and Psychiatry at the Menninger Foundation for his consultation throughout the year's research and his continued interest and support as I brought it to a conclusion. To the others at the foundation, Alice Moriarty, Marie Smith, Joseph Morgan, Julie Palmquist Fewster, and to Grace Heider (formerly of the Child Study Project), thanks for their advice, support, and help in understanding the children and in gathering data upon them.[1] To Mary Elizabeth Brown for her assistance in typing the original biographical material, and to Mary Banks for typing the body of the text, I also am grateful. And finally, many thanks to my adolescent son, Mark, who assisted in data tabulation, and to my wife, Alma, for her constructively critical eye as she read and read again the emerging copy.

I hope the study will be useful to the college and seminary students who wish to learn something of youth's quest for meaning and identity in today's world. There should be a useful frame of reference here for teachers of youth in school and church which may enable them better to hear youth's questions about beliefs and values. Ministers and priests should also find the study valuable since the age group dealt with is the typical confirmation class age (twelve-sixteen).

The census makers now predict that by 1970 roughly half the nation's population will be under twenty-five years of age

[1] The major longitudinal data were assembled under the support of USPHS grants, M 680, M 4093, and contracts from the Division of Children's Mental Health, NIMH; other support for the longitudinal studies came from the Louise and Gustavus Pfeiffer Foundation and the Menninger Foundation.

(111,000,000). Mass media, particularly television, movies, and the magazines, are busily beaming their sounds, pictures, and print at the teen market. In a society in which the role distinctions between the young and the adult-teachers are being blurred by the mass media, some careful examination needs to be made of what is effective and what is not effective about the teaching. Where teaching fails, the fault most often is a communication blockage. I discovered in the study that in simply listening for an hour to what a youth thought and felt I was filling a vacant spot in his life left there by an absent parent or pastor. I was thanked several times for helping a young person think through his beliefs when all I did was listen responsively. Listening is not a new technique, but it may be the missing link in the breakdown of awareness and responsiveness between youth and their elders.

The manuscript was completed one summer day to the tune of a teen-age serenade, a six-hour concert in the neighbor's garage by a Beatle-maned and electronically equipped band. Youth do express themselves forcefully, dramatically, and with emotion! But, as one father confessed, it was not until he took time to listen to the words of a rock-and-roll song that he understood his son's fascination for the music. If this writing enables the reader to get inside the young adolescent's world, to live through his struggles, and to understand how faith helps him cope with his emerging world, I will consider the whole project worthwhile.

"There's a place for us, a time and place for us," the tragic lovers of *West Side Story* sang when faced with insurmountable odds. Their place is the new world being born, and their time is now. This is a secular hope, founded as always on a deeply religious faith.

July, 1966   Charles W. Stewart

Contents

1

Understanding Adolescence

Youth is absurd; adolescence is vanishing;[1] the former ways of understanding adolescent religious experience are outmoded. If we grant the validity of the reports of social psychologists and sociologists today that many youth are no longer directed toward a tradition nor toward the inner voice of conscience but are outer-directed, seeking adjustment with the peer group, of necessity their religious experience is affected. The consensus of current studies is that contemporary youth have established themselves in an "adolescent society" with their own values, norms, and styles. This is

[1] "I believe that adolescence, as a developmental process, is becoming obsolete. The kind of personal integration which results from conflict between a growing human being and his society is no longer the mode of maturity our society cultivates." Edgar Friedenberg, *The Vanishing Adolescent* (Boston: Beacon Press, 1959), p. 133.

"In the great society they are certainly uprooted. But in the gang their conformity is sickeningly absolute; they have uniform jackets and uniform morals. They speak a jargon and no one has a different idea that might brand him a queer. . . . It is a poor kind of community they have; friendship, affection, personal helpfulness are remarkably lacking in it. They are 'cool,' afraid to display feeling." Paul Goodman, *Growing Up Absurd* (New York: Random House, 1960), p. 44.

13

not in rebellion against their parents directly but represents a fairly easy passage from conformity to the ideals, norms, and beliefs of the parents to conformity to those of the teen-age group. The usual rebellion against the authority of parents and the storm and stress which youth experiences at this time appear to be lacking. Playing it cool and not sticking one's neck out are said to be the primary values, and if young people can obtain what they want without rebellion, without going through authoritarian struggles, without conversion from disobedience to obedience, this is the way they will behave.

The early studies of adolescence were primarily viewed from the world of the adult and saw youth undergoing crises and learning experiences in order to become adapted to the world of the adult. The studies of adolescence and religious experience beginning with G. Stanley Hall and Edwin Starbuck and reaching their zenith in William James' classic *The Varieties of Religious Experience* spelled out the relationship between the *Sturm und Drang* of puberty and the crisis experience. James, in particular, was able to distinguish the several kinds of religious experience—namely, the conversion experience, the gradual growth experience, and the mystical experience—and saw these dependent upon the kinds of temperament which the individual possessed. His contribution to psychology of religion was to relate religious experience not to outside norms established by the church and society, but to relate them primarily to certain inner dispositions which predisposed the individual to particular kinds of experience. The studies following James, namely, those of Anton Boisen, George Coe, Henry Wieman, Gordon Allport, Paul Johnson, and Walter Clark, have followed this lead. The study has been primarily of the individual's religious experience in relationship to psychological development, his learning experiences, or the crisis, nodal points in his life, and relating the noetic states to this development.

Religious psychologists have not studied the tremendous social and cultural changes which have been influencing youth to the extent that the kinds of religious experience which they undergo have drastically changed.[2] It is apparent that many adolescents themselves

[2] See William McKeefery, "A Critical Analysis of Quantitative Studies of Religious Awakening," unpublished thesis, Columbia University, 1951. See also, Merton Strom-

14

no longer report a storm and stress kind of puberty but are entering the teen years without a critical decision-making, value and guilt-oriented disposition. Margaret Mead discovered in her anthropological studies of young people in the South Sea islands that culture itself has a great deal to do with whether the youngster experiences storm and stress.[3] In certain primitive cultures youth pass quite easily from childhood to adulthood through "rites of passage" without the violent crises which American youth in the first part of this century were reported to have undergone. Although we do not have a culture similar to the primitive cultures, we have entered a different kind of situation in which the passageway of puberty may not be functioning in the same way that it has heretofore, and because of this we need to look at the religious experience of youth from a different vantage point. As Joseph Adelson says after a prolonged study of over fifteen hundred youth,

The traditional idea of the adolescent's experience holds that the youngsters become involved in an intense concern with ethics, political ideology, religious belief, and so on. Our interviews confirm a mounting impression from other studies that American adolescents, on the whole, are not deeply involved in ideology, nor are they prepared to do much individual thinking on value issues of any generality.[4]

Without admitting that the conclusions of the sociologists and social psychologists hold the interpretation which we would want to make of these facts, one must grant that the kind of culture in which youth find themselves today does directly influence the kinds of experiences which they are undergoing with respect to the church and with respect to their religious beliefs. The earlier studies are lacking in categories necessary to understand contemporary youth's experience. It is necessary to undertake new studies, to find new categories, which will encompass more of the factors in-

men, *Profiles of Church Youth* (St. Louis: Concordia Publishing House, 1963), which indicates the decline of the conversion experience and other experiences related to storm and stress; August B. Hollingshead, *Elmtown's Youth* (Science Editions; New York: John Wiley & Sons, 1949) and Murray Ross, *The Religious Beliefs of Youth*, New York: Association Press, 1950, which put young people in a particular culture and show the relationship between the culture and their religious ideas and struggles.

[3] *Coming of Age in Samoa* (New York: New American Library, 1961).
[4] "The Mystique of Adolescence" *Psychiatry* (1964), p. 4.

volved in their experience, the better to understand the kinds of religious orientation which they display and the religious behavior which they undergo. This study will attempt to break some new ground so that those interested in the religious activities and beliefs of young people may have more data and a contemporary framework by which to understand them.

An account of junior high school society by a member of this adolescent group points up these characteristics quite dramatically:

Interviewer: What about some of the ways kids act nowadays when they're together?

Greg: Well, kids can be pretty terrible, and I don't know—they're pretty much divided up into classes—well, not classes, but groups.

Interviewer: How's that?

Greg: Well, there are the kids that are no good—I mean they're just kind of no good. I don't know—I don't like to say this about anybody, but they're really just not very nice at all, you know, and not very many kids like them. And—

Interviewer: You mean their morals aren't very good?

Greg: Yeah, and well, they're just not very good anyway. They don't make very good grades, their morals aren't good—I think they're pretty terrible. And then there comes the, oh, there's the pretty nice kids, and then—and I don't really think—and then there's the nicer than that, and then there's the high-class snobs. And I don't know, every social class is divided up into two classes, and in between that is the nice kids and the not-so-nice kids and everything and so it's a big mess.

Interviewer: Where do you put yourself in there?

Greg: Well, I hope I'm nice—ha ha—and I think I am. I put myself among, if you divide it up into high class, middle class, and low class, I'm just kind of middle class, because I know a lot of the kids that are real popular, and I'm fairly popular, I mean—I'm not "it" or anything, but I don't pretend to be because I don't think that's really fun.

Interviewer: Well, are the "it" kids the snobs?

Greg: Well there are a lot of "it" kids that are snobs, and there are a lot that aren't. Some of them become "it" and become snobbish, and aren't "it" very long, because when you're a snob it's pretty hard to have friends. There are some kids who think they're "it" that are snobs, that are way past being "it."

Interviewer: Uh-huh.

Greg: Uh—usually the person everybody likes—I mean everyone—is the person who's nice to everyone, no matter who they are. And this type of person is the sophomore class president and you know those type that they're nice to everyone, no matter who they are.

Interviewer: Why wouldn't you want to be "it"?

Greg: It's too hard. (laughs)

Interviewer: How do you mean?

Greg: Well, I've made some social efforts, this year, and just making the ones I did it's terrible—you have to party every other week, and a lot of times every week, every Friday night at school and you have to go to those and go to all the games, and by the time you've done all that you don't have any money left and you're tired—too tired.

Interviewer: Well, what about "making out" and things of that sort? Do you have group standards or are these pretty much individual?

Greg: Oh, uh, I guess you decide—well, you decide when you're in that group. I mean, those kids with low morals—a lot of times they're trapped into those places because of their parents and their health. Uh, their, uh, you know, position. But, I mean, if you want to be an all-out good guy, you can come to school in rags and if you're really an outstanding student and everybody likes you, you can be the most popular kid in school and you know a lot of kids don't have a lot of money and are really popular, but that's because they try and they have good parents. But, uh, I think parent influence can do an awful lot with their attitudes and their behavior, and the kids will go as far as they think their parents—if they think their parents don't care, they'll go the limit—they'll do anything—because their parents don't care, so why shouldn't they—and everything—but the way you act puts you in your class.

Several characteristics of "teen society" are evident from this short dialogue. *It is a conformist society.* Conformity is necessary in order for society to function according to law and order and to divide the work necessary to keep the life of a community going. The conformity we shall deal with is youths' *conformity to peers* for judgment and taste, rather than their forming independent choices from an autonomous center. Riesman makes this point clear in distinguishing between the inner-directed and other-directed. For the first, "the source of direction . . . is 'inner' in the sense that it is implanted early in life by the elders and directed

17

toward generalized but nonetheless inescapably destined goals." For the second, "their contemporaries are the source of direction . . . — either those known to him or those with whom he is indirectly acquainted, through friends and through the mass media." [5]

The young adolescent's teachers are not the primarily adult world of teachers, pastors, and parents, but the "taste makers" of the mass media. Since the group between thirteen and nineteen now make up twenty-four million people or one eighth of the population of the United States and they spend over twelve billion dollars a year,[6] one can understand why the teen market is of such importance to clothing, record, cosmetics, and sports manufacturers. "Just look at youth," says Eugene Gilbert, a youth market researcher. "No established patterns. No backlog of items. No inventory of treasured and, to many adults' way of thinking, irreplaceable objects. Youth . . . is the greatest growing force in the community. His physical needs alone constitute a continuing, growing requirement of food, clothes, entertainment, etc." [7] And the marketers have rushed to meet the requirements of this child of affluence.

The adolescent's response to the lures of his society—popularity, influence, leadership, pleasure—are evident also in Greg's account of the class structure of his school. Some youth make it and some don't, depending upon the sensitivity of their "radar" and their competence among their peers. Those who make it are "adjusted leaders of their set" but still filled with anxiety lest they take a wrong turn. Others apparently don't aim so high but "follow the leader" as copycats or echoes of the crowd. Still others are "outsiders"—too intellectual, too "religious," or too uncouth to make it. These young people may make subgroups who resent the others but try within their subgroup to find acceptance. The "collegiates" and the "greasers" are two such designations for the kids who aim for college against the leather-jacketed predelinquent crowd. Apathy, or what Riesman calls anomie (lack of meaning), may be the symptom of the youth who are not able to keep up with the crowd, drop out of high school for intellectual, socioeconomic, or other reasons, and who then become "beat" or delinquent or mentally ill.

[5] David Riesman, *The Lonely Crowd* (New Haven: Yale University Press, 1950).
[6] *Time* (January 29, 1965), p. 56.
[7] *Esquire* (July, 1965), p. 68.

Sociologists state that the approach of adults to adolescents as trainees for a role in a traditional church or conscripts for inner-directed values is bankrupt. Adolescents are the influencers of their parents. Their tastes in clothes, in music, and dancing are taken over by adults. And the moral and religious confusion of adults make it imperative to listen to youth, to their needs and desires, their struggles, their attempts to cope with their world—not to imitate but to translate the lore of the past to today's language and to correlate its truth with the questions which our whole generation confronts—race relations and peace, work and automation, creative leisure, and a contemporary world view.

SOME DEFINITIONS

What do we mean by puberty? By early adolescence? What are its characteristics and its tasks? What do we mean by religion? What are the religious issues youth must face? How can we understand development from birth through adolescence to adulthood so as to put our questions in some kind of perspective?

Puberty refers to the biological changes through which a young man or woman goes whereby he acquires the primary and secondary sexual characteristics which enable him to reproduce his kind. Irene Josselyn chronicles these changes:

The sequence leading to the mature body structure is in general orderly. In the girl, breast development is one of the earliest signs of sexual maturation. This begins before the appearance of pubic hair. Axillary hair develops later and often grows only after the first menstrual period. Pubic hair is the first masculine secondary sex characteristic to appear, coming shortly after the primary sex organs, the penis and the testes, show evidence of increased size in comparison to the total body. Axillary hair and then facial hair follows. At the time of the development of axillary hair, there is often some breast enlargement in the boy. . . . Voice changes in the boy have traditionally been the criterion for determining the onset of adolescence, but actually this occurs relatively late in the period and usually indicates that the typical bodily changes are fairly well advanced.[8]

[8] *The Happy Child* (New York: Random House, 1955), pp. 116-17. See also, Rolf E. Muuss, *Theories of Adolescence* (New York: Random House, 1962), for a comprehensive survey of definitions.

Early adolescence refers to the period immediately following the first menstrual period in the girls and the first seminal emission of the boys to a midpoint, age sixteen. It can begin about eleven and a half to thirteen in the girls and twelve and a half to fourteen in the boys, depending on one's hereditary growth pattern. Adolescence is a psychosocial phenomenon, as well, and as said earlier may be negotiated with more or less conflict and stress. If we take Goodman and Friedenberg's argument seriously, the task of adolescence may be changing because adults have lengthened the time before assuming jobs, and patterns of conformity have tempted youth to play it "cool." Seeley pinpoints the crisis:

In the 12 to 15 year level, therefore, the child himself, for the first time, becomes seriously aware of what the society demands of him, if he is to become adult. Both home and school impose high standards of performance. The child, at the same time, must adjust to the demands of his peer group, which frequently run counter to those of parents and teachers. At this age, too, the child must form the heterosexual relationships which later lead to courtship and marriage. The achievement-in-isolation then of the culture deepens and strengthens as the child is expected to achieve more and more in the competitive academic life which leads to university entrance. Self-reliance must be developed through experience at summer camp, or, more rarely, the part time job. The girl, while expected to prepare for a career of her own, must also assimilate the idea of renouncing it for marriage; and the boy must, in the absence of close or clearly defined masculine models, learn what it means to play a man's role in the society. These are the difficult tasks of early adolescence. [9]

The purpose of adolescence in our culture has been *self-definition* which involves finding identity, integrity, and faith. Who am I? What is the center of my being? And to what persons, things, and ultimates am I committed? These are questions posed to the adolescent by his living within nature and society, and he seeks some existential answers. To what extent youth does use this period, particularly the early junior high years, to settle questions of faith and value is open to question. We can subject the questions to empirical testing from our own study.

[9] J. R. Seeley, *et al.*, *Crestwood Heights* (New York: Basic Book, 1956), p. 112.

What do we mean by religion? We are defining *religion* not in normative terms as right belief or correct ritualistic practice, but as the individual's relationship to whatever he holds ultimate and the shared ritualistic and ethical response which ensues from that belief. Ritual involves him in group worship, and ethics involves him in action within the society. Within American society religion as practiced means relationship to the Judeo-Christian tradition [10] and the institutions of the church and synagogue. Moreover, religion as expressed involves theology: the symbols, myths, and doctrine about ultimate reality. That is, although relative in its capacity to communicate, theology does attempt to find the purpose of human life, the destiny of man's life on this planet, and the clue to the enigmatic mystery of his birth and death. The motives of religious actions, the dynamic determinants of religious beliefs and feelings, are not examined with any thought of explaining them away by the religious psychologists but rather of providing some further data to theologizing about ultimate issues. We shall attempt to do this in the chapter on faith.

A COPING MODEL OF ADOLESCENCE

Let us look at Greg again as we present a "coping model of development" with emphasis on adolescence. You would describe Greg at fifteen as a young man of medium height, with black curly hair, blue eyes, and round handsome face. He wore "sharp ivy-league sports coat and slacks and loafers, with pink button-down shirt and black knit tie." He is a bit exaggerated in his gestures and effusive in his language, with many adjectives and colorful, dramatic expressions. The first focus is on Greg's *organism* which has proceeded according to a ground plan of growth from the time of his conception by father and mother. His body is the *matrix* from which proceed all activities for body nurturance and growth, and now reproduction. Greg has grown to his present height and weight by ingesting food

[10] This does not exclude other religions as having integrity as means of relating to the Ultimate, although we shall limit our understanding to the Judeo-Christian faith since this orientation is the one taken by youth in this study. The author's allegiance to the Protestant Christian faith is acknowledged—recognizing the basic strengths and weaknesses of its expression of religion.

21

and oxygen, gaining proper rest, and getting exercise which has developed his muscle structure and kept its tonus. However, growth is not explained simply biochemically by the diminution and restoration of certain body fluids and temperatures to maintain an equilibrium. Growth also proceeds through the release of body energy through certain channels, the satisfaction of which the organism seeks. These "drives" are random in the infant but are soon channelized or "canalized" as hunger, thirst, mobility, rest, sex, etc. Greg's *drives* vary from other youth as does his *ground plan of development,* and therefore he confronts puberty at a specific time and with specific organic vulnerabilities (openness to stress). He may have particular difficulty with the explosion of the sex urge, depending on its intensity, his feelings about it (autonomic reactions to it), and the particular way his energies have been mobilized up to this point in his life. He has an "innate" intelligence, moreover, by which we mean his innate intellectual endowment. Although this relates immediately to learning, his ability to learn, to understand, and to communicate with his "world" depends on his intelligence. The fact that some children are retarded, slow learners, or not adequately socialized by adolescence is related to relative intelligence. Moreover, Greg's temperament and mood, one of intensity and apparent cheerfulness, is related to his physique and the functioning of his endocrinal system. Although one would not want to tie his temperament entirely to his being an ectomesomorph (Sheldon's category) and his sensitive skin and hyper-alertness to visual and auditory stimuli, nevertheless they play a part. The *organism* must be recognized not only as the receptor but the reactor to stimuli within this young adolescent.

The second focus is upon Greg's *environment.* He is the only child of a dentist and his wife. His real father, a professor, died before his birth. His mother remarried when Greg was eight and a half. He has not played in team games, is not interested in sports but rather in horses and models. He does not use all his intelligence and throughout elementary school was an under-achiever. He is from a fairly affluent, middle-class home, although before the second marriage the mother had to work and she and Greg had things a bit harder. They now live in an upper middle-class neighborhood. He has his own room and a fair amount of stylish clothes. He attends one of the best junior high schools in town and a large Protestant church, in which he is an active member. Greg's environment is made up of the natural and social setting in which he finds himself. It is midwest America, a state capital, an upper middle-class home, school, and church. More specifically the environment is his family— for eight and a half years his mother; now, after her remarriage, his vigorous father. The environment changed drastically before his birth when his blood father died. It changed again with the advent of a stepfather. Being so close to mother may have complicated the development of a masculine role. (See chapter 13.) It has meant some identification with the mother, and more taking over of attitudes of his mother than some other boys would have absorbed.

What Greg has learned has been the English language, his manners, and elementary social roles from his parents, particularly his mother. He has learned the three R's, the tradition and history of his nation and culture from the school. He has learned to play, the law of the group, and some basic give and take from the juveniles he has known. He has learned the tradition and worship of the Christian faith from the church. He has been socialized up to the "passageway of puberty." He has learned the signs of the race by conditioning and its symbols by association; interpersonally he has developed some sense of selfhood by unconscious mechanisms of identification, introjection, etc. The press of the environment upon his growing organism has provoked and challenged him to learn. Which brings us to the third factor—"coping" or mastery.

How is he doing with what he has against what he faces? One Freudian model places the organism with its sexual-aggressive drives against the environment which tries to inhibit or crush him. Other biological models emphasize the strength of the drives which determine the organism's course. Behavioristic models focus on the shaping force of the environment which molds the organism and pushes him in certain directions. We must admit the partial truth of these models but then point out that they do not allow enough place for the individual's capacity to shape himself and his environment. Particularly by adolescence does a boy such as Greg have this possibility. He has the capacity now to cope with the challenge of his environment and with the stress of his own drives. This has the force of another drive or motive—the drive to master problems

23

or cope with seemingly irresolvable stress.[11] Lois Murphy and Alice Moriarty have designated two kinds of coping as discernible in the children observed and tested in the Child Study group at the Menninger Foundation.[12] Coping A is fundamentally problem solving, i.e., the capacity to bring one's resources to bear upon an obstacle or frustration in the environment. Coping B is basically ego-strength, i.e., the capacity to maintain inner integration or to find ego-unity under stress or difficulty. The capacity to cope with problems means one does not remain passive under stress from the environment or from one's organism but actively goes out to meet it. The problem may be solved, but even if it isn't one rolls with the punch, is sensitive to the resources within and around one to sustain and strengthen oneself, and eventually "masters" himself in relation to the stressful challenge. Others have spoken of compensation or sublimation, but the active use of the ego to maintain an inner balance and positive orientation to life is what we are recognizing. Referring to Greg again, he lost his biological father, but he "managed" with just his mother; now the challenge of heterosexual relations will force him to "cope" with his own drives as well as his sexual identity in adolescence. Thus we have the three factors held in dynamic tension in the young adolescent's life:

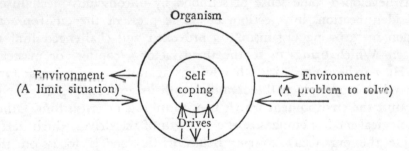

The relevance of the coping model to faith is apparent, and we shall spell it out in chapter 13.

[11] Abraham Maslow indicates the difference between deficit motives and mastery motives, the former being to satisfy a need such as hunger, the second to *master* a difficulty in the environment. András Angyal further states the difference between homonomy (joining oneself to larger wholes) and autonomy (becoming a whole self). *Foundations for a Science of Personality* (New York: Commonwealth Fund, 1941).

[12] See Lois Murphy, *The Widening World of Childhood* (New York: Basic Books, 1962).

"God has a special understanding for teen-agers who don't quite understand everything," said a thirteen-year-old girl in an interview. It is necessary for adults who work with youth to develop a special understanding for them through empathy and through getting within their frame of reference—the better to see the world through their eyes. Admittedly this is difficult, because they desire a certain distance from adults in order to get their ideas straight and achieve some autonomy in their life. But as Erik Erikson says, at this period youth turn the tables on adults and begin to be their teachers.

In youth the tables of childhood dependence begin slowly to turn: no longer is it merely for the old to teach the young the meaning of life, whether individual or collective. It is the young who, by their response and action, tell the old whether life as represented by the old and as presented to the young has meaning; and it is the young who carry in them the power to confirm those who confirm them and, joining the issues, to renew and to regenerate, or to reform and to rebel. [13]

This study asks the reader to sit at youth's side and listen to him and learn from him.

[13] "Youth: Fidelity and Diversity" in *Youth: Change and Challenge* (New York: Basic Books, 1963), p. 24.

2

The Plan of the Study

With the exception of Gordon W. Allport, the Elkinds, Leon Salzman, and Carl Christiansen, and the unreported work of Edith Cobb, [1] very little intensive study of the religious experience of youth has been carried through since the pioneer work at the turn of the century. In particular there has been no contemporory longitudinal study [2] of adolescent religious experience. In fact, the study of normal lives rather than neurotic or psychopathic lives represents a major gap in our understanding of religious experience.

Robert White, who has engaged for over twenty-five years in such study and whose book, *Lives in Progress,* gives us many clues for this work, said in 1952:

Individual lives moving forward normally amid natural circumstances have received almost no scientific study and have played almost no part

[1] See bibliography, pp. 305-9, for their studies.

[2] Longitudinal studies are being carried out by the Gesell Institute, University of California, the Fels Institute, University of Maryland, and Harvard University, as well as at the Menninger Foundation.

in our current understanding . . . : it is a gap at that point where it becomes necessary to consider the continuous development of personality over periods of time and amid natural circumstances. [3]

The possibility of interviewing a selected number of youth from the Normal Development Project [4] who have been studied at birth, preschool, latency, and prepuberty and are now young adolescents, opened the door to this important neglected area of investigation. Approximately nine tenths of the sixty pubertal youth have active church ties. These include thirty-six Protestants, of whom five belong to intensely evangelistic or fundamentalist denominations while the remainder belong to the main-line Protestant denominations. One third of the churchgoing youth are Roman Catholic, and most of these attend parochial schools. Dr. Povl Toussieng interviewed approximately forty of the youth at age twelve and discovered that religion played an important part in the problems and the adjustments of a substantial number of youth. My presence at the Menninger Foundation as a Fellow in Theology and Psychiatric Theory presented the opportunity for an intensive study of the religious experience of these youth. The particular questions we posed in the last chapter have some chance of being answered by such research.

RESEARCH PROCEDURE

A careful pilot study was initially proposed and undertaken utilizing the longitudinal material of just six children. Using Grace Heider's Categories of Vulnerability, [5] which were developed on infants and preschool children, I read through the prepuberty records on twenty-two children; i.e., psychological tests, psychiatric reports, parent interviews. Each one of these original children was ranked as to his vulnerability at age twelve and along with this ranking a synopsis was drawn up of each child, with reasons given for the rating at the puberty period. This ranking was considered in relation to the infancy and preschool ranking. It

---

[3] (New York: Holt, Rinehart & Winston, 1952) , pp. 3 and 22.
[4] The Normal Development Project, formerly called the Child Study Project, located at the Menninger Foundation, Topeka, Kansas, is directed by Lois Barclay Murphy, Ph.D.
[5] See chap. 10, pp. 212-13.

27

was possible then to select three initially high vulnerable and three initially low vulnerable adolescents for intensive study. The biographical studies which appear throughout the book are of these particular youth.

Each youth was seen for two periods of an hour and a half in length. The youth were interviewed in the familiar office where other interviews of the Normal Development Project had taken place. This office is electronically equipped with multiple microphones for optimal tape recording and the group already knew about and were accustomed to this equipment. Introductions to me were made by Dr. Murphy or by Mrs. Smith, both familiar to the youth. I then explained in some detail the purpose of the study of youth's ideas and feelings about religion, which frequently engaged the quick interest of the boy or girl to be interviewed. The importance of their responses in understanding youth in general, and of its application to help in the training of ministers, was also stressed. Generally, however, I began where the youth were and "fished for their interests" before beginning to probe directly into their beliefs or attitudes. The first period consisted of a depth interview in which the adolescent's religious practices and beliefs were investigated, with the focus on current church relationships and beliefs about God, Jesus Christ, church, prayer, immortality, and right and wrong. The interview was in the nature of a nondirective inquiry, i.e., a question was posed around a certain belief, and feelings surrounding the ideas followed up. The second period was spent in testing, using the Godin Religious Projective Test, a Q-sort test about God concepts, a Likert-type God-concept scale, and a "hymn selection" test designed to explore emotional needs satisfied in religious experience.

The mother of each youth was also interviewed, the focus being on the mother's beliefs, attitudes, and uses of religion (as in the use of prayer at times of stress), and her imparting of these to the child. Early childhood training and the strength of the family's connection with the church was inquired into. The pastor of each child was also seen, with the exception of the one family which does not now attend church. The focus of the interview was on the pastor's impressions of the youth, whether he had known him in a membership or confirmation class, what he had taught him concerning the religious beliefs of the church, what part the youth played in the life of the church, what he felt the church meant to him. Where he had expressed interest in full-time religious service (e.g., going into the priesthood), this was also investigated with regard to his pastor's knowledge and understanding of the youth's motivation, needs, and the relation of this interest to the development of his personality.

The mode of analysis was to ask certain key questions of the material and to search for trends and to document these from the material where they were found. For example, in the case of one youth the central question might relate to the problem of identity and the manner in which religious experience aided him in discovering his sense of self over this period of his life. With another it might relate to his motivation for entering a religious vocation and to the psychodynamic factors and needs relating to his desire to "give his life to God's work." Consultation with Dr. Lois Murphy and with Chaplain Thomas Klink as well as with other psychologists and staff consultants was carried on during this period of gaining an understanding of the evolution of the youth's religious orientation and its relation to his developmental needs and adaptational style. Finally, a correlation and integration of the material attempted to provide an intensive study of the religious motives and experience of each particular child.

The second phase of the study was an enlargement of the first. Twenty-four more children were interviewed and tested, bringing the total group to thirty. A graduate student in psychology was employed who visited the parents and pastors of these thirty youth, plus thirty more, completing the total group of youth currently in the Normal Development Project. The results of this larger investigation are reported in chapter 4, "Religious Beliefs," and chapter 6, "Religious Practices."

THE USE OF BIOGRAPHICAL STUDIES

Gordon Allport, twenty-five years ago, explained the tremendous advantage of using personal documents in the study of lives. [6]

[6] Allport, Gordon, *The Use of Personal Documents* (New York: Social Science Research Council, 1942). Allport makes the case for the idiographic approach (study of individual lives) over against the nomothetic approach (study of statistical popula-

It is possible to move from theory to experience and back again, checking one against the other. Moreover, it is possible to ask the biographical data certain questions and to see if they yield answers. Having a cross section of the child's life at the various stages is better even than having the fragments of memory and fantasy available to the psychoanalyst. Natural observation, testing, the play situation, and the interview can come about as close as possible to reporting the youth's actual world as he perceives it.

For the student who desires to study these lives intensively, three methods are suggested: First, one may study the developmental progress of each child into adolescence with the convergence of the organic, motivational, environmental, and coping variables into his unique personality. The questions listed below, which I have adapted from Erikson, are suggested for such a study.

1. What is the "fit" of the mother's nurturance to the child's temperament?

2. What is the connection between the life tasks, sensed and met during the child's development, and his group identity?

3. What success did the child have in abandoning the narcissism and autoerotism of infancy for the acquisition of skills and knowledge during latency?

4. How adequately did the child solve the oedipus conflict within his social setting? In childhood? In adolescence?

5. How well did the young adolescent relate his ego-identity to his opportunities for education and interpersonal relationships?

6. How well did he find a "faith" to be loyal to, beyond his parents and church, and how well did he relate to realizable ideals to make him a creative coper?

Second, one may study one life at a time, in particular to get at the dynamics and development of religious faith. Thus, in the case

tions). Paul E. Johnson uses this approach in *Personality and Religion,* and Allport in *Letters from Jenny.*

of Helen, one may ask: How did she develop her strong sense of empathy for others? How did she develop controls over her strong urges? Where did she develop her sense of religious identity? How did she develop her present stance toward religious reality? These questions may lead to others as one studies the biographical material.

Finally, in the sections on confirmation, vulnerability, coping, and faith, the reader may refer back to the six biographies and, reading them afresh with these concepts in mind, may find the areas illuminated as well as discover how the concept has vitality and relevance to contemporary youth's experience.

CONCLUSION

This study, although completed and now being reported, is in reality incomplete. The reasons for this are several. In the first place, time and money ran out, and the amount of basic empirical research was, therefore, curtailed. With a minimum of staff, and by utilizing the work of many of the Menninger Foundation staff, however, I accomplished a great deal more than would have been thought possible without this available method. In the second place, these youth are in transition and the kinds of struggles they are going through have not reached a terminus. They are now sixteen and seventeen and are now right in the middle of the adolescent struggles. Thirdly, the results must be qualified since the group is of a particular geographic region and represents largely lower middle (blue collar) and middle middle (white collar) classes. Finally, the study did not gain access to the social grouping of youth directly, as in school classes, youth groups of secular and religious kind, nor, in particular, informal groupings. In order to answer some of the questions posed in the first chapter, this kind of participant-observation would have to be done by a trusted young adult. Although the responses to the interview are candid and often tremendously revealing, the youth's response to certain adult expectations of performance are intrinsic to the situation. The preschool parties, reported in the materials in records of direct observations, need to be repeated for youth—with all the peer expectations and conformity patterns in evidence. It is to be hoped such studies will be made in the future.

31

3

Helen
the Study of a Protestant Girl

The reader is invited now to enter the world of one young adolescent girl. I entered this young woman's world myself one warm summer's day in 1962. She was the first person interviewed, so her study became the model of the others. The interview proceeded fairly easily over a number of topics, including her religious beliefs and practices. After the interview she underwent the testing procedure. I then spent a month reading through the longitudinal materials on her and consulting the staff about her. Fortunately, Anna Freud was at the Menninger Foundation at the time, and Helen [1] was presented to Miss Freud, who analyzed and reviewed her history.

As a result of the study, certain questions were formulated to serve as a basis of the study of Helen's religious development, namely: (1) How did Helen become so empathic and develop an awareness of others as persons with needs such as herself? (2) How

[1] Helen is a pseudonym. The elements of her life are real, although persons and places in her biography are disguised so as not to reveal identities. No real names or identifying features appear in any of the biographies or other reports in the study.

did she develop controls over her strong drives which buffeted her so fiercely in infancy and childhood? (3) Where did she develop her sense of religious identity?

After the materials of Helen's life are presented, it will be possible to draw certain conclusions. However, the reader is asked to do some formulating and concluding on his own behalf. It will then be possible to continue with the more general chapters on belief and practice with some specific understandings of development. That the young person does not become religious in a moment, in the twinkling of an eye, is obvious. How he does is the problem which shall occupy our attention through this case study and throughout all of them.

Helen Warren is a young adolescent girl of thirteen and a half. She is medium in height and slight of build, having naturally curly dark brown hair and blue eyes. Her face is animated, and when she smiles she shows one broken front tooth which detracts from her beauty but not from her outgoing warmth. She wears an attractive wash dress and loafers with bobby sox for the interview. She does not yet wear lipstick, but her face is fresh and clean and free of blemishes. She seems rather shy and anxious upon meeting, but later during the interview she moves out toward the interviewer in continuing conversation. She appears anxious to please and to give of herself openly in establishing a contact. However, just as quickly she closes off a contact and withdraws behind a thin adolescent mask. She seems to like adults and to try to court their approval, as though she hopes someday to achieve their poise and to explore their world.

Helen comes from a large family, being the third in a family of seven. Her older sister Louise is married at seventeen, and her brother Bill is in high school. The little boys—Greg, twelve, Dick, eleven, Tom, nine, and Bob, seven, are all in grammar school. She is now in second year of junior high school. She is also active in community affairs, a member of the Girls Scouts and the 4-H Club. She takes piano lessons as well. Last Easter she joined the church and now sings in the church choir and serves as president of the junior high fellowship. She likes to ride horseback, but because of her parents' limited means, she does not get to do much of this. She is interested in people of other nations and says she would like to travel. The family did make one trip to California when Helen was ten, visiting Disneyland and other tourist attractions.

The family is in the lower middle class, Mr. Warren working as a skilled laborer. Previously they lived in several four to five bed room houses in Capital City, but in 1960 they bought a lot east of town and began to build their own home. The entire family helped on the project, but since Mr. Warren works full time, the living room has not yet been finished. However, everyone likes the new place, even the grandmother who says there is plenty of "yelling space" in the country for the many children. (GH, 1960) [2]

1. RELIGIOUS PRACTICES

Helen is a practicing Protestant Christian. Her parents were free churchmen and had attended several different churches in Capital City. But when they moved to the country they joined a small church served by a college student. The entire family now attends this church, with Helen and her mother and father perhaps being most active. She goes to Sunday school, sings in the church choir, and for the past two years has been a member of the youth fellowship. She is evidently thought highly of by the rest of the congregation, for when they collected money for a wedding gift for their young pastor, Helen was treasurer of the project.

She prays regularly, but now quietly to herself. She feels that prayers for oneself should not be for material blessings but for spiritual improvement. One should pray for others and in an attempt to get closer to God. She feels the need to pray for forgiveness and may often pray repeatedly for this if she does not feel forgiven. She has been to Protestant youth camp, and during evening prayers with a group of girls, by candlelight, she had the experience when she felt closest to God. She feels it is in a small close group, when everyone is concentrating on communion, that the presence of God makes itself felt. This is described as "wonderful," as "something you don't want to end."

---

[2] The investigators' names, abbreviated in the text, are included in the appendix, pp. 299-300. I am indebted to their observational reports for the longitudinal material.

She describes herself on the Godin test as leaving the "noise and fractiousness of the family to go out in the woods alone to seek refreshment." (CWS, 1962) She is able to do this through contemplation in the out-of-doors. The noise of the family may make her upset, i.e., angry, tense, or fearful of her position with her mother and her family. Prayer is a means of getting herself in balance again. Again, alone on her bed, she can pray and ask forgiveness for things she has done wrong. She may have to beseech God for this, but often she falls asleep at peace with him and with herself.

2. RELIGIOUS BELIEFS

Helen has recently finished a course in church membership and has had this additional introduction to Christian beliefs to add to the teaching of the church school, youth fellowship, and her own reading of the Bible. She shares orthodox beliefs, though these are, of course, reflected through the uniqueness of her personality and her development. Although she leans on her pastor to support her beliefs and to refer to in case of confusion and doubt, some of her ideas and attitudes are developed in response to her own need systems. We shall look first at her formal beliefs and in the next section turn to her religous attitudes.

God, for Helen, is an invisible Presence, with whom one can talk and on whom one can depend although others fail one. Ultimately he bears you up in life or death. He is seen in absolute terms: divine, omnipotent, eternal, and sovereign. But these terms are to keep him in focus as Lord transcending man and earth. He is not inaccessible or impersonal but guiding and fatherly in his approach to man. (Q-sort, 1962) His perfection is in the moral realm and this perfection is angered by sinful acts, although he is not wrathful in a human sense. He is a just judge, but also a forgiving father. His ultimate power will protect the righteous, but allows men freedom which may bring disaster on themselves. His control over things is not mechanical but saving, in that he can turn bad things into good and in death calls his own to himself. Helen's stance toward God is found in her motto: "With him

nothing is impossible, without him nothing is possible."
(CWS, 1962)

Jesus, she describes as the "best living soul that has ever been on
the earth." He was almost God on earth—only he was in the form
of a man. She sees his incarnation first in terms of his birth: angels
told Mary she was to bear the Son of God. She sees it also in his
possession of God's understanding and love. She sees it finally in
his being "chosen of God" to show people the way God wanted them
to follow. She uses an interesting symbol here. "It would be hard
to drive a nail with your fist. . . . You'd have to use a tool like a
hammer. In a sense, he's like a tool." (CWS, 1962) She feels she
is meant to be a daughter of God, but that Jesus had a special
mission which distinguishes him. The Crucifixion made God angry
at his persecutors, but he used it for his purposes and brought good
out of evil through the Resurrection. She felt Jesus' triumph was
in not showing anger, except at the time of the cleansing of the
temple.

Sin, she feels, is more an interpersonal breach than a direct
disobedience of God. Specifically, she feels sinful and guilty when
she gets angry at her siblings. She feels specific things are wrong—
such as smoking, drinking, cheating in school, hitting a brother
or sister, or a sexual breach in conduct. These make for complications in interpersonal relations and produce the need for forgiveness.
This means asking God for pardon, and it also means going to the
person and making up. One should talk things over if there has
been a misunderstanding and next time seek some way of controlling
one's temper. Sexually, Helen feels one should keep out of dangerous
situations with a boy. When one's temper boils up, Helen says she
thinks "running around the house may keep one from boiling over."

Heaven and hell are also thought of in interpersonal terms. Although she has not seen death at firsthand, except for animals, she
has thought a lot about it. She thinks that those who die and who
have lived righteous lives will go to be with God. This is not a
place in space but is extra spatial and beyond time. Those who have
lived wicked lives will go to hell, described as constant sin and
temptation. It is not constant fire, but going outside of God and
then being aware of judgment and guilt for one's sinful life. She
distorts the parable of Lazarus and Dives a bit to picture sinners

able to see the righteous enjoying God's presence and longing for it too late; however, the righteous ones cannot see the plight of the sinners, "for there wouldn't be any evil or bad in heaven." She believes that she will go to heaven for she knows God and thinks of herself as his child. For Helen the church is the entire people who worship and believe in Christianity, old as well as young. The church is a supportive place for her, a kind of second home, where all ages have a place of importance. For her the pastor is the one who represents God and Jesus to the congregation, not just by his preaching and teaching, but also particularly by his example. She has felt quite close to the student pastor and wants to be like him in living the Christian life which he not only talks about but lives.

3. RELIGIOUS ATTITUDES

We shall use in this discussion of adolescent attitudes Krech's and Crutchfield's [3] distinction between attitude and belief, namely, that a belief is motivationally neutral but that an attitude is dynamic and goal-directed. One finds in an analysis of Helen's interview and her psychological tests certain attitudes which appear to be at the core of her religious orientation. These are: (1) empathy, (2) moral controls, (3) religious identity, and (4) a positive relation to religious reality. Let us examine them as they appear at the time of the adolescent study.

Helen is described as a girl who is responsive and outgoing toward others and who is able to feel into their position with warmth and genuine emotion. She is aware of the tester's difficulties, of the plight of the mentally ill, and of how her serving as a subject of a normal child study may help sick children in the future. Her pastor believes her to be the most genuinely interested religious person in her family, and also the most "religious" in her peer group. She seems to sense the pastor's interest and to want to help him in an outgoing fashion in his work in the church.

She is also a girl who has developed strong ideas of right and wrong and controls for her emotions which enable her to keep from being

[3] David Krech and R. S. Crutchfield, *Theory and Problems of Social Psychology* (New York: McGraw-Hill Book Company, 1948).

flooded with anxiety. She sees the difference between alternatives in almost absolute terms. Some relative situations color the response she makes in a situation but the response must be in terms of a higher good. In the instance of Jesus' dining with the publicans, she sees this not as Jesus drinking wine—for her a wrong—but as going to sup with them in order to help them to salvation—a right. She does not think it right to express strong hostility, though she feels it at times. She uses the strategy of "running around the house" to dissipate the angry feelings which her brothers might stir up, or talking things over when a disagreement comes up between siblings, or imposing strong regulations on herself when she feels parents don't care enough to, or keeping one's distance from a boy who may have amatory ideas about her. She is aware of the strength of her impulses and is not one to bribe her conscience in order to gratify the impulse and pay with guilt later. The norms of her church have been used to reinforce her own ideas of right and wrong, some of which even outdistance those of her mother and father.

So far as her identity is concerned, Helen feels that she is set apart, chosen, so to speak, to be the *good girl* of the family. This comes out in her identification with "Elsie Dinsmore," a Sunday school heroine of former days. Elsie was not like the other members of the family, rowdy and quarrelsome, but was loving and charitable and sought her consolation in religion and the identity of the Christian. This identity is of one "alien" to the family, but one who turns this negative to a positive in becoming the one good girl of the family. Helen has a positive identification with Jesus, the Son of God. She realizes she is not like Jesus in that God had a mission for him unique in history. But in a sense she can look to Jesus as the one who gives her courage to face adversity and deprivation. As she said in reply to what she saw in the blank TAT card, this is Jesus who takes her and the other children into his arms in a gentle and loving way. (AM, 1962)

Her relationship with religious reality is one of firm anchoring. There is no evidence that she questions God for the tragic side of life or that she doubts God's goodness. She has a strong faith that whatever comes, whether good or ill, it will be ultimately providential in nature. This is not rational nor well thought out but is a faith. One might suspect her faith to be callow or Pollyanna-like but it appears to be a "courage in spite of." She has been disappointed in parents, in sister, in friends. But she feels that she will never be let down by God. If troubles come, things will work out, or if they don't work out, even in death one's life is centered in God. Her relationship with God is also intimately personal and revelatory. God not only reveals himself in the quiet moments of altar time in the church or cabin devotions of a camp. But she can reveal something of herself to him when she prays without the usual reserve. This recoups her energies and enables her to face the trying times of living in a large family and suffering frustration in having her emotional needs not gratified.

4. QUESTIONS

There are certain questions which one must ask of the developmental history in order to understand how Helen got this way. Granted that she has certain beliefs, practices, and attitudes at this juncture in her life, what are their antecedents and determinants in the life history? How much can one discover by reviewing the longitudinal material? Also what can her pastor and her mother tell us about how she became the kind of religious girl we see at adolescence? The questions which come to the forefront about Helen are:

1. How did she become so empathic and develop the awareness of others as persons with needs and difficulties similar to her own? What are the antecedents in terms of her organism, her response to the environment, and the mode of coping with stress which she developed from birth to this period? And what is the relation of empathy to her religious life?

2. How did she develop controls over the strong urges which she displayed as an infant and as a child? How has the "religion of law" helped her? How, if at all, has she been able to move from law to grace, and what were the experiences which helped her make these moves? What were the determinants of Helen's conscience as she developed? Has adolescence brought to the fore any conflicts which were delayed, suppressed, or denied in the earlier periods, and is her religion helping her with these?

3. What is the background of her sense of identity? It will be

recalled that Helen spoke of herself as a "stranger in the family." Where did she develop this sense of oddness and difference? With whom did she identify at the various stages of her development? Where did she get her sense of religious identity? Where did she get her sense of sexual identity? Is adolescence as an identity crisis going to be heightened, or will she seek some resolution of the crisis through religion?

4. Helen does not have the questionings and doubts of late adolescence, yet she has passed the parroting of Bible verses and "sleeping innocence" of childhood. How has she developed her present stance toward religious reality? How did she develop such a positive belief in God and such an ultimate feeling of dependence on him? What were the antecedents of her feeling of the presence of God in prayer? And are there any lacunae in her present stance which may give her difficulty in later adolescence and adulthood?

5. DEVELOPMENT OF HELEN'S RELIGIOUS ORIENTATION

Empathy. The most distinguishing characteristic of Helen at twenty-eight weeks was her social responsiveness. Though not particularly attractive physically because of her large mouth and large bags of skin under her eyes, she was able to attract the observer by her cooing and smiling responsiveness. (ML, 1949) She was possessed of a strong oral drive. Her mother breast-fed her for four days and then gave her a bottle. She drained this quickly and engaged in sucking and mouthing behavior which indicated continuing oral needs. She sucked her thumb; in fact, the pediatrician told Mrs. Warren, Helen must have been sucking her thumb *in utero,* for it was red at birth. Grace Heider ranked her a vulnerable child because of easy fatigability, a proneness to infection, marked sensitivity of the skin, and autonomic difficulties shown in colic which developed right after bottle feeding while she was in hospital. (GH, p. 88, vulnerability study.)

Her mother, though efficient, was not entirely compatible with such an active and hungry child. She resisted feeding her when Helen cried, causing her to wait fifteen minutes or more. Mrs. Warren held her aloof, feeding or changing her quickly and putting her down without cuddling her. The mother had lost her second daughter and having undergone a slight depression went to a psychiatrist at the time. The mother did not let herself get too close to her children from that time on, lest something happen to them. (CWS, 1962) Two months after Helen was born the mother conceived again and had the problems of another pregnancy besides caring for this baby. She was described as a good manager by Grace Heider—this mother who did not have time for extras such as giving affection to the hungry Helen, who wanted contact and love as much as food from her mother. This combination of orality and a depriving mother seems to be the substrate for Helen's empathy.

At the preschool period Helen's need for affection was even more marked. For example, at the preschool party she accosted her observer with the demand, "You come with me wherever I go." She impressed the observer as a combination hoyden and urchin. "It was as if she had to hold on to me for dear life and she behaved as if she had known me for many a month." (ME, 1954) Another observer was watching her ride a tricycle around the garage and hit the wall, yelling "Kerplunk." Helen stopped near the observer taking notes and shouted, "Write down that Kerplunk" (MS, 1954) She used situations to bring the adult down to her level and to interact with to her heart's delight. This "affectionate" quality worried the mother somewhat because Helen wanted to "love strangers" who came to the house. "One time there was a salesman who started up the side walk and she wanted him to pick her up and love her," said the mother. (GH, 1955) The mother dealt with this quite firmly, and it tended to lessen.

With adults, particularly the testers and observers of the Child Study, Helen practiced role reversal many times. The psychiatrist at one time was left alone when Helen and the psychologist left suddenly. Helen came back and offered to come and live with "poor lonesome me." (PT, 1954) She would shift roles with the psychologist, insisting that she close her eyes and respond to questions similar to those just asked Helen. Once she stood on her chair and called out, "I'm bigger than you people, and I can turn around in back." (AM, 1954) At times she used role reversal to gain control of her strong drives. After threatening to hit the examiner, she controlled herself saying, "I don't like other people to do it to me, so I'd better stop doing it to them." (AM, 1956) This is, of course, a growing feeling that others have feelings and are sensitive to hurts as she is. One observer summarized Helen at age five: "She was likely to appear too demanding and insatiably so in her receiving." (WK, 1954) Even with her sensitivity to people, her own needs and impulses dominated her relationships with others.

There was during latency some modulation of her demandingness. She developed a bladder difficulty which necessitated exploratory surgery when she was seven and a half. She had to take pills for the condition following this. The prolonged discomfort and the special attention seemed to temper her feeling of needing more from her mother. Furthermore, Greg, the next youngest son, was involved in several delinquent episodes which upset the mother quite a bit. Her fears were communicated to the children, and Helen tended to be quite upset. She became more subdued as a result in her own mood. The projective tests she took during latency reveal the shift in Helen from one who receives and takes affection to one who gives. The partner in the CAT (Children's Apperception Test) was pictured as one who is helpless, deprived, or ill so that she, the protagonist, is expected to give. (AM, 1956) Roles were reversed in play sessions. At one time she asked both observers to pretend that they were frightened of being examined by the doctor. Helen then comforted them saying it would not hurt and gave one of the adults a "shot" in the buttocks. She then went to the other observer and said, "You laugh, he's scared, you're three and he's five." (AM, 1956)

At age eleven there was the emergence of a new quality in Helen which enabled empathy to develop more fully, namely social distance. The impression she gave the observers was a radical modification of earlier aggression and demanding toward social skills. Says one psychologist, "I experienced Helen as a warm, bubbling gay child with considerable insight into affective processes and remarkable social skills. Helen's aggressive affectionateness has become modulated and her flighty movements have almost entirely disappeared. . . . There was no need to draw Helen out, because practically from the moment we met, she initiated conversation at a mature level." (AM, 1960) It was noticed that with her peers at school she did not participate in the giggling and yelling. She now stood apart somewhat in almost a shy manner. She seemed to distance herself from relationships and see them more objectively before entering them, and to then stand apart from them again.

At the prepuberty period she also was noticed to side with the underdog. During latency she pictured her heroes as "dead end dogs and children who knew poverty both physical and emotional." (AM, 1957) Now at eleven she sees the need for understanding healthy children so as to help the sick. She sees the roles of nurse, teacher, and airline hostess as ones she would like to assume. She can understand the deprived, having herself known hunger for affection. She can put herself in place of the sick, having been ill herself. She can even see how the criminal and mental patient got that way, having lived side by side with her siblings who got themselves in "hot water."

The religious side of empathy is also apparent. Her religious ideas have provided her a frame of reference in which to make sense of the developing feelings of empathy. She has developed certain controls for her demanding emotional needs from others. In latency there has come a shift from a "Give me" to a "Let me help you" orientation. She has observed the examples of Jesus and of her pastor as persons who gave themselves so as to be of help to the sick and the emotionally distressed. This has tended to provide a religious framework for this growing sensitivity to suffering of others. Besides this has come a new trend—that of emotional distancing—enabling her to stand apart from the distress of others so she could be of more genuine help to them. Whether it entirely defends her against her tendency to overidentify with the sufferer, we shall have to leave unanswered at the moment.

Control. How did Helen develop controls over the strong inner urges which she felt from infancy? She was described not only as an oral infant but a vocal one as well, "accompanying almost all her activities by expressive and quite well differentiated sounds." (MM, 1949) She had difficulty with autonomic stability as well. This became apparent at the time of toilet training. The mother had been quite strict with the two older children, but with Helen she softened a little. Helen was started in her training at fifteen months,

43

but at first she did not care. The other children made fun of her and her mother aked, "Don't you want to be dry in the morning?" Helen replied, "I just don't want to. I don't care." (PS, 1954) She was trained for the day by twenty-six months, but she was enuretic until past four and a half. She was proud of her training pants when they were put on her. She wet the bed again at the time of her bladder trouble, and this gave her a lot of anxiety. By then, control had evidently become important to her.

There were conflicting reports about her expression of hostility at the preschool period. She told one psychologist, "I be naughty most of the time." (LBM, 1955) However, upon being questioned by the home visitor, her mother called her the least naughty of the family. "She usually is a very good girl. Helen is usually not noisy, not often." (GH, 1954) As she developed she had strong needs for affection and her aggressive drives were expressed only if she was pushed to extremes. If the little boys dumped her dolly things out "then she really tells them. It is in extremes that she hits back; she then runs because she does not want to be hit in turn. She recovers quickly from this kind of disturbance. She will go to mother and stand around and hang her head and then put her arms around mother until she asks what is the matter." (GH, 1954) Her only naughty behavior at this age reported by the mother was messiness in the bathroom, spilling water out of the sink and tub.

Her principal target for aggression at the preschool period was mother, mainly for not giving her enough time, attention and affection. She displayed this in a play session with a woman psychologist and male psychiatrist. She called the psychologist a "poor little woman," but then checked her hostility with the psychiatrist. She let the puppet kiss him in an aggressive fashion and associated this act of love with spitting candy. (PT, 1954) She used talk in aggressive ways trying to force others to pay attention to her. Her father could not rescue her either at this time because of his long work periods, so that she had to "act out" her need for love in aggressive ways with mother.

At the preschool period she showed considerable amount of sex interest and sex role concern. In the doll play with the psychologist her interest was in the holes in the So Wee Doll and in Bobo and

Bugs Bunny. Part of this was her concern about control of toilet functions, but part of it might have been her concern with her own sexual organs. The psychiatrist observed, "She appears quite concerned about being handicapped by being smaller than others and being a girl." (PT, 1954) On one occasion at a party she engaged in lifting games with two other girls which may have been erotically stimulating.

How did Helen form her conscience or superego? Her mother reported Helen's early conformity at home. Later Helen seems to have turned from her father in disappointment much as Elsie Dinsmore did from her father at the end of the oedipal period. He was not the white knight who would rescue her from the loveless mother. At the preschool testing she responded to a picture on the Stanford-Binet, pointing out a witch who "stands behind the mother and behind the girl." (AM, 1954) Mother was not bad to her, but Helen felt she was not good enough either, and so the witch stood behind the both of them.

At age eight Helen was constantly preoccupied with "good" and "bad" themes. She attributed naughtiness to boys and goodness to girls, although she was ambivalent about this, for one time in play she called one girl a stinker. With the psychologist she asked that she be put in jail for putting a small mark on the table. When the psychologist demurred, Helen scolded saying, "You're in jail for letting me out." She used fantasy as a means of gaining control. The superego was represented as a protective mother figure and the unruly drives by a child. At times the mother was associated with badness when proved inadequate or disinterested in helping the child check her strong urges. Her fears of punishment could only be mastered with the help of the protective figure. And when the mother was not there, more anger was felt by the little girl. Her hospitalization brought out many of these fears and they were acted out by the psychiatrist. In role reversal she instructed the doctor to say, "Mommy, am I going to die?" Helen then played the protective mother and reassured him, "Of course not, they just snip your hair off." "Why do you worry about these things?" he asked. Helen answered, "Maybe it's because I'm little." (KB, 1956)

An interesting shift began when Helen was about eight, centering in her competition with her rebellious sister, Louise, for the mother's allegiance. Helen was disturbed by her sister's badness, but she also used the occasion of Louise's escapades to get closer to her mother. On the last occasion she went to her mother and promised her, "I will never do anything like this to you," and asked, "Why did Louise do it? Is there something the matter with us that made her want to do it?" (GH, 1958)

Both the mother and Helen were quite concerned about Louise and suffered the shame reflected upon themselves. Helen's reaction was to conform more strongly with the standards of the family, particularly the mother's. Her ego ideal became more clearly apparent as the good girl, who does not cause mother concern but who does the right thing and controls her drives the better to please her parents. At latency Helen developed the typical "rules consciousness," even though one would have thought in terms of her earlier development that she herself might have been more rebellious and naughty at this time.

An incident took place when Helen was ten which helped her to modulate her overfriendliness with strangers. She was terribly frightened by a threatening approach of a boy who was, however, frightened off by her friends. But she recovered enough to tell the mother and to have the mother explain this kind of danger to her. A friend's sudden marriage was the final act which brought Helen, at adolescence, a realization of the need to control her impulses. She made what Erikson calls a "moratorium" on sexuality and became reserved in groups of boys and girls. Heterosexual responsiveness is kept for later life. Since she reports that she wants to marry and have a family, she knows she will have to deal with it later.

Are her standards and means of control a part of a religion of law or a religion of grace at this period? That is, does she do her duty for duty's sake or is there an inner motivation of love? As will be spelled out in the last two sections, her emotions seem to be successfully sublimated into the area of religious activity. And there is evidence even before latency that Helen controlled her sexual and aggressive drives so as to be good as her mother wanted her to be. She is no longer raffish and rough, but allies herself with the ego ideal of properness and goodness, which she feels will win her mother's praise as well as that of other adults. One might say that she is not completely free in that she cannot act completely spontaneously with others without the rigor of her superego keeping her in line. On the other hand, she can reason about right and wrong, and, particularly, through her application of the formula "What would Jesus do?" bring her behavior under the criteria of an ethic of love. She may still have to face the strength of her drives in later adolescence and a more complete integration of her faith and ethics.

Identity. Erik Erikson has called the "identity crisis" central to adolescence. That is to say, the crisis is one of finding a core self, which has some sameness from day to day, and whose inner face (revealed to oneself) matches its outer face (the one others see). We want to discover how Helen got to see herself as she does in adolescence. And furthermore, we want to investigate the role of religion in helping her find her identity. We shall trace Helen's growing sense of self back to infancy, and look particularly at her emerging autonomy and sense of sexual identity.

Helen was an autonomous infant at two, against a mother who was always there physically but to Helen "not there" emotionally. She was, as we have seen, a lusty, emotionally hungry infant, who kept reaching out for affection which she did not receive. Her pushiness and loudness made her feel like a "bad girl," but these means were the only way she could hope to catch her mother's attention or, if not her mother, some stranger from whom she could steal affection. In addition, Helen needed someone to help her set boundaries, to help her understand the limits of her selfhood. She did not have many possessions, but her dollies were *hers,* and she fought for them against a pack of brothers.

At the age of five and a half she was struggling with the problems of sexual identity. The nearest siblings were boys, with Greg just eleven months younger than she. It may have been that mother found it difficult to distinguish the two children in her mind. Helen at this age was a combination of tomboy and little girl. She climbed over the car seat, flounced her dress around showing her panties, and appeared to be a tomboy. On the other hand, her mother reported, "She gets dirtier than the boys yet she doesn't like to wear jeans. She likes sunsuits in summer but they must have a sash or ruffle and not look like boys' things." (GH,

47

1955) She also reported that "Quite often a whole bunch of boys Bobby's age come into the yard. The games get too rough and Helen comes into the house. She does not go in for rough stuff at all." (GH, 1955) Helen seemed closest to Tommy, the baby, at the time. Though she roomed with Louise, the age difference meant that the girls did not have too much in common then. She was therefore forced to struggle with the sexual difference between boys and girls and to feel, perhaps unconsciously, that the boys had the advantage. At least she revealed to the psychiatrist a need to draw boundaries between boys and girls, between adults and children, and between the big and the little. Along with this, the psychiatrist surmised that she felt handicapped in being a girl. (PT, 1954)

The image the mother had of Helen at this time was of the "odd one" in the bunch. (GH, 1955) The boys were reported to look like their father, while Louise looked like her mother at that age. But Helen did not look like anyone except perhaps the great grandmother. This "oddness" may have added emotional distance between Helen and her mother; it certainly was communicated indirectly to the little girl. Later, in adolescence, when Helen told the story of Elsie Dinsmore, she seemed to identify with the little heroine, "who was not at all like the rest of the Dinsmores, noisy and raucous, but gentle, loving, and good." (CWS, 1962)

Helen's sex role conflicts continued into latency. She did not successfully resolve the oedipal conflicts, carrying into latency the confusion as to her sexual role. She became sensitized to body functions through the bladder difficulties until age eight. Her enuresis made her dependent upon her mother for control, but her mother was not "present" to help her with what it meant to be a little girl. During the hospitalization period, she again felt the need for a nurturing and protective mother, and was somewhat satisfied by the mother during this time. She has a heightened interest at latency, however, in body openings, the mouth, anus, and urethra. Her Rorschach responses reveal this in particular. She sees two men dancing on card III. She further sees a lady's halter on another part of the blot and the men carrying the halter to the lady. (AM, 1957)

Her thoughts about girls are ambivalent at the time; sometimes girls are nice, and sometimes they are stinkers. By the time of preadolescence she uses emotional distance with boys, attempting to hold them at arm's length. Boys are not just boisterous, but dangerous. Sexuality for her is still a mystery. She remembers her first menstruation with little trauma, after witnessing a Girl Scout movie on the subject and having her mother prepare her with sanitary napkins. But she has declared a moratorium on sexual activity, with some real struggles ahead for her before she has integrated these body urges into her self-picture.

Helen has finally formed a synthesis in puberty of two separate self-pictures which she has carried with her from childhood—namely that of the strange one and her ego-ideal of the good girl. She felt "different" from the rest of the family, by her mother's designation. She also learned that if she were to claim her mother's love and attention she must be a *good girl*. There is played out in Helen the drama of the way of Ruth with Naomi. Ruth, even though from an alien tribe, will be the good girl and stay with the mother and her religion. In the story of Elsie Dinsmore she sees the merger of identity of the strange one and the good girl, and she adopts it for herself. Her strangeness now becomes an asset, a means of finally getting the coveted goal, her mother's love. Curiously enough, her mother discloses a similar self-image on her Rorschach. There is a feeling of being on a pedestal, of having to measure up to a level of goodness above the crowd. However, the feeling of rebelliousness is there, too. Helen has, on the other hand, responded to the "pedestal" side of the mother and ultimately identifies with the "reserved and good girl."

A final question needs to be asked concerning Helen's religious identity. When questioned about her belief in Christ, she told the Elsie Dinsmore story to show the difference of this little girl from the rest of the family. She also used it to show the mediating role of the good girl for those in the family who might need forgiveness and the largess of God. She tends to take this role for herself, identifying with Christ as she understands him. Christ controlled his anger and did not show it, except in righteous indignation against the money changers. In identifying with Christ she asks herself, "What would Jesus do?" but must realize there are occasions which a girl in this century faces which Christ did not. She thinks of satisfying her needs for dresses and for things for which she is

49

deprived in a large family. Here she has the bounty of God at her fingertips through Christ, and she mediates this to her family. An example is her sharing of candy which she gets from the project. This is done through her, in an unselfish way, but a mediating way.

Christ is mediated for her through the identity of the young pastor and the church. She sees him as someone she would "very much like to be like." She admires him for his friendliness with people of all levels, with his ability to make the Bible understandable, but most of all for his genuineness and sincerity of spiritual purpose. There may be some hero worship here, but it appears to be a sublimation of affection. Finally, she has identified with a church group and found herself as a member of a group which shares her values and ideals. This is found most in small groups of adolescents her own age. She is somewhat aloof and perhaps differs from them in that she takes the teaching more seriously than the rest. But she does feel the support of the pastor and the group (a larger family) in becoming the person she pictures for herself. There will no doubt be disappointments for her in putting all her emotional investment in this kind of group, but for an emotionally hungry girl it does provide a satisfaction of intense needs for the present.

Relation to Religious Reality. The previous tracing of Helen's development comes to focus in looking at the development of her relationship with religious reality. How did she become so firm in her stance toward God? We have intimated that she has had several emotional awakenings rather than a particular crisis experience. What were these and how did they help her in her awareness of, and hold upon, religious reality? What were the experiences during these growing years which helped her know and understand God, prayer, Jesus, and the beliefs of the church?

Helen was from the beginning a questing child. An early movie taken of her with her mother (four months) shows her looking about, rubbing her hands together, sucking them, rubbing her feet together, etc. She appears to be reaching out with all her senses to gain contact with her environment. Before school she was an "elaborator and multiplier of the modes of satisfying her needs." (LBM, 1962) She was active, not passive, in reaching out to her environment. When the mother proved ungratifying and did not satisfy her physical and emotional hunger, she reached out to find means of satisfying herself. (In the development of empathy we have traced how she modulated these needs in her development.)

The search for religious reality, however, took place in a family where religion was practiced and where this means of satisfaction was ready at hand. She, like the other chldren, was taught her prayers as soon as she could talk. Her mother, consulting the baby book, said that Helen knew "Now I Lay Me" at age two and a half, saying it alone at age three. (CWS, 1962) She started Sunday school, going with Louise, when she was three. The family taught the children graces when they were small, but this practice has dropped out since the children have grown. At holidays there was extra churchgoing, but the mother, in particular, with a music sense, found the playing of religious records, such as Handel's *Messiah* would set the atmosphere for the season. Someone would get the Bible and read the story of the birth of Jesus from it at Christmas or would read from one of their Bible books. "Last Christmas, Helen got the Bible down and read the story to the little boys," said the mother. (CWS, 1962)

Church, therefore, seemed like a second home to Helen in growing up. She told one of the observers, "That's my church" on going by at age six. (LBM, 1955) It was a place the entire family attended and was a part of their family pattern and texture. The learning must have been difficult for her, particularly when the classes were large and noisy. She told the psychologist, "Ya don't learn much. All the babies do is get up and yell. . . . Even with the minister, the boys yell." (AM, 1956) Helen reported that she felt the noise of the class kept her from learning what she wanted in the Capital City church. She was perturbed by the "Paper wads and undiscipline of the boys" in the class, even at age nine. It was not until she came to the country church where the classes were smaller and the attention more personal that church began to mean much to her.

As we have discussed previously, however, she felt that she had to snatch "fire from the Gods" as a little Prometheus in her childhood years. She felt this as early as preschool. The oedipus conflict was never resolved for her—for she found on turning from mother to father that father also was incapable of satisfying her tremendous needs. Should she keep pressing her father for some affection and

51

attention, or should she resign herself to her lot? Dr. Escalona discussed a difficulty of this choice at the preschool stage:

It had been anticipated that Helen would inwardly accept and apply to herself standards of right and wrong that had been taught her. This was true so far as it goes, but what the predictor had no way of anticipating was that this would be the one point where resignation might apply. Helen (at 5) saw herself as a child who could not hope to be "good," by the standards she herself held to be valid. With unusual clarity she expressed a self-concept of someone whose activity, noisiness, occasional awkwardness, and hostile impulses stand in the way of genuine acceptance by the social environment. In the judgment of the writer at any rate, Helen was a child who lived up to the role which she thought had been assigned to her: that of a person who has to take by force those vital satisfactions which she cannot expect by right. [4]

What one discovers with the modulation of drives (which we have already traced in Helen's development of empathy and controls), is a change from an "Olympus-storming" to a "resigned stance." She became interested in her own beliefs one day, reports the mother, when the family lived in Capital City. She was age nine at the time and played with two little Roman Catholic girls along with a Lutheran girl and a Jewish girl. The two little Catholics insisted on talking about their beliefs and how superior their church was to the others. Helen, along with the little Lutheran girl, got quite upset about this and reported it to her mother. The mother did not know what to do about the problem, until one day this experience was repeated when the father was working on the screen door on the front porch. The little girls expounded doctrine until he had taken all he could, and then he spoke out, "Who'd want to go to your church anyway? We're happy with our own." (GH, 1958) This evidently stopped the discussion. One can guess that it must have helped Helen know that her previously silent father had some convictions here.

When the family moved to the country, a major crisis ensued for Helen. At first she was most unhappy in school, since she had no friends. She did not concentrate on making one friend or two, but

---

[4] Sibylle Escalona and Grace Heider, *Prediction and Outcome* (New York: Basic Books, 1959), p. 221. (Different pseudonym for Helen is used here.)

she wanted every person in the class as her friend. Her mother tried to explain the cliquish nature of the class, but this did not satisfy Helen. One night the mother counselled her to seek God's help in prayer for the difficulty. Helen did pray that God would help her understand this and help change the situation if it be his will. She did get along better after this, she reports. This is an example of how the mother, with so many children, did "throw this one to the universe." And she found God an answer to her tremendous needs.

There was a quickening of religious interest when she was twelve. She had previously been given a Bible when she became a member of the junior department, but now she decided, with her church school teacher's help, to earn a Bible. She learned the books of the Bible and where specific sections such as the Beatitudes were. She learned special graces and prayers, spending extra time with this. Finally a year and a half later she was awarded her special Bible. She and her brother Greg spent special time reading the Bible. Her pastor, Tod, encouraged her interest in religion and at altar time, she was able to throw herself on God's mercy and feel his attention and his love as a satisfaction of her needs. She attended a youth camp at age thirteen, and, she says, during the cabin devotions experienced an intense awareness of God, in the closeness of communion with the girls.

If Helen had a special period of commitment, however, it came in a solitary experience at age ten. She reports that she had questioned the business of celebrating Christmas by getting presents and not giving any. She thought long and hard about this and thought she would like to give Jesus some present this Christmas. She went to her room—probably away from the hubbub of the rest of the family, and there resolved that she would make a little ceremony of giving Jesus a present. And in Christina Rosetti fashion she thought,

> What can I give Him
> Poor as I am?
> If I were a shepherd,
> I would give Him a lamb,
> If I were a Wise Man,
> I would do my part,—

> But what I can I give Him,
> Give my heart. [5]

She came out and no one knew she had done this, but the season took on a special meaning to her that year. She felt she was God's child and Jesus' disciple.

The Lord's Prayer and even "Now I Lay Me" were meaningful for the first time. And now she practiced daily prayer time as a means of keeping this flame burning. As she expressed it, baptism was a pledge for her at age thirteen, but not a pledge for her parents to bring her up right as much as for her to live as a Christian. Communion was engaged in meaningfully for the first time, in a candlelight service, after she became a member of the church. It meant that she knew what Jesus' sacrifice was, and that she was one of Jesus' disciples, a group to which she really belonged.

The religious themes are very similar to the family themes as discovered on the Godin Projective Pictures and the hymn selection test. They are: Injury, pain, and consolation; vital belonging to someone who cares for you and loves you; satisfaction of deep needs without feeling greedy or envious. One Godin response shows a little girl being told by her parents that she is adopted and that they shall have to send her away. A wealthy friend, however, intercedes and enables this poor family to keep their foundling. Helen still feels "different"—adopted—with a need to have her sense of belonging reinforced by the family. One would also infer that prayer and worship accomplish this task for Helen religiously. She feels that she belongs and has a sense of participation in God's family this way. The second picture that adds to this impression is the one in which Helen sees two girls, sisters, praying in the church for forgiveness. One sister is sincere and receives an answer to her prayer; the other, less sincere, must hear the words of the preacher in a sermon on forgiveness before she believes. Supposing these two girls to be Helen and Louise, one can say that Helen is more sincere in her approach and, at least in the religious realm, outdoes Louise. Helen's concern for Louise following her episodes turns up here as well. But it takes more than Helen; it takes the minister to help her find real forgiveness. (CWS, 1962)

[5] "My Gift," from "A Christmas Carol."

Helen's favorite hymn is "Blest Be the Tie That Binds" and here she states that she likes it because it gives her a sense of belonging. She finds that she is not isolated nor alone but a part, and that this is reassuring to her. Another favorite hymn, "I Would Be True" bespeaks her drive for integrity and for feeling special and good in her mother's eyes as well as God's eyes. She states that this feeling of being watched as a model comes out also in school, and, one would suppose, in church. She now has the reputation of a "good girl," and she needs the reinforcement of prayer and worship to maintain her integrity. One finds in Helen's favorite hymns, however, a balance of activity and passivity: she finds the stirring strains of "Onward, Christian Soldiers" and "Sweet Hour of Prayer" equally helpful in maintaining her devotional life.

This brings us to a partial answer of the question of whether Helen is active or passive in her faith. She no longer feels she can storm the heights of Olympus to get the love and affection she wants—neither from father, nor especially from mother. She has turned to religion to provide her consolation and a sense of identity. She does this because it is "the way we look at things," she says, and also because her Mother pointed her in this direction when the mother felt she could not satisfy this girl. This is not resignation—as though she could never find the deepest satisfactions of her needs—nor is it fatalism—as though her sister had won and she has to be willing to take second best. It is an active faith—she has reached out for and anchored in a dependable God who provides for his devoted disciple.

She has come to a feeling that she must work the works of righteousness and not depend on a magic helper to get her out of troubles. Thus on her projective tests she sees hard work and cooperative planning by a family group as the means of overcoming illness, poverty, and trouble. No doubt she has learned this in the web of family relationships. But she senses that ultimately she must rely on the dependability of God, that he will make things work for good in his time. Interestingly enough, the mother also believes this. Mrs. Warren believes that "God is the force that keeps us going." She believes that one must learn to live with damage and hurt and that one ultimately becomes a better person through enduring tragedy. Helen has come to this belief not by talking to the mother but by observation and by empathy. The mother has influenced the daughter by example and by pointing to God, the source of her own strength.

This brings us to a final evaluation of Helen's religious strength. She asked on the final interview if I thought it was all right for her to go to someone else besides God to talk over her troubles. What she wanted to ask with the question was my opinion as to whether I thought it possible for her to talk to her mother about her adolescent questions and conflicts. Helen still has to make some resolutions of undiscussed problems with her mother: Is it all right for me to be a woman through conceiving a child? Do you really love me as I have become the "good girl" of the family? Is it all right for me to gain my independence by becoming a self-sufficient young woman? But these are problems of later adolescence of which Helen just now has but the beginning feelings. She knows that she has come a long way from the "harum-scarum," child she remembers. She knows that her "Christian faith" has helped her grow. But something of the questing, searching character of this young girl is bursting out again in the adolescent. And I would predict that her religious faith will continue to be a source of strength to her as she seeks a creative and mature life.

The reader is now better able to answer the questions presented in the opening paragraphs. He may differ from the interpretation which I have given of Helen's religious orientation and attitudes. As a matter of fact, some of the psychologists and religious consultants differed from me in the interpretation which I made of Helen. However, discussion of her development and life experiences with some other person or a group of persons should add insight. The reader is particularly asked to give the question of religious identity adequate attention. Is Helen another Holden Caulfield, a "Catcher in the Rye" to save the other members of the family from destruction? Is she a self-appointed savior, or has the family chosen her for this role?

Her beliefs were briefly discussed at the opening part of the chapter. They were obtained by interview and test procedure. (See chapter 4 for a presentation of test procedure.) Similar results were obtained from thirty other young adolescents, both Protestant and Roman Catholic. To formulate how Helen's beliefs appear when compared with other adolescents, we shall have to look at the test results more nomothetically. Do her beliefs serve personal-need systems? Do they reflect parental teachings? Do they represent her Protestant church, or do they reflect the pastor whom she idolizes? To get answers to these and other questions we shall now turn to the religious beliefs of the group.

4

Religious Beliefs

An intensive study of the religious-belief systems of young adolescents needs to be undertaken. Although this group makes up the largest percentage of those who are confirmed in Protestant groups and although the conviction still lingers among evangelical groups that the "storm and stress" period is the time to win them to Christ and the church, the nature and quality of the beliefs of the group from twelve to fifteen has not been researched to any great extent. The Normal Development group from which this study is made is small and geographically localized to a midwestern community, yet the opportunity to study their beliefs over against that which parents and church had taught does offer us significant data.

Previous studies provide a framework through which we may view these youth. In a 1944 study of 547 adolescents in the sixth, ninth, and twelfth grades, Raymond Kuhlen and Martha Arnold through questionnaire and problem check lists discovered that: (1) many rather specific beliefs which were taught to or rather picked up by young children are no longer held by most of them in the late teens; (2) a greater tolerance with respect to religious beliefs and most practices is apparent at the time of adolescence; (3) with respect to certain beliefs, the issues are far from settled by eighteen years of age. There was more wondering about belief than not believing in their population.[1]

Arnold Gesell, using an embryological model of maturation, found the belief systems of young adolescents responding to their psycho-physical growth. He characterizes thirteen years as an age of "inward-ness and anxiety." "But this inwardness is not confined to itself. It takes in the outer world. It is linked and interlocked with an exter-nalizing awareness." [2] Gesell finds that the adolescent at fourteen is able to accept the world pretty much as he finds it.

A pivotal year . . . he presents a fine constellation of maturity traits and potentials, which are in propitious balance. . . . He has a fair measure of wisdom and philosophy. . . . His group loyalties are strong and sensitive, but normally they do not distort his person-to-person relationships in the home circle, at school, and within the community. . . . His spon-taneous attitudes make him tremendously educable in the realm of human values and social obligations. [3]

Fifteen again is an inward period, according to Gesell, and the adolescent is preoccupied with "inner states of feeling" and rep-resents "an almost effortful refinement of the patterns of feeling." There is a "respect for the spoken word" and for "details of thought and feeling." [4]

The conclusions of August Hollingshead in his study, *Elmtown's Youth,* in the 1940's still find a lot of the traditional viewpoints holding sway over young people, although for the majority there is evidence of slow attrition in late adolescence.

Religion to the vast majority is an amorphous body of beliefs symbol-ized by a number of awesome words, God, Jesus, Christ, Sin, Salvation, Heaven, Hell. It is given form in a book that embodies all sacred truth, the Bible. The church is built on *the* Bible and Sunday is *the* Lord's

---

[1] "Age Difference in Religious Beliefs and Problems During Adolescence," *Journal of Genetic Psychology,* LXV (1944), 291-300.
[2] *Youth: The Years from Ten to Sixteen* (New York: Harper & Row, 1956), p. 140.
[3] *Ibid.,* p. 181.
[4] *Ibid.,* pp. 214-15.

Day. One can believe the Bible without reading or understanding it; just to know about *the* Bible makes one religious. To the great majority, the sacred words associated with religion through long usage have taken on a magical quality, and one respects them for this reason. To a few, God, Soul, Heaven, Hell, Sin and Salvation are real entities that surround them at all times like the air they breathe; for them everyday experiences are manifestations of spiritual reality, and life is a testing ground of Hereafter. But to about 90% of the boys and about 80% of the girls, religion does not have this compulsive quality. These youngsters believe that a person ought to be religious, but the word does not have any very specific content or meaning except a vague belief in God confirmed by the assertion that they are Christians and belong to a church. [5]

The most recent study of a denominational group, Merton Strommen's study of Lutheran high-school-age youth, reveals even among this rather strong faith and ethnic group some confusion and spiritual uncertainty. Although three fourths of Lutheran youth hold to the faith as described in the ecumenical creeds, there is confusion and contradiction about the concept of justification by faith. "The lack of clarity shows in the almost half who accede to the tenets of a generalized religion." Strommen says the widespread concern of Lutheran youth over questions of doubt and uncertainty ranks second only to their concern over self-acceptance. About two of three Lutheran youth experience some awareness of spiritual lonesomeness. Among approximately one half there is a hesitation over what is being taught by the church. Strommen links this directly to parental beliefs and what is being taught by the congregation. [6]

These studies are generally of late adolescence, with the exception of Gesell, whose study only incidentally concerns youth's religious beliefs. Here we are attempting to examine carefully the belief systems of a group of thirty young adolescents, ages twelve to sixteen, with the majority in the thirteen to fifteen age range. We shall examine their beliefs in general, obtained by interview and test, and then focus on their specific beliefs about God, Christ, the church, prayer, the sacraments, right and wrong, and heaven and hell. Specific quotations from the youth themselves should add

[5] *Elmtown's Youth,* pp. 244-45.
[6] *Profiles of Church Youth,* pp. 68 and 143.

richness and depth to the various aspects of belief. Then, we shall focus on the beliefs about God and look in explicit detail at the source and motive of these beliefs in the lives of the young people. Finally, we shall draw some conclusions about the total group and project some problems forward for later consideration.

1. THE BELIEFS THEMSELVES

The religious beliefs of early adolescents both clarify and confuse. They show the tradition, but always through the kaleidoscope of the child's life—with parents, priests, pastors, and peers bouncing off their beliefs against the youth while he is trying to bring bits and pieces together to make sense of his life's experience. With regard to the group's beliefs in general, the table on page 62 shows the specific kinds of beliefs held and the percentages of the group which hold them.

Beliefs About God

It will be noted there is more confusion about God than any other concept, perhaps because of his spiritual nature, perhaps because of other reasons which shall become clear in a later section. In this group we can notice first a latency view of God (a quasi-physical view).

Nobody knows what he's really like. I mean he's powerful and he's strong and he's visible or invisible, I really don't know. [In questioning her about whether he is a person] He's got a lot stronger powers than we do. . . . Well, I don't think he's as tall as a mountain but I think he's got a lot of powerful ways, I mean he made this world. I mean, I don't know, he's got strength and power over us. [In answer to question about the fact that Eve was created second, did this mean women were a little less than men] Yes, I think so, in a way, because Eve was looked at [in a whisper], let's see, how do I want to say that, well, it was something—it said something about he made Adam and he made Eve for something to help Adam or something. . . . I think that man should have the right over his family but I think the woman should have a part in it, too, but, I mean, well, it's hard to say. The man should be top of the household. (CWS)

Table 4-1
Group of Thirty—Basic Beliefs

God	Quasi-physical	6	20%
	Person	5	16.6%
	Power	8	26.6%
	Abstraction	3	10%
	Confused	6	20%
	Unreal	2	7%
Christ	Mystical reality	5	16.6%
	Historical model	7	23%
	Theological abstraction	8	26%
	Distant story	7	23%
	Matter of indifference	1	3.3%
	Matter of hostility	2	7%
Church	One true church	6	20%
	Mediator, God and men	6	20%
	For "saved" believers	5	16.6%
	Fellowship of growing Christians	5	16.6%
	Social group	4	13.3%
	Indifferent	4	13.3%
Heaven and Hell	Geographical place	5	16.6%
	Reward and punishment	9	30%
	Relationship with God	5	16.6%
	State of mind	6	20%
	Uncertain	2	7%
	Unreal	2	7%
Right and Wrong	Law of parents	5	16.6%
	Law of church	7	23%
	Peers standards	7	23%
	Thoughtful codes	6	20%
	Confused	2	7%
	Rebellious rē authority	3	10%
Prayer	Person to person	8	26.6%
	Harmony with power	5	16.6%
	Reflective planning	3	10%
	Rote recital	7	23%
	Indifferent (no practice)	5	16.6%
	Hostile to idea	2	7%

Another young girl is confused, although she did begin to question the tradition. The older person whom she asked felt it inadvisable to help her at the time.

[Concerning the conflict between science and religion] I asked my science teacher . . . when we were talking about cave men and things like that. I don't know if I should have or not but I asked him who really came first—Adam and Eve or the cave men and he said, "Well, I can't answer that," and I said, "Well, okay," you know, just went about my business because I guess he couldn't say anyway, because according to science the cave man was first and on the other hand in religion Adam and Eve came first so I'm kind of confused about that. (CWS)

Another girl has a sense of God as spiritual presence, and for her the definition is not so important as the reality of him at the moment.

You can't even beat him. He's perfect. [About his presence] Well, you know you'd feel funny if you were pretending you were talking to someone who wasn't there—like maybe you were talking to your aunt and she wasn't there, you'd feel kind of funny about it afterwards. But you don't feel funny when you're talking to him. (CWS)

For a boy going into the priesthood, the providential—even predestinarian—character of God is most important. The thoughts are those he has been taught, but he applies them now particularly to his struggles about religious vocation.

I think he has a plan for everybody's life. I think that every evil that happens in the world that eventually some good will come of it. And I think that in every person's life there's a set plan for each person and that the person can go against the plan because he has free will. [Concerning God's nature] He's a supreme Being, higher than the rest of us and he knows everything and has control over everything. He can destroy anything and he's so much higher than any of us it's really hard to understand really all about him until we get to heaven where we can see him, but we know he really is and that he created the world and that he always has been and that he's higher than us. (CWS)

Belief About Prayer

It will be noted there is a variance between those who list God as quasi-physical and spirit and those who pray to him as person. The explanation is that there are some who think about God but who do not pray to him personally, and there are some who pray but who are not reflecting about God. There are fourteen, almost half, who either simply say their prayers by rote or are indifferent to praying or hostile to the idea. This may reflect the fact that their parents no longer hear their prayers (one fourteen-year-old boy did have his prayers heard) and when left on their own they do not pray daily as they once did. Or if they do it is a quick rote prayer before going to sleep.

One must add, however, that with the other half there is either a person-to-person type of experience recorded with prayer (an attempt to bring themselves into harmony with a power) or a use of meditation as a time to reflect and plan.

Even with the Roman Catholics, a spontaneous prayer is seen as of more benefit than a formal prayer.

Well, prayer is a talking to God. There are certain prayers that we have like the Hail Mary and the Our Father and—but I think a better prayer is just talking to God in our own words, like when you're in a church and instead of reciting all sorts of Hail Marys and the rosary and—they're all good prayers, but I think a person if he just sits in church and talks to God in his own words, I think it might give him a little more grace than if he just recited these prayers and kind of rattled them off and didn't really get the meaning of them. (CWS)

There is also a strong tendency to deny petitionary prayer as important or even Christian. One notices this with Helen, though she feels it is all right to engage in intercessory prayer.

I don't think you are good enough to ask anything of God . . . unless it is to take care of someone else . . . or someone who is sick. That would be helping someone besides yourself. But if you were asking for something for your own benefit, . . . it is almost like if you were greedy. If you were Christian you wouldn't ask for things you really wouldn't need. . . . If everyone asked God to take care of someone else, then everyone would be taken care of including himself. (CWS)

A boy, who has not faced many doubts as yet, is aware that much of his prayer is by rote, and that it would be better for him if he did not pray this way. Note also a feeling similar to Helen's about petitionary prayer:

I don't pray too much during the day, but I pray every Sunday. But of course at the time I'm supposed to go to bed I recite a prayer—it is not the same one though. I sort of make it up. I don't especially like to say the same prayers. They would even mean more if I did this, because I would pray for whatever I was thankful that happened that day and I might be thankful for my parents, sisters, and friends. [In answer to what other kinds of prayers] Lots of times when I do something wrong I ask for forgiveness, but most of the time I just thank him for what I have. [In answer to whether he prays for a fishing rod] No, I'm sure that is not right. Well, when you're asking for a new fishing rod it is more or less selfishness then than anything else. . . . I mean it doesn't have any real meaning. All you're interested in is the new fishing rod. (CWS)

Prayer as thoughtful reflection comes out in a few (three). Teddy perhaps reflects this best. He does not always have to bow his head, but he does need to seek quiet, away from the flood of stimuli and the sensations of a crowd.

[Is it helpful to withdraw in prayer?] Yes. Well, I've gone in my room and just thought and read in private and I don't really have too much seclusion from mankind but it's almost impossible to withdraw for any length of time. Man has the ability to reach anywhere in the world. [In response to how God influences him] It's just when I'm more or less in private. . . . I can be reading a book, and I can't think of any relation between it and God—I mean I don't see any relation—and all of a sudden something hits me. Well, I don't see any relation between what I'm doing and God but then something just hits me and I stop and think about it a second. (CWS)

Beliefs About Jesus Christ

Jesus Christ has more reality than God for both Protestant and Catholic youth in this sample. Thought about God requires abstract and philosophical speculation, but Jesus is a human being whom they have heard about since kindergarten. In this part of the Midwest, the region H. Richard Niebuhr once called the "Jesus Belt," Christ is spoken of more than God in some churches. Added to this, as we shall discuss more in chapter 8 on confirmation, is the identification figure which Christ becomes for this age. When the interviewer questioned the young person closely about his belief in the Incarnation or the Atonement, he got unique answers, some of which were orthodox, others which reflected the youth's individual struggles.

I asked, "What differentiates Jesus from other men?" and from Greg got at first a mediatorial type of concept and then a more thoughtful answer regarding Christ's mission.

I think he was given all the things that humans had, except that he had something a little bit more, too. I mean he had to. . . . He was kind of the only extra special human, because the way people put him. He's way below God, but way above the people, the regular people, because he had all the advantages of being a person—because he could reach other people. Yet even when tempted, you know, he always managed to do good. [Concerning what makes Jesus special] He was made special because he had to have special things about him—I mean he just couldn't—I mean he was special in that he was bearing a new and different type of message. . . . Jesus preached simplicity and kindness, you know, repaying evil with good. (CWS)

Chester, who was undergoing doubts about the reality of God, had done some interesting and imaginative thinking about Jesus. He is a boy who, on the tests, showed a need for a shepherding person in his life.

I think there might have been a man or something, you know . . . from an advanced race and he came in from outer space or something like that and went back to the earth. . . . There's one thing I don't see how anybody can explain—how he rose from the dead, if he could. . . . There's a lot of weird ways he could of done it if he did come from an advanced race. [Concerning the virgin birth] "It might have happened. In fact, it had to happen because he just couldn't have been placed there. . . . How do you know Mary wasn't some space woman? (CWS)

Teddy spoke of the reasons for Jesus' crucifixion particularly in terms of moral example.

God sent Jesus, his son, down here to be an example to us, to show us how to live, and it was a way of showing, well, how to go through the hard times like the Crucifixion. . . . We each of us have our own personal crucifixions during our lifetime and it shows for us to stand up before them and not to give in in your faith and beliefs. . . . I'm sort of creating my own religion. That's the way I believe it. It's my interpretation. (CWS)

The substitutionary atonement of Christ was reflected in Roman Catholic answers but not to any extent in the Protestant answers with the exception of three fundamentalists. The focus of the saving work of Christ was personal in the lives of several of the youth who had faced crisis and suffering. Adele, whose mother died when the child was nine and whose alcoholic father put her into a foster home, reflects this attitude most clearly.

[In response to reason for Jesus' death] I don't know. I guess to save us from—I mean, doing things that we shouldn't do. Save us from different things that, uh, we shouldn't do and save us from, uh, really destruction of ourselves, I guess. (CWS)

Beliefs About the Church

Youth's belief about the church divided in this group pretty much according to whether they were Protestant or Catholic, with only about eight holding conventional or indifferent viewpoints. The Roman Catholic young people held that their church represented "the one true church," the mediator between God and man (40 percent).

Ronald's belief reflects catechetical teaching with almost no change.

I think it's his greatest instrument for the salvation of mankind now, because in it we have the mass and mass is . . . a form of worship wherein the church officially adores and glorifies God and draws men to God. And I think it's his greatest instrument now because it draws men to God and they have a tendency, if they go to mass regularly, they have a tendency to lean more toward his ways instead of evil ways. [In answer to question of whether there are many churches] Well, I feel that the

67

Catholic church is the true church because Christ had said to Peter that "Thou art Peter and upon this rock I will build my church." Peter meant well and he established the true church on him, which was the Catholic church, and then as the true church grew older, men didn't like some of the ways and teachings of the church, so they broke away from the church and established their own. [In answer to question of whether other churches are outside salvation] No, they aren't . . . those outside the Catholic church who through their own fault do not know that the Catholic church is the true church can be saved if they really do God's will and love him . . . and so if they are connected with the church by desire, they want to do God's will, and so they are saved in that way. (CWS)

Stewart has thought about the teaching, but what he learned in parochial school remains the springboard for his own views.

It's the gate to heaven. It's the thing that Christ founded to organize all his followers into one thing and it's the way to heaven. It's the way we wrote all the teachings of Christ and it's—mainly, it's to get every one of his followers to Heaven and to convert the world. (CWS)

On the other hand, the Protestant young people hold varied views of the church depending both on the length of their confirmation class and church school exposure and on the quality of the relationship with the pastor. Greg, for example, has had a good relationship with his pastor and, as a result, has a positive attitude toward the church.

Well, there's two types of repentance, and I think our minister is pretty good on the type I would prefer. There's the type that these ministers get up, you know, and they raise all—they raise the roof by telling everyone how terrible they are, and I can't stand—if we had that kind of minister, I'd just leave because I don't—I don't know, I just don't like that. I prefer just being told. You know, just break it to us gently or something. And he makes it quite obvious, you know, but—and I just don't like the way some ministers get up and yell and scream and everything and I don't think that's necessary. Well, you see again, screaming and everything is by force. It's putting fear into the people and that's just another one of those old tricks. Whereas the way our minister does it, I'm not sure—he doesn't put any fear in men, he just

68

instills a want to repent, just because he leads off and you finish it up yourself or something. (CWS)

Of all the young people interviewed, Helen had the strongest "community view" of the church, reflecting a strong tie to the minister but with awareness, too, of the ministry of the laity. She has assumed responsibility in the "adult society" of her church. Further, she sees youth and adults working together, even when adult attitudes are opposed to youth's views.

I mean the people make the church. I think the younger generation has to know what it's all about because they'll be the church after the older generation and they'll have to take over. I think you ought to pay attention to what's going on. (CWS)

We shall investigate the gulf between pastors, parents, and adolescents when we look more closely at religious behavior. Suffice it to say that beliefs about the church come not just from intellectual teaching, but also from what youth observe adults doing—whether they attend, pray, support financially, and serve. Among the more thoughtful young people, religious beliefs appear to be a synthesis of both the precepts and examples of adults screened through their own reflection and experience.

The mystical reality of Christ is felt at the serving of mass by some Roman Catholic girls, and his mystical reality in prayer by a minority of Protestants, both boys and girls. We should be aware of the fact that even in the "Jesus Belt" for one third of the group Jesus Christ is a distant story or a matter of indifference.

Beliefs About Heaven and Hell

This group of youth lives in an area where heaven and hell are often talked about in sermons and confirmation classes and church school. The fundamentalists and some Roman Catholics hold the "hereafter" to be a geographical place. The remaining Protestants and Catholics hold heaven and hell to reflect one's relationship with God and the state of mind of the redeemed. By and large the Roman Catholic youth associate heaven with reward and hell with punishment. (Note the study below of ideas of God and punishment by parents.)

Looking at specific youth one finds the belief transmitted through their unique personalities. Diane reflects a fundamentalist viewpoint which is being seriously doubted but which still causes her much anxiety.

Hell is a place of eternal destruction and heaven is a place that I can't dream about because there are so many things I don't know about it. Will we eat in heaven? You know—stuff like that—what's heaven going to look like? Will we float around on clouds or have our own mansions, or solid ground, or solid trees and where is heaven? [In response to a question about the reality of hell] Well, you just, just go down there. You're being tormented forever and when I think about forever and forever and forever, it sort of rings and it sounds bottomless and it is, for that matter. (CWS)

Darlene, a fundamentalist who has been saved, still fears an avenging God and, although she knows she is saved one moment, feels that she could be damned another.

[In answer to a question about whether she would go to heaven] If I died right this minute, I feel that I would go to heaven, because I have accepted Christ as my personal Savior and he's in my life and he's real to me and I don't feel I have done anything wrong against him to my knowledge that would keep me from going to heaven. If I did something wrong, I shouldn't wait until I got home to ask God's forgiveness. I should do it right there on the spot because I might never get home and I might never get another chance and I should ask forgiveness right there on the spot. [showing a fear of God's judgment] (CWS)

Claudia, a Protestant who has had to grow up rather quickly because of a divorce in the family, affirms heaven but denies hell because she believes in a forgiving God.

I think all people go to the same place and that no matter how good you are or how bad, everyone is treated equal. And the bad, they try to correct and the good help the others and everything, but I do believe that you are all in the same place. In a way I am kind of confused but that he just doesn't let all the lives go to waste. If you've been bad, you go to hell, as you say. But that he'll try, just as here on earth that they try, to make 'em good or something and go through stages. [In response to a statement that those who love God are with him] Well, I think everyone is with him, 'cause well, his sons and daughters, I don't think he'd turn away anyone. (CWS)

Greg, another crisis-prone youth, has thoroughly divested himself of a physical viewpoint, but thinks of the hereafter in relational terms. Even so, he ends in mystery.

Well, I don't think it's a place in the clouds or anything like that. I think it's all over the—I mean kind of all around us, maybe. Some—I mean it's like God, it's kind of all around us and it's just there. [In answer to whether it is like the presence of God] Well, I know I try to think about space and everything. They say it goes on and our minds are so now that it's impossible to comprehend this, how something goes on, because everything we have just stops, you know. And it's very irritating just to think how space can go on and on because how can it, you know? This is the way with everything, because well, I don't think we're really supposed to know too much about this and I think we're getting too nosey for our own good. (CWS)

One will note the close relationship between young people's viewpoints of heaven and hell and right and wrong. They have associated reward and punishment with the reward and punishment of parents in preadolescence. This still remains with many adolescents, particularly when the church reinforces the teaching. As we shall examine later on, the punishment experiences of the child in growing up directly influence his idea of God and, of course, colors the idea of eternity, the dwelling place of God.

Beliefs About Right and Wrong

When the interviewer probed ideas of right and wrong, he came straight up against the young people's struggle with authority. Some 80 percent of them were still dependent upon their parents and/or their pastors for their beliefs. Even in the 10 percent of the cases where the young people were rebelling against authority, parents still influenced their code, although in a negative direction.

Darlene is an example of one who is rigid in her ideas—solidified

71

almost into a Puritan ascetic by fears of her drives. Her mother has particularly taught her these ideas about dancing.

There are words that I think are wrong that the kids at school go around saying all the time and they don't think anything about it, not a second thought. I don't think we should wear jewelry or anything such as this because in the Bible it says that thou should not adorn thyself with costly jewels and costly array. And I don't think you should drink or smoke because God intends for us to keep our bodies strong and healthy and in the best condition possible and if you do this you're not. And it's dirty and filthy. And it's in the Bible that it's a sin to drink. [With respect to dancing] I feel that that's a sin. There have been kids at school that say, "What's wrong with dancing?" and *they* say, "Well, whatever you do, you are supposed to do in the glory of God." Is that to the glory of God, really? And can you witness there? I've heard many kids that have tried it, and I know some have and I've tried to witness on the dancing. They ask when they dance and so on, "Are you Christian?" and they say, "No, are you?" and then they would say, "Yes," and they would say, "What are you doing here then?" And I don't think that it's right. [When asked what is wrong about it] It's not to the glory of God. There's no place in the Bible that I know of that says anything against it but it is not to the glory of God. You can't witness anything. And the crowd that you get into, it can lead to things of sin. (CWS)

A Roman Catholic boy, Delbert, shows the excellent training he has received in moral theology in his religion classes.

[In response to where he learned moral values] Well, they, the sisters, educate us pretty well, I suppose. . . . If we didn't have it we'd be almost impossible for us because a—right and wrong is undoubtedly different for different people. The same thing as for evil. Evil is one thing to one person, another to another. That's why there has to be a basic knowledge or conscience in a person to know right from wrong. [Concerning the ten commandments] It's a guide and it . . . explains more or less what our conscience is and what it's based on when we think of right from wrong. It's basically on ten commandments because God put this knowledge in us and it's the same basic knowledge that's in the ten commandments. (CWS)

A sizable group, about seven, show that peers are influencing them with respect to setting their standards. Roddy is an example of a young man, who, though he sounds inventive, underlying it all betrays that the group influences his standards.

[Where do you get your idea of right and wrong?] Through your brain, through what you think . . . maybe your life is run off on a tape recorder and then as it's played back you go through; but whatever is down over in this reel will transmit what's going to happen to you, and what's over on this reel will tell what you have already done. [In response as to where his conscience comes from] Maybe through what somebody—you saw somebody else do it, so your eyes transmit it back here on this little recording machine so you keep that stored away and then you come to it, "Hmm, should I do this?" Then you recall somebody else doing it on that little tape recorder—"Hmm, I'll do it," so you open the door. [His teachers appear on the face of it to be his peers.] (CWS)

Boys and girls are at different stages in their thinking about sex codes. Some have not done any conscious thinking at all; others, particularly the girls, are working out codes using what their parents, the church, and their peers have brought them. Martin, for example, denied he had thought about sex relations and showed immaturity and some fear of the opposite sex.

[Concerning sex relations] Well, I mean, gosh, that's kind of rough. Well, that's all some boys date for, but I don't think that's the way it should be. If you want to get married or something, well, then you should—you should kind of date a girl, kind of. Well, I mean if you meet a girl at school or something you just see her good side, sort of like, I mean. Then after you're married, she might start beating up on you or something. But that's one thing. I think you should date, if you're gonna marry her. You should date her a few times to see what she's really like. She might turn out to be totally different than when she is in school. (CWS)

Milly, on the other hand, is dating a college boy steadily, but has learned most from the experience of her sister's having a child out of wedlock.

[When asked if her parents had taught her where the limits were] Oh, yes. You see, I had a sister that had to get married. . . . I really learned my lesson. Well, I knew all along. Well . . . she got married a year ago . . .

73

and I saw how it really hurt my parents. Of course, I never would—I mean she's completely different than I am. . . . She's always—you know, she didn't like to listen to Mom and Dad which is normal. [She related that she had learned the commandments at church.] I mean, my mom and dad were—I mean, they taught us—but I mean, I really didn't completely understand these until—I really didn't understand a lot until I got up into my later years of grade school. (CWS)

It is significant that in this group of young adolescents there are only 20 percent who by this age had achieved a thoughtful moral code. It would appear that morality might be an area where youth might need to wait until late adolescence, when more of the data are in; or when they have removed themselves away from the powerful influence of parents and perhaps church before they can begin to work out their own standards. We shall look at this problem in more detail in the chapter on religious behavior.

2. CONTENT OF BELIEF IN GOD

We shall now look at the content of the belief in God of thirty of those who were interviewed intensively by a pastoral interview and tested using the battery of tests indicated above:

Table 4-2

Idea of God			
	Quasi-physical	6	20 %
	Person	5	16.6%
	Power	8	26.6%
	Abstraction	3	10 %
	Confused	6	20 %
	Unreal	2	7 %

More than one fourth of the group saw God as a power which we defined as an invisible force which underlies and sustains the universe. However, it is significant that one fifth still carry the childish view of God as a giant man, and with some he is not a giant but a very human man, with magical powers. And even more so, one fifth are confused in their thinking about God; he is not physical nor can they understand him as spiritual. This may represent a breakup of the latency view. Only five saw God as person, using biblical personalism as a reference, that God has created man in his image and therefore, even though Spirit, has will and purpose. Three saw God as abstract, like a principle or law, but having no personal reality. And for two God was unreal, though only one of these claimed to be an atheist.

When one clusters the belief systems of each adolescent, synthesizing the Likert Questionnaire, the Q-sort God Concept test, and the results of questioning the adolescent by interview, the following results obtain:

Summary—God Concepts

Barbara—Not a father but a holy, just punishing God who threatens her.

Helen—A father who is just, who impersonally punishes but personally supports.

Terry—A power who is not a father but a shepherd spirit, holy and just, transcending all, and does not harm.

Diane—Ambivalent—an abstract principle who used to be a shepherd father but who now is 'not supporting or intimate or forceful.

Roddy—Remote natural law which is impersonal and not all powerful.

Teddy—A personal shepherd, all just, who transcends, supports, and does not punish.

Dennis—Quasi-physical person—near but not all powerful, like man in his character.

Donald—Quasi-physical yet all powerful—who punishes impersonally, like a shepherd.

Delbert—A just and holy spiritual power, impersonal in his dealings with men.

Rachel—Quasi-physical; like a shepherd, not a father, who is all powerful—his control to be feared.

Ron—A power, like a father or shepherd, who impersonally punishes but does not support.

Greg—A personal father or shepherd who is not all, but who impersonally controls us and of whose power he is afraid.

Darlene—A personal father-shepherd-spirit who transcends us and impersonally controls and punishes us justly.

Vernon—A holy power, not a father, who supports and impersonally governs.

Martin—An abstraction—holy, impersonally transcendent, beyond man.

Melvin—A powerful force who may have some personal characteristics yet who governs and punishes us impersonally.

Claudia—A remote, yet just and transcendent, force—confused.

Adele—A remote power, not holy or just, who is above her, yet she desires his care.

Milly—A personal father-shepherd-spirit who transcends her, yet supports her.

Sally—A remote being, impersonal and no support, yet whom she fears.

Lenny—A remote being whose many attributes confuse him.

Janice—A person—ambivalent about his impersonal control, his holy law, and his personal concern.

Corliss—An unreality—she fears the punishing impersonal force which is the universe.

Maurice—An abstraction—who transcends all and whose fatherly and spiritual reality has been assented to.

Stewart—A fatherly, shepherdly spirit who supports, transcends, and impersonally controls.

Ray—A quasi-physical being who, like father, supports, transcends, and punishes.

Daryl—A quasi-physical being (just) whose support and acceptance she needs.

Vivian—A quasi-physical reality who confuses her, is remote and of whom she is afraid.

Chester—An unreality, he nevertheless desires a shepherd who would support, accept, and discipline. [7]

Confirming the data above, it comes as no shock that only five see God as a father, the predominant Christian concept. One should add, however, that we do have another five who see God as a shepherd who has a Christlike character. There are only two who blend Father, shepherd, and spirit into a trinitarian concept, and these are Catholic who have had perhaps the best theological training. One of these is studying to be a priest. The impersonality

[7] The clustering of beliefs comes froma a factor analysis of Q-sort and Likert God-concept scales, to which has been added my rating of the portion of the interview dealing with God. See "Religion and Prejudice: A Factor Analytic Study," by Bernard Spilka, Philip Armata, and June Nussbaum, *Review of Religious Research*, VI (1964), 28-36.

of God, his distance and punishing character, come out clearly for eight and lead to fear. On the other hand, there are an equal number who experience the support and justice of God, even though they do not acknowledge any personal quality to him. The quasi-physical character of God is held by those who evidently have not entered into adolescence intellectually, and therefore have not thought about God, or if they have they have become confused and retreated to a childish concept. One atheist is fearful of the punishing impersonal quality of the universe; the other is wistful, and, though he does not believe, he desires a shepherd who would accept him.

One might say on the basis of the preceding data that one finds a wide range of ideas about God in the group, some of which have been taught by parents and church, others of which appear to be the result of their own thought and experience.

3. QUALITY AND INTENSITY OF AFFECT REGARDING GOD

Table 4-3

	Very Shallow	Shallow	Moderate	Intense	Very Intense
Doubt				2	1
Awe	3	2	2		
Respect		5	3		
Identification			2		3
Dependence				4	1
Union					2

In the group of thirty the boys were either moderate (five) or intense (six) in their feelings about God, with only three expressing shallow feelings toward the deity. On the other hand the girls were either shallow (seven) or intense (five) in their feelings about God, with only one expressing moderate feelings. Perhaps this indicates that in this area of mid-America, with fundamentalists and lower socioeconomic strata represented, the boys still find faith in God a strong emotion. For the girls it is weaker, perhaps partly because the girls are still tied to their mothers and fewer have declared independence by turning toward the church.

The boys' strong feelings were identification with God (four); the girls' strong feelings were of dependence or union with the divine (eight). Strong feelings of doubt were shared by two boys and two girls. One boy (judged by the psychiatrist to be on the effeminate side) had strong feelings of union with God.

When one looks at the results of the coding denominationally, one notices other differences. The Roman Catholic youth generally showed awe and respect toward God, with the exception of two. One girl who is sixteen and rather mature desired union with God, and one boy who is studying for the priesthood identified with God. The fundamentalist youth generally showed feelings of dependence or union, with doubt showing up in two cases. The mainline Protestant youth, like the Catholics, showed awe and respect toward God in general. Three identified with the divine: one girl and two boys. One might draw the conclusion that, with the exception of those to whom relationship with God assumed primary importance (seven), the young people felt distant from God. Both Protestant and Catholic youth were of this description; the fundamentalist group were the ones who showed both the most intense feelings and the ones whose feelings were of the primitive level of dependence and union.

When one refers to Table 4-2 and examines the fact that for eight of the youth God was a confused and unreal concept, the emotion associated with doubt must be included. Further it must be admitted that for some the tradition has not been felt emotionally, and that confusion exists regarding the whole idea of God.

4. CONVENTIONALITY OF BELIEF IN GOD

The majority among the Protestant and Catholic youth (eighteen) were conventional. This "Conventional" group approximated the group who had moderate to shallow feelings toward God, according to the former coding. Ten of this group accepted the authority of their parents and church and eight were in conformity

Table 4-4
Conventionality of Belief [8]

Acceptance of authority	10
Conformity with peers	8
Reflective selection of beliefs	7
Rebellion against authority	4
Rejection of authority	1

with their peers, believing what they heard and what their friends agreed to. This coding also correlates with the content of belief, with 36 percent of the youth believing in a physical/personal God, and 36 percent believing in God as an abstract power.

On the other hand, five were in the rebellious and rejecting group and represent those who doubted conventional beliefs but who in a sense were still bound negatively to the authorities. Rebellion and rejection are similar trends displayed, with rejection being the end state of rebellion for the young person. One might also expect that following a stage of rebellion, the youth might begin to deal creatively with doubt as displayed in the next group.

Only seven of the total group—three girls and four boys—in the eyes of the raters appear to be reflecting on their beliefs and selecting those which help them cope with emergencies, which appear true to their experiences, and which help them make sense of their lives. These believers are among those previously listed as intense or moderately intense but whose quality of emotion ranges from identification to dependence to union with God.

One might say on the basis of the preceding data that the youth were by and large conventional in their beliefs, with some meeting the authorities of parents and church with rebellion and rejection. It was the minority (29 percent) who were actively working with their tradition and using it selectively to serve as a framework for coping with their experience.

[8] Professor Gale Jensen of the Department of Adult Education, University of Michigan, checked the reliability of this coding and agreed with me on the meaning of the categories. In fact, in three instances out of four he and I placed the youth in the same category.

5. ROLE AND USE OF THE IDEA OF GOD

On the basis of the study thus far, it appears possible to understand how these young adolescents function religiously. An appropriate way to do this is to hypothesize how they use religion and the place of God in their faith. We may begin with a general hypothesis: *Religious belief tends to be related to central coping tasks experienced by the youth at his particular age and in relation to his particular environment.*

Particular hypotheses related to this central hypothesis are:

1. Those youth who are emotionally deprived of love and acceptance by their parents in childhood or who are over-dependent upon them in early adolescence will think of God as a controlling power or may have trouble believing in God at all.

2. Those youth who are afraid of their burgeoning impulses of sex and aggression and feel a need of external controls will think of God as ruler or lawgiver. The parent who controls such a youth will provide an image in which he "creates" God, the predominant emotion felt in the presence of God being fear.

3. Those youth who are anxious about their powers and their relations to authority—parents, teachers, ministers, police, etc.—tend to think of God as a savior from the evil powers. The youth may consider the evil powers within himself, keeping him from creativity, or he may consider the evil powers outside himself in nature or society. However, for him to become productive, an outside agent must come into the evil situation, pluck him out, and put him in a new place.

4. Those youth who intellectualize their world in order to distance themselves from it emotionally, tend to think of God as an abstraction. These youth do not respond to God as a personal reality but simply as an idea. For them God may be hidden or dead, until a crisis or new stage of growth enables them to respond to the symbol from a different level of need.

5. Those youth who fear their peers' opinions and desire their approval above all else tend to think of God as an approving or disapproving group authority. Many youth may not call this authority God, but it functions in the manner of law-giver or arbiter of behavior. On the basis of the entire study it appears that over

half the youth, despite their religious affiliation and creed, operate by this "religion."

6. Those who seek self-identity and mastery of life tend to think of God as the life-force sustaining them and their world in and through the self. The conceptualization of God may be personal (for the majority it is) or impersonal or superpersonal. However conceived, God is responded to as immediate, supportive, and within the nexus of personal relationships and sustaining events.

Youth will probably shift from one use of religious belief to another as a careful study of the biography of Helen will show. However, our hypothesis is that the inner-personal dynamics, the environmental challenge, and the coping task together condition his framework of belief, in particular the belief about God. In chapter 12, "Faith and Coping Styles," we shall examine these variables in more detail.

Let us look more closely at the second hypothesis with data from the Child Study Project which studied the strictness of parents in punishing the child, and the data from our testing, particularly the Q-sort data, which uncovered the child's feeling regarding God as punisher and as one who needs to be feared.

Relation of Belief in God and Parental Discipline

Those who say father is stricter parent	Idea of God as punishing
Teddy	father does not punish
Susan	no response
Greg	fear of father's power
Terry	no response
Diane	no response
Ray	punishment is personal
Vernon	no response
Daryl	no response
Vivian	fears impersonal punishment
Rachel	fears personal punishment
Lenny	no response
Donald	punishes impersonally

Those who say father is stricter parent	*Idea of God as punishing*
Helen	punishes justly
Ron	impersonally punishes
Delbert	impersonally punishes
Corliss	fears impersonal punishment
Milly	fears impersonal punishment

Those who say mother is stricter	*Idea of God as punishing*
Darlene	punishes justly
Sally	fears impersonality
Dennis	no response
Maurice	no response
Melvin	no response

Those who say neither is stricter [9]	*Idea of God as punishing*
Chester	no response
Stewart	impersonal control
Adele	no response
Martin	no response
Janice	impersonal control

In the total group nineteen were concerned with punishment or control of their impulses, and as a result tended to think of God in punishing or controlling terms. The fear of this aspect of God's nature came out clearly in five of the tests, and in one there was a denial of fear, saying God does not punish in this way. In seven of these nineteen there is a belief that God's punishment is impersonal; in the rest the idea of a personal God is linked up with his justice, but in all instances it is in the cases where the father is the strictest parent. In those instances (five) where neither parent

[9] Even though punishment is not accepted in the last group, impersonality is and the feeling of emotional distance.

is considered stricter, one might conclude that there is a lack of discipline. In no instance is this the case. In fact, in three instances the parent is severe in discipline, and for this reason the youth may have denied the question. The impersonal control mentioned in their cases may be a response to the fact that they have no recourse to justice, to God, or anyone else.

One might conclude that the hypothesis is conditionally proved in this group of thirty youth. One should add, however, that the desire for a lawgiver is not the only variable in the framing of their idea of God; but the kind of discipline that they receive, the parent from whom they get the strictest discipline, whether they have recourse to justice, and whether the law is meted out impersonally or personally may play a part in the way in which they conceive their world, and the God who governs it. A corollary of this hypothesis might be that the early adolescent does not yet have enough emotional distance from his parents, with the exception of a few of the faster maturing ones, to think of God as more than a law-giver. These data appear to show that thinking about God is by and large in childhood terms, where morality is spelled out as rules which parents have set down and where infractions are punished. It would appear that the early maturers are overcoming this "religion of obedience." By the process of identification with the parent, priest, or Christ-figure, these selves are becoming more clearly identified. The ego ideal now operates instead of the punitive superego as the force of conscience, and the youth is becoming more independent of rules. The relation of parent figure to the youth's concept of God is for many a very close one.

Father André Godin, a Belgian Jesuit psychologist, has investigated the latter problem, not just with adolescents but with a Catholic population ages seventeen to fifty-seven. In the study he has replicated the Q-sort technique first used by Nelson-Jones and Strunk in studying Protestant youth. His results substantiate the earlier studies and show that "where there is a marked preference for the parent of the other sex [than the subject] the evocation of God is strongly drawn in that direction." [10] In other words, if the youth prefers the mother, God is imaged in maternal terms; if the father,

[10] "Parental Images and Divine Paternity," in *From Religious Experience to a Religious Attitude* (Chicago: Loyola University Press, 1965), pp. 75 ff.

God is seen as a father. The harsh or permissive discipline, as well as who administers the rules, does have a telling influence on the child's thought of God. The adolescent must further distance himself from the parental authority and find some balance of immanent and transcendent in them and the Ultimate Authority. This coping with the new situation we shall explore further in the next biography.

Conclusions. Looking at the entire group, one may say that with only two exceptions the young people have had some exposure to the Christian faith and are reflecting that exposure in both positive and negative ways. For the majority of Roman Catholic youth the source of beliefs is mother church, reflecting parochial school education as well as confirmation practices. For the minority of Protestant youth the church is an influence on what they believe. So far as parents are concerned, the mother is twice the influence that the father is. In fact, the peer group appears to be as influential in what youth in this group believe as the father. The source of religious beliefs will be further analyzed in the study of religious practices.

As far as the beliefs themselves are concerned, it was noted that the group held clearer beliefs about Jesus Christ than about God. About a third of the youth hold God to be quasi-physical and personal. About a third hold God to be an abstraction and power. 20 percent appear to be confused about their belief in God, which is a rather large percentage in a group all of whose parents had some connection with the church. That two found God to be unreal in this predominantly religious region is also held to be significant.

The beliefs about right and wrong and heaven and hell reflect moralistic teachings. It was noted that the younger adolescent is still pretty much under the control of his parents, and the authority which is felt is that of parents. There is some questioning of this moral authority and considerable struggle in moving from strong superego controls to the inner control of the ego ideal. The majority of the youth, however, are still too close to the parents to break away from their authority. The ideas of heaven and hell closely parallel the ideas of right and wrong. The fact that God is still perceived as law-giver and judge probably reflects the strong authoritarian character of these parents and the youth's reaction to authority.

Regarding the motivation for belief, the majority of the youth felt an emotional distance from God. Only seven of these thirty youth had anything approaching an immediate experience of God. The emotions were generally not strong with either Protestant or Catholic, and the quality of emotion was awe or respect for God. Doubt was a strong emotion among three. Identification was the strong emotion for boys and union for girls. However, the majority of the youth were conventional in their beliefs, with just a few showing rebellion or rejection of traditional beliefs. The minority, seven in number, were actively working with the tradition, reflecting upon their experience and beginning to form their own belief system.

The overall impression is that the largest number of youth is traditional, that is, accepting the forms and systems of the church with small question, little reflection, and a rather weak integration of these in their lives. The next largest group are conventional, that is, they are motivated to say what they have heard from the pastors, priests, and parents, with it making very little influence on their lives. In the conventional group one expects a childhood orientation and one finds it. The third group is conformist to the beliefs of the peer group, many of which are not spelled out in this section because they are not a part of the traditional or conventional belief systems. Finally, there are those who hold intrinsic beliefs, i.e., holding to religious beliefs which bear the hallmark of their struggles to cope with their environment.

Many questions arise as a result of this survey of religious beliefs. How does the youth develop intrinsic or extrinsic religious values? What is the relationship between his beliefs and those of his parents? What influence does the church have upon him—in the church school, confirmation class, youth fellowship, or by direct contact with the pastor? If so many are conventional and conformist, where do these attitudes arise? In what manner do peer groups influence what youth believe and what they value? In order to answer these questions and others, our plan is, first, to look to the biography of Terry with these questions in mind. Second, we will focus on religious practices with data coming to us from the larger group of fifty youth, to get a more adequate cross section of the institutions of the home and the church.

5

Terry
the Study of a Catholic Boy

It is quite natural to be introduced to religious activity and practices by observing Terry, for he is a religious activist. The questions about intrinsic and extrinsic religion can be explored through his biography also. Terry conforms with parental expectations surely, and he does his duty to the church, but in such an excessive way and with such fervor one must question his motives. He is an institutionalist, but he appears to serve the institution for deeply personal reasons.

The questions which the reader is directed to will help him understand the religious practices of the entire group more clearly. (1) How did Terry develop such strong controls over his sexual and aggressive drives? (2) What about the balance between fantasy and reality-testing in his personality? (3) What are the sources of his identity as a person? (4) What are the psychodynamic factors which motivated him toward the priesthood?

Terry is a Roman Catholic and the non-Catholic reader is invited to enter the Roman Catholic world without bias or distortion.

Terry is a very accepting young man, you will discover. The ecumenical relations between Protestant and Catholic will take on new dimensions when seen through the eyes of a young man. Moreover, Sullivan's remark that "we are all more human than anything else" will become more significant as you attempt to understand someone from a different religious group.

Terry Bowen is a tall, thin, energetic adolescent boy of fourteen years and five months. He has brownish hair cut short in a flat-top, blue-gray eyes, and his heart-shaped face is covered with freckles. He wears glasses and was attired in a red and white sport shirt, tan chino pants, with the usual white sox and brown loafers when seen by the interviewer. He walks erectly, but sits in a slumped position and nervously fiddles with something—a pencil, a key chain, or something else—while talking. His face has no blemishes; he has entered puberty; according to his mother, this happened in the summer of 1961. He talks with a push of speech and on rare occasions cannot pronounce a word because of his rapid-fire delivery. He is rather shy at first but warms up on acquaintance, so that he does not want to stop talking at the end of the hour. He is forthright on meeting and leaving you, shaking your hand vigorously and politely.

Terry is now in the freshman year of high school, a parochial school which is operated by the parishes of a midwest city. He previously had graduated from a parochial grade school, having attended it for all his school life. The previous school was related to his parish; however, the present school takes in students from all over town, including some Spanish-American, Indian, and Negro students. He is now, therefore, thrown into contact with more lower-class children than was the case in his lower-middle-class parish school. He has three siblings, Ben, age twelve, Chet, age nine, and Jean, age five. His father and mother have had to struggle to keep their financial heads above water. They began in a one-room apartment, moving to a low-rent apartment when Ben was born, and finally finding a house which they have started to buy in a housing development. This house has two bedrooms, but they plan to build onto it in the future; these plans having to wait for the money. The father is a ward attendant in a rest home; the mother, an occupational therapist, works half time on special duty in a state mental hospital. The father formerly had a second job working part time in a drive-in theater, taking a night shift in his other job. He still works nights, and the mother days, one of them attempting to be there with the children at all times.

1. RELIGIOUS PRACTICES

Terry's family is described as a practical Catholic family by their priest. By that he means they are not apostolic—one that goes to mass daily—nor are they nominal—going to confession and mass once a year; they are weekly attenders, receiving the sacrament regularly and keeping up their religious obligations as they should. One should note, however, that the mother came from a strong Catholic family and saw to it that the children were enrolled in parochial school. Mr. Bowen came from a mixed marriage, and though reared a Catholic was not baptized until his marriage. Terry is described by his priest as "ordinarily religious," by which he means he did not stand out in catechism, though he was always prepared and did serve mass and participate in religious activities. His mother, on the other hand, describes Terry as always intense about religion, until he entered high school. By this she means he took it up with his characteristic gusto and has always displayed more interest in religion than the other children. Which of these pictures more nearly fits Terry will be one of the problems of the study.

Baptism at birth, first communion at eight, and confirmation at ten—these are the prescribed steps for entering the Roman Catholic Church, and Terry took these steps at the proper age. He felt he was practicing his religion before he went to parochial school, for he knew his prayers—the "Hail Mary," "Our Father," and "Apostles' Creed." He was not going to mass, because he would be a bother to his mother, but he was interested in what he heard— especially the Bible stories on television and radio. His mother fed his interest and was only temporarily stopped when he equated the Bible stories with the Santa Claus myth.

Parochial school was taught by sisters, with an occasional visit by the parish priest to question the children on their catechism.

Religion was taught daily, with an elementary catechism used in the first three grades; a harder one was used as he took his first communion, and learned the Ten Commandments and the six commandments of the church; a still harder one was used as he prepared for confirmation. At the confirmation service the archbishop from a nearby city came and confirmed the large class of almost three hundred children. In this group Terry was one who was asked a question by the archbishop and answered it correctly. The thing he remembers though is failing to use "Your excellency" as a mode of address and being terribly embarrassed.

In adolescence he is a member of the Knights of the Altar, a group of altar boys who help serve mass. He attends a parochial high school, where he goes to confession on Thursday and mass on Friday. His religion class now is taught by a Jesuit, who uses a standard text on Genesis correlated with science theories and the doctrine of Creation. Of most interest right now is his interest in becoming a Roman Catholic priest. This interest began when he was ten and began to serve holy communion; it has waxed and waned ever since. The past two summers he has taken a week-long visit to a Benedictine monastery, and after the last trip had a talk with his parish priest about his interest. He was listened to sympathetically but told that he was still too young to make a decision, and to use the high school years as a time to test it out. How he came to this feeling about the priesthood and what function the vocation of priest serves in his religious belief system and orientation toward life will be another area for study with this young man.

2. RELIGIOUS BELIEFS

Terry could be said to hold orthodox Christian beliefs—it is impossible to see how he could do other than believe as he does with his educational background. However, even in a boy who has had as much religious training as he has, he does hold to certain beliefs and slights others. This could be called characteristic of him. The reasons or motivations for this, the relation of belief to attitude we shall explore in the next section. First, let us look at the way he phrases his beliefs.

God for him is real, as opposed to mythical. He is present in the world but revealed particularly in the sacraments of the church. The distinction between nature and grace, though not articulated in Thomistic terms, is a part of Catholic thinking even down to the first catechism. God is described in more than human terms for Terry. "I used to think of him as a big man," he said, "but I know now that isn't possible." The adjectives which fit God are "absolute, all-wise, kingly, and forgiving." God is not "meek or jealous or avenging or damning"—these for him are too human for God. Above all God is not remote, but he is a power which guides and corrects, even disciplines. He created the world—but not in six days, as in Genesis 1, nor like "Leonardo da Vinci with a brush or a sculptor with a tool"—he created with a word. Terry does not believe God is simply a spirit, but must be enfleshed. "What you can't see, you don't know, and what you don't know, doesn't exist," he replied to my query about God as invisible. God's evidence is found in revelation and in the deposit of doctrine in the church. He has had no mystical experiences of God, though he knows that this is something that persons such as St. Francis or St. Teresa d'Ávila have had. If he were to have such experiences he would have to be a saint, he believes.

He believes that Jesus Christ came to earth "to open up the gates of heaven, to create the sacraments, and to die for *us* to save *us*. He is God in man." He is very well-versed on Christ, though he has not thought much about the doctrine of the Virgin Birth or the Resurrection. He has thought more perhaps about the death of Christ. "He died for our sins, not at his enemies' decision, for no man is his enemy, but at God's command. Thereby he showed perfect obedience." Terry does not think that he has anything of the nature of Jesus, for Jesus is of divine nature. The absolute cleavage between God and man, which Jesus tries to heal on the cross, is apparent in his thinking. The crucifix makes him sorry for his sins and helps him do right. The Resurrection is Christ returning to life for us, proving he is God, and ascending to open up the gates of heaven for members of his church.

Heaven is eternal happiness, and hell is eternal punishment. If one is in a state of grace, he goes to heaven with a short stop in purgatory. He feels he is going to heaven, because he has the assurance through the church he is in a state of grace. Terry said,

"Where God is, heaven is," which gives the impression of eternal life being a quality of life here on earth. He denies this; he would rather hold heaven to be the presence of God in time and eternity.

Terry holds to the Catholic belief in an age of reason, which begins about age seven. When asked about right and wrong, he explained that he believes the conscience to be "instinctual." When questioned about where his ideas of right and wrong came from, he gave his parents as the teachers, but the church as the institution which has defined these things for people on earth. He explained his ideas of the influence of a peer group as follows: the kids who do things such as drinking and smoking and destroying property are trying to act like big-shots, to impress the group. But he goes with a group of Catholic boys and one Jewish boy who do not do these things and think it "stupid" of others to act this way. One gets the impression that Terry has strong ideas of right and wrong, and that at present he is testing these ideas largely taught by parents and priest against what he finds in the high school community. He believes basically what he has been taught so far, however.

The church is, for Terry, the "go-between" for God and man. The power of the church resides in its organization and its sacraments. The most meaningful sacraments for him right now are holy communion and penance, since he has already been confirmed and is not yet ready for marriage or unction (last rites—which he called "excommunication"). The meaningfulness of confession is found in its being a means of gaining God's forgiveness through his agent, the priest. One is then not held responsible for his sins. In communion one receives God through the bread and wine. The result of taking communion is not a thrill in an emotional sense, but an assurance that one is "headed in the right direction," by which he means in a state of grace. The strength of the church as an organization which guides, gives the sacraments, and holds the "keys of the kingdom of heaven" is apparent in this boy's statements. His personal experience of God or of the Savior is not important; what is important is that the body of beliefs and sacraments are held in trust by the church of which he is a part, and one felt, quite literally, the "gates of hell would not prevail against it." He would argue with me, a Protestant, but one gets the impression he accepts the statements of the priest quite literally because he has the authority of the church behind him.

3. RELIGIOUS ATTITUDES

Terry has a curious blend of belief and doubt, displayed on the tests and during the interview. He holds an intellectual assent to Catholic doctrine, and this faith must be correctly stated. His doubt, however, extends to the emotional substrate of his faith, that which was laid down in infancy and childhood in his relationship with his first Gods, his parents.

He holds to a similar ambivalence between distance and presence in his relationship with God. God the Father must be real and not mythical; God the Son must be real in his sacrifice and his presence in the Host; yet they must not be entirely in human form or they would be imperfect. And so Terry must hold God in transcendent terms, with a nature other than man's and see Jesus with a divinity about him man could never attain. Even the Catholic saints are able to experience the Holy Spirit in a way which he cannot, because of his distance from God.

Another dichotomy in Terry's religious attitudes is that between conformity and rebellion. He conforms to the church's teaching about right and wrong—he behaves as a good Catholic should. In fact, when he has an opportunity to build up his "merit," as in the Knights of the Altar which he joined, he goes to work with characteristic energy and gusto; for example, he became a First Knight as soon as he could. His five-hundred-word essay on "The Sufferings of Christ" was excellent, said his mother, far beyond his age group. (GH, 1960) His rebellion, however, comes out in anger when he is held down by rules about what is possible for his age— as, for example, an Eagle Scouting award, for which he was ready at thirteen but could not receive until he was fourteen. It also is currently coming out in some adolescent cursing around the house. This has shocked the mother and brought on some lectures about the example he is setting for his brother.

The predominant religious theme is that of sacrifice—taught by the church as the once-for-all atonement of Christ upon the cross for the sins of the world. The brokenness of Christ appeals to him in his own feelings of brokenness; and the need for suffering in order to bring aright a messed-up situation. He identifies with the dead Christ and the sacrifice which he made, but he also finds in the Virgin Mary an appeaser of the wrath of God. Perhaps the basic theme for him is that of the Pietà—the broken Christ in the lap of Mary. In this theme he sees most dramatically the struggle to conquer sin as finished and the anguish of the Virgin over the dead Savior. On one of the Godin Religious Projectives, he sees the priest dying and being held by the woman who had loved him, but the death was to save the religious community and to straighten out a messed-up situation. One wonders if in Terry's mind there is not a linkage between sacrifice, death, and redemption, and an eventual anguish of the mother, represented by the Virgin.

Finally Terry's religious attitudes should be related to his desire for a religious vocation. On the one hand, he feels that he is not worthy, since he has not had a religious call. (For the Roman Catholic this is not a prophetic call, but a priestly call, i.e., given by the church and sealed by the church upon ordination.) On the other hand his perfectionistic drives, whose origin and development we shall trace in the next section, make him desire to aim for the highest goal. This goal, in so nervous and energetic a boy, is not a life of contemplation but one of action. Moreover, his need for lines and structures makes him look to an organization which can order his life and bring chaos out of his drives. The church, perhaps more meaningful to him than the home, is the logical society to do this. Here again, the theme of sacrifice may be seen, as he says "One gives of oneself, but one also receives the self-giving of God in return." I should point out that in Catholic families, as in Jewish ones, it is appropriate for the oldest son to go into a religious vocation. There is no pressure from his parents or from the church for him to do this; nevertheless, it is a calling which is held in high repute. In fact, the life is of a different order than a secular profession. For that reason, in addition to the religious instruction given by nuns and priests in the parochial school, a Catholic boy cannot grow up without giving the thought of priesthood some consideration. Why Terry has done this is another theme that will need tracing in this study.

4. QUESTIONS

We have certain questions to ask of the developmental material to help us understand how this young man has attained his current religious orientation. Some of these questions may have to be given partial answers because of the lack of data available and the indefiniteness of the subject himself. However, the basic personality trends can be seen most clearly in the developmental material and will show in a decisive way the interrelationship between maturation, maturity, and religious stance.

1. The first question centers around the development of Terry's strong controls and his oversensitive conscience. How did he develop these strong controls, particularly in the light of his intense drive systems and his seeming inability to stop once he has got started on something he wanted to do? How did he learn to handle the aggressive drive? What did he do with his strong sex drive? We shall be particularly interested in the years four to seven in looking for an answer to these questions.

2. What about the balance between fantasy and reality-testing in his personality? How can one trace his coping procedures at the various levels of his development on both an imaginative level, with its religious themes, and on a problem-solving level, with its scientific and intellectual themes? What are the interpersonal roots of his religious themes, and what intrapsychic conflicts do they attempt to solve?

3. What are the sources of his identity as a person? What does one find in his sexual-role identity, and what are the means he has used to establish who he is? What are the current conflicts he has about identity, and what are the religious means he uses to deal with them?

4. The preceding questions lead quite naturally into the final questions about his vocation: What are the psychodynamic factors motivating him into the priesthood? What function does he see it serving in the integration of his personality? Is the priesthood as a vocation a lifetime job for Terry, or is it an attempt to resolve his interpsychic and intrapsychic conflicts? In other words, what is defensive and what is active coping in Terry's consideration of the priesthood?

5. DEVELOPMENT OF TERRY'S RELIGIOUS ORIENTATION

Before beginning our developmental study, we need to trace out the givens in Terry's life, i.e., his constitutional organism and his environment. Terry was born to a young Catholic couple, the first-born of four children. With a high school education, the father, following service experience, planned further schooling, but upon marriage he settled down to a job as a ward attendant which he has held ever since. His mother, with O. T. training following high school, was more ambitious than her husband and more frustrated by their low socioeconomic status. They live in a standard two-bedroom housing development, crowded and cramped, but livable. The home visitor mentioned television and magazines in the home, but no books. (GH, 1955) It was dull and dingy, even though new, perhaps the result of two working parents trying to keep it up with small children around.

At thirty-two weeks Terry was observed to be an infant with high motoric drive, a low sensory threshold, and low frustration tolerance. Documenting this statement is the fact that he developed colic soon after coming home from the hospital. The observers' comments were: "unbelievable and untiring vigor of movement" (SE, 1948); "strong affect, especially anger, explosive motor discharge, temper tantrums, stamping, kicking, etc."; "if humans had more than two arms and two legs, he'd use them all." (PT, 1955)

The interaction between this highly active child and his mother was most uncomfortable. She must have expected a child that behaved like a doll, for she reacted to his nervous energy with sharply stimulating activity of her own. She would whack him when he was vigorous or fretful at the time his diapers were being changed. She would say "O.K., you're going to settle down to business and take this bottle and go to sleep." He would react by more activity and determination, only to get his mother's back up. Both parents had read Spock, but the father handled him in a relaxed fashion, while the mother would be provocative. The mother started back to work in three months and the father took care of Terry in his time off in a creditable fashion. But the difficulty of knowing just how to react to a stimulating environment was not confusion

95

but attack on Terry's part. It is better to fight than to be overcome, he soon learned.

Controls. Terry developed quite early, therefore, as a "stubborn, vigorous, emotionally labile child." (SE, 1948) "He was prone to push too far, and to become victim of overstimulation, and to resist the interference of the mother or any other adult in his own freedom of movement." (MM, 1948) He broke a number of things at the crawling stage—a rattle, a bottle, his father's glasses. His first word was in fact "Bwoke." At nine months Dr. Escalona called him "the most impatient little fellow you ever saw." He was driven, he ate on the run, with meals developing into a contest with the mother. He resisted diapering, and after the struggle was over he would rise to his feet with squeals of triumph.

With such early drives for autonomy, it is understandable that the toilet-training period was a struggle with the mother. She began, as do many lower-middle-class mothers, at nine months, but he was not trained for bowel and bladder until past the twenty-seventh month. In fact, he developed enuresis after the second child was born and slipped back in his training. Enuresis remained a problem for him as we shall see into his tenth year. The mother states he was more difficult to train than any of the other children.

He was rated as one of the highly vulnerable children by Grace Heider on the basis of his high motoric discharge and his extreme sensitivity put alongside a mother who overstimulated him and did not help him withdraw or defend himself against his environment. Dr. Escalona predicted that he would have difficulties either in speech or in the oedipal stage of his development, that he would have nightmares or enuresis. As it turned out her predictions were all fulfilled in this boy. He had a good intelligence and was able to use his motor skills in mastering difficulties in his environment. However, the "driven" nature of his attempts became highly manifest as he reached the age of five. At a preschool party he was given a pair of stilts by an observer. He spent a good deal of time trying to master them. His defense was "I can't. I'm too big." Then correcting himself, "I'm too little." (WK, 1954) He displayed a lot of jittery, surface anxiety, which he attempted to discharge through play. He would not stop once he had started but would push himself way beyond his limits. It is this "drivenness" which kept him so highly vulnerable to stress.

This drivenness came out most forcefully in his speech difficulties. His mother reported to the pediatrician that he did not speak words until eighteen months or phrases until thirty months, and that these were understandable only to the mother. When at five years it was obvious that he was not articulating or pronouncing words distinctly, he was started at a university speech clinic. His trouble was described as functional, the result of hurried and jumbled phonation which leads apparently to the substitutions and omissions. (RLS, 1953) His speech had improved by the time he was in first grade, but the "push of speech" continued to be a characteristic of him, and even in his teens he would stumble over a word or transpose words in a sentence in his hurried way.

Control for a boy of this high drive could be expected to be a problem, and it was. The battle for control was begun during toilet training and continued into the preschool years. He threw temper tantrums at eighteen months and was still having them at five. He resented his mother's working and would become alarmed that she would not return from work. He would not fight with the other children; however, his brother Ben, being more aggressive than he, would. He did not develop affectional bonds with Ben either, preferring his mother's company. His father took a second job when Terry was five, so that the mother could work only part time. The mother began a practice of letting Terry climb into bed with her at night or in the morning until the father returned. This provocative, sexually stimulating behavior at the time when Terry felt an intense desire for her surely added fuel to the flames of his oedipal conflict. The father was home, but he was absent a good deal of the time, which also must have led Terry to imagine that he might possess the mother for himself alone. The fears which this aroused in him were fears of being hurt or having something broken, or at least being cast out of the family. The themes in his fantasy were of danger, of enemies, of big people doing things to little people, and of brokenness. The kidnapping murder of a small child in a nearby city brought on an anxiety attack expressed in continual concern that someone would kidnap mother or daddy. He handled this with humor, however, after talking it over with his mother, saying "Do you think they will kidnap the chair tonight, mommy?" (GH, 1955)

Terry was therefore still highly vulnerable at the preschool age. He experienced the oedipal conflict with great intensity, and, as was apparent in infancy, he did not know how to escape overstimulation. He was still anxious over "brokenness," and he would not "eat a broken cookie or play with a broken toy." He defended himself by "being on the go all the time," and by action solutions. "Now you give me a real hard one," he ordered the psychologist (LBM, 1954) as if he preferred a structured test better than a free, unstructured situation. He had a bravado front and the beginning of compulsive mechanisms usually not seen in a child this age. (PT, 1954) On the positive side, the psychologist said, "He could with considerable skill and resourcefulness utilize perceptual acuity and motor capacities in deep concentration and direction toward a goal. This was especially true with new or difficult material. He sometimes tried to avoid, postpone or substitute but was quite amenable to limits once they were definitely established." (AM, 1954)

The formation of Terry's conscience, therefore, came following the oedipal period with the introjection of the mother's demands. He had previously been moving in the direction of compulsivity and perfectionism. But without an identification figure in his father, he could not deal with this side of the family triangle. Rather he had to meet the mother on her own grounds and defend himself against her "nagging" and "pressure to conform" by outdoing her at her own game. To handle his fears of brokenness—whether his own or his mother's—he would not have anything to do with a broken toy. He once spent a good deal of time rearranging the ladders of a toy fire truck so that they would set just right. (LBM, 1954) Messiness in the bedroom was a real irritation to him, and he would gripe to his mother about it. (It is to be remembered that he shared a bedroom with his brothers.) He demanded more of himself, and incidentally of the family, than she did. The mother said that the parents are moderate in their ethical behavior— swearing in anger, gambling a little, drinking a little. But during latency Terry would admonish his father if he said "Damn," and he felt that any drinking or gambling was wrong. (CWS, 1962)

How did Terry learn to control his drives, his aggression and sexual drives? It has been intimated earlier that he handled his aggression by attacks on things in his environment, but he feared attacks on people. He was not a bully but rather retreated from open conflict with other boys. He feared that if his anger were expressed openly against father or mother they might abandon him. He therefore developed compulsive and perfectionistic strivings in activity. When tested, if he failed on a performance task, he would want to continue until he completed it perfectly. (AM, 1954) He would project his failure upon the test or the tester and become critical of both. He would not fight back openly but would do so in an indirect fashion, as in passive resistance. As we shall see in prepuberty, when he found an activity in which he could excel, such as Scouts or the Knights of the Altar, he would not be satisfied until he had mastered the highest rank and then might criticize the adults for not allowing him the rank because of his age. The anger is beneath the surface, but he is afraid to express it openly for fear of counterattack. One would expect "controls" to be a continuing problem for Terry in adolescence.

Reality Testing. Fantasy has been an avenue of escape for this boy particularly in evidence in the preschool period of testing. We have already discussed how hearing about a kidnapping and murder of a child his age threw Terry into an anxiety attack. This incident must have tapped some of his own fantasy life, so that it released some of his fears about an attack on his own wholeness or that of his mother. His play centered around bigness and littleness (themes of power) and of damage (the big person hurting the little one). On the Miniature Life Toys he was preoccupied at first with the broken toys, moving back and forth in a jerky, irritated, and frustrated way for the first hour. The second hour, he found most satisfaction with structured games, with impersonal give and take. In a family type doll-play he was concerned about the mother and said, "I wonder where the daddy could ever be," recalling the oedipal struggle. With Dr. Moriarty he fantasied on the word "brave," to tell the story of "The Brave Little Indian." And brokenness again bothered him, saying when given a puzzle to solve, "Hook, what the mattah? Am you teasing? I can't believe this. There's no horsey. This was never a cut-up horse." (AM, 1954)

On the Children's Wechsler Intelligence Scale, he saw the "body of a woman in the eye of a man on the face puzzle"—a rare occurrence. He responded to the shipwreck item on the same test with the explanation that women and children are saved first "Because they're the most important item . . . because the women have babies and children got a good life ahead of them." We shall look at this remark again when considering his identity crisis.

In the fifth grade he had an anxiety attack over the approaching end of the world. One can imagine certain reality overtones to this, with the imminent dangers of war in various parts of the world. However, the fantasy was that his world was in danger, and because of something he had done or thought or felt. He encapsulated his fantasy life, and it became a means of his getting distance from an otherwise threatening environment. He used fantasy not just emotionally but intellectually in terms of plot creation and manipulation. This is seen in particular in his use of the Thematic Apperception Test and the Godin Religious Projective pictures. On the TAT he used the Peter Pan story to tell of a little boy who did not want to grow up, but who lost his shadow (his identity?). On the Godin test he used at least three movie plots, all of which had distance to them, but which he embroidered in quite a bizarre fashion.

In summary fashion Dr. Moriarty says,

Terry shows the capacity to shift from secondary to primary processes easily—but he clutches to reality as long as he can, as a measure of security and tries to take it along to the deeper primary process too. Conflicts, emotions and affect shatter this hold and Terry is lost, his concentrated energy gets diffused, his play activities become disrupted, loose and incoherent; and he needs an external authority or control to get him out of it. Once he lands in fantasy play, he seems to cling to that; one gets the feeling that he is like a baby who is reluctant to give up anything that happens to come in his grasp. (MLT, PT, WK, 1957)

In adolescence the sex-role conflicts and the identity diffusion are very apparent on the projective test. Reality is presented as something to "get lost in," or "to fade into." (CWS, 1962) It is no longer presented as something to be fought or struggled with, but as something threatening and fear evoking. Says the psychiatrist of Terry, "Eleven is the privileged age for him. 'The oldest is best, I get to grow up first.' He tended to look back on eleven as a golden age, in contradistinction to Helen who continually looked ahead." (PT, 1959) The psychologist interpreting his Rorschach at pre-puberty found him to be

expansive and ambitious. . . . He is also strong in the trait of conformity. In spite of his conformity, however, he shows strong oppositional tendencies. He protests, argues, apologizes but conforms. He seems to be unsure of himself, reluctant to commit himself and at the same time distressed with his difficulty. . . . He seems particularly vulnerable to his inner doubts and misgivings, seeking new answers for his own reactions and dissatisfactions with the given propositions. Reality-testing suffers from his tendency to be expansive and perhaps a need to be original. The test shows an admixture of the impulsive child and self-critical adolescent. (PH, 1961)

Terry is therefore aware of reality—of the necessity to grow up— but in fantasy he is still *Peter Pan*. He looks back on the golden years of childhood and would return to them if he could. Yet there is also something of the restless search to make sense out of confusion, to "straighten out the family situation" (as he reports on the Godin, [CWS, 1962]) and to find sincerity among sham—even the sham and pretense of his own family "trying to look like a real family." (CWS, 1962) In fact, the big change in him from twelve to four-teen—when he entered adolescence—is some recognition of the folly and futility of trying to possess his mother even in fantasy. He is critical of the do-nothingness of his father, having turned from him as an identification figure early in life. But he knows that the family should have more to it than he has experienced—more controls, more structure, more genuine feeling. He feels robbed, though he won't let this feeling into awareness. However, he peoples his stories with priests who are disguised bandits, with mothers and fathers who wear a facade, and with lovers who play act rather than actually relate to each other. (CWS, 1962) One feels his defense of intellectualization is still prominent, but the unrest and the insecurity and the doubt are being turned now toward his experience in the family. If he can turn his intelligence to solving interpersonal

101

problems he will begin to face reality outward—as an adolescent must face it.

Identity Struggle. One becomes aware of Terry's struggle to discover who he is, as he enters adolescence and is involved in the "identity crisis." For him it is more of a crisis than for Helen. As we have observed, he did face the latency period without an adequate identification figure in his father and had to introject his mother's standards. Earlier he had undergone some sex-role diffusion in being cared for by both father and mother, because of his mother's starting to work three months after his birth. One should say, however, that his mother has meant most to him, even though she has been nagging and sexually provocative. His father has until the past year been an "absent parent." Even when he was around on Sunday or a holiday, he appeared to want to watch TV rather than play with the children. (GH, 1955) He is not as intellectual as the mother, nor as ambitious. Terry resembles her side of the family, says the mother, rather than the father's. (GH, 1955)

The sex-role diffusion has led to some question about his own masculinity. Although highly motoric and bursting with nervous energy, he has tended to fight with his hand tied behind his back, because mother wouldn't allow it. The mother herself was concerned about this, feeling he tended to be a sissy at the time he started to school. (GH, 1955) The figure of Peter Pan is an identity figure which is asexual, that is not worried about becoming a man and having to assume the tasks of a man. One finds the role of the priest also as one which is asexual, that is, it is a means of being a father to a flock without having to go through the storms of sexuality and the responsibilities of biological paternity. When we examine his vocation we shall see how this appears to Terry as a means of solving the sexual role confusion.

The second identification which Terry carried into latency is of a fragile person, even an injured one. Vulnerability was felt in all its deep physiological counterparts by this boy—when he stuttered, when he wet the bed, and when his high energy bumped him against an unyielding environment. One can understand how, after he took to his crutches with an ailing hip and then stumbled on them and broke an ankle, he could feel fragile. It is on the Rorschach that this "brokenness" of self-image comes out in psychosomatic

102

preoccupation. Terry's body had not been adequately integrated into his feeling for himself, though he has been motoric in his attempts to accommodate to his environment. Dr. Moriarty points out that in the Wechsler IQ test he shifted from a higher score on the performance in latency to a higher score on the verbal in prepuberty. (AM, 1960)

When he was evaluated at the clinic, there was some feeling that the parents rewarded a nonidentification with the father. As his doctor stated,

At one and the same time the mother seems to tease him into action which she has already tabooed and follows this up by stopping his mode of adaptation. Somehow this whole family seems to take pleasure in deprivation. They seem confused as to what they want to withhold. In one sense Terry does not have a mother since she is gone so much of the time and when she is home her role is so interchangeable with that of the father that no clear sex differentiation is perceptible to the boy.

His attendance at a parochial school provided him with an identification figure in the person of a priest. The only other ambition he had stated was at nine when he said, "I'd like to be Jesse James or like Jesse James." The priest came into classes and reviewed them on religon. One, according to the mother, Father Dunn, was quite controversial, asking difficult questions to stir up discussion in class and demanding perfect performance of the children as altar boys. (CWS, 1962) One can imagine, even though Terry reacted bitterly to his freedom in the classroom and his perfectionism at the altar, this young man stirred his admiration. Another priest, Father Dowe, even though quieter and more passive, was his football coach and sponsored his Scout troup. The father, though a Scout committeeman, did not have time for him while he was passing his achievements, though he did become Scoutmaster when Terry was fourteen, after the achievements were accomplished. Terry's image of himself as an altar boy, in which he made it to the top, and as an Eagle Scout, in which he excelled, has given him confidence that he can be aggressive and succeed in what he sets his mind to. The highest profession in the church appears to him as an identity, in which many conflicts can somehow be resolved.

Religious Vocation. All of which brings us to the central focus in this boy's life: the ambition to become a priest. He has not clearly made up his mind, but at times seems certain and at times indefinite, says his mother. Whence came this desire, and what are its psychodynamic roots? The family, according to the priest, are practical Catholics, which he says means they are not extreme in their religious devotion. The father, in particular, came from a mixed marriage and did not begin to practice his faith until his marriage. The mother admits that she too has not been extreme in her religious practice, but she did notice this son's early intensity about religion.

Terry remembers he practiced his religion before he went to school, by which he meant he knew his prayers. At the age of five he had three statues from the dentist for being a good soldier: a pig, a cow, and the child Jesus. During this period he decided not to pray any more because he thought it to be childish nonsense. But a year later in the first grade he was annoyed when the sisters would not allow the noisy pupils to pray at school. (GH, 1955) Religion was a habit system for him evidently through latency, for he said his prayers faithfully every night. He wanted to join the Knights of the Altar when the opportunity arose and learned to parrot the Latin responses. He worked so eagerly on the requirements for the Commander Knight that he "stimulated the whole class" his mother said. (CWS, 1962) It was the activity which attracted him, particularly the service projects. One notices the same thing later when he works for the Eagle Scouting award—he passes the achievements and gets his merit badges and lacks simply the opportunities to get the award.

In evaluating his religious interview and the questionnaires about belief the striking thing to notice is the absence of emotional commitment or involvement in the ideas. He knows the correct doctrines and is able to assent to them. He is even able to argue about certain fine points of doctrine, but he denies any feelingful response to the mass or any subjective aspect to his belief. He has taken first communion and become confirmed because this is what a good Catholic does. However, feeling is looked on as something to be held in check.

There is a story which comes out of his childhood in which one learns of his being profoundly moved. This concerns a wild bird which someone had found and which he and the whole family pitched in to help pull through its weakness. Terry cared for it as he had not done for anything up to then. The third day Ben gave it to the baby who, unbeknownst to anyone, choked it. When Terry discovered this, he was hurt and took the bird out and buried it early in the morning alone. Terry has served mass at funerals and known of his grandparents' death. This was the one sorrow his mother can recall which he expressed openly, and the one time he showed open caring. (GH, 1958)

The emotions which are operative in Terry are, therefore, not a desire to help others or to serve God, but conflicted emotions which come out of the family. One sees the priesthood not as a vocational calling so much as a paradigm of his interpersonal and intrapersonal conflicts and a means of resolving them to some degree of satisfaction. One sees these around the conflict between himself and his mother and father. Internalized, these conflicts can be seen as centering around sexuality, aggression, anxiety, and guilt. We have seen Terry's struggle for some kind of control of his tempestuous drives; we have discussed his use of fantasy and reality in some attempt to come to grips with his environment; we have followed his search for identity. How do all these trends come to focus in his vocational choice?

In the first place, Terry has discovered in the parochial school and the church necessary lines of authority, the boundaries and the structures which keep his unruly drives in some kind of order. The problem of control for him is central, and the sublimation which he has attained as he enters the teens is in large part the result of such boundaries. He sought it from his parents, but because of the turmoil of the home with mother on one shift and father on another, with too many siblings in one room to break one's toys and keep things messed up, with contradictory means of handling him, he has wanted a structure in which the lines of authority are clear. And he has found it in the church. The church can provide him with rules; in particular in the priesthood it can provide him with an order of life and a discipline under which he can live. His two visits to the Benedictine monastery, though not appealing so far as to what kind of priest he wants to become, have shown him the

105

ordered life. Here is a place for a "rebel with a cause," appealing to his need to conform.

Again he has found in the organization a way of channeling his aggressive drive. He is intensely ambitious, and motorically oriented. He can in the church live an active, busy life as demonstrated to him by the priests he has known. He has achieved already in the church, by becoming a Commander Knight, making Eagle Scout, passing his ad altare Dei. He knows he can succeed in this way, and the hierarchy of the church offers him a means of sublimating his aggression in constructive action. One wonders if there is guilt hidden behind such intense drive, particularly the compulsive side of it. In answer to the question, "Would being a priest be a way of doing penitence?" he said,

No, I don't think so. 'Course it is somewhat of a penitence because you give up everything, public life, family, but it's some type of penitence. Well it's not like—well, you get more out of it—it's not really a penitence, you receive more than you give . . . you receive special graces and you never have to worry about socks or belts or anything that normal people have to do. I mean other people in other walks of life have to worry about, and then of course, in the religious life you get a hundred-fold. Christ said that any person in the religious life will get a hundred-fold when they reach heaven and they will be much happier than the average person when they reach heaven. (PT, 1961)

Which leads us to his intensive struggle with the sexual side of his nature. It would be one way of controlling his sexual drive if he were to renounce marriage and take the vow of chastity. There exists in him a split now between woman on a pedestal, as the Virgin Mary, and woman in the gutter, as a prostitute. This split would be perpetuated in the church, one would guess, with whatever love he feels coming out in a sublimated way in his devotion toward Mary. If there is any devotional feeling in him, it appears to be expressed in the mother-son relationship involved in prayer to Mary. However, he is aware that taking the ordination vows would not still the voice of the devil. He says,

In fact, they (the priests) need more prayers than normal people do because they have more temptation and they have much more trials than a normal person meets in life. . . . The devil is always trying to make them sin more because they're in a place of God on earth and so they try to make them sin and then of course then you have to say your rosary every day and then in mass, there's certain part in mass that if you forget one word you have to say—in Concentration, if you leave out one word, then you commit a mortal sin because the bread and wine is the body of Jesus Christ and a mortal sin develops . . . if you leave out the word. (JM, 1961)

He is aware of the sin of masturbation now and the guilt it inspires. He feels in penance some means of grace in mastering the guilt. But it was in the talk with his mother that he got some relief that it wasn't as bad a sin as the church teaches. In a real sense the masturbation storms are a part of the old oedipal problem, and it is significant that he would confess this to his mother.

It is in the oedipal triangle that one finds Terry's deepest motivation. The priesthood offers him a socially acceptable and available solution to the conflict-laden relationship with his parents. His mother wants him to take this solution, probably to answer some of her own ambition and striving for status. She said to the interviewer with her face lighted up, "Maybe it's something I'm hoping for too much, for I would love for him to be a priest." (CWS, 1962) Father is mystified by the whole thing; he is not sure what he would do if he had a son who became a priest. The mother is not pushing him, except subtly, in this direction, as she worries over his drop in interest in the church or fears his excursion into adolescent swearing. She may unconsciously feel this to be a way she can keep him from another woman and yet see him go on to success and glory in mature life, and find some reflection of this glory. Terry no doubt feels this unconsciously in his relationship with his mother, that being a priest is a way he can please her and get her undying praise.

In the interpersonal relationships of himself to father and mother, however, the priesthood may appeal to Terry for certain unconscious reasons. For it appears to have the means of keeping the proper distance from his father, an established closeness with his mother, and setting himself in relationship with the community in a role which will have status but will not demand too intensive

107

relationships. Terry's mother thinks he would make a better priest-teacher than a parish priest, for the reasons that he would be too demanding of his parishioners and too perfectionistic with them. (CWS, 1962) This remark is significant on several levels, in that it shows the mother's awareness of Terry's drives to perfection on the one hand, and it shows her conception of the priesthood on the other. Realistically she wants the best for her son and does not want him to be unhappy in his profession.

Terry, on the other hand, would be able to please his mother and to relate to her as the ideal man, while keeping his father at safe distance. The father's confusion at Terry's ambition shows how he may feel outflanked by Terry's competitive bid for the mother's heart. On the other hand, he may feel that he has failed the boy in not offering him a suitable identification figure. Terry would desexualize the whole conflict, in that he would rise above the sexual level to the ascetic level. And in the mother-son relationship seen in Jesus and Mary he would idealize his relationship with his mother. In addition he would be able to keep emotional distance from people from the higher level of the priesthood and yet have status in their eyes. He may not be aware of the demanding character of the priest-parishioner relationship here but may have romanticized this in some regard.

One needs to ask in conclusion whether these motivations for the priesthood betray defensive maneuvers or coping procedures on Terry's part. It would appear that the motivation to resolve the oedipal conflict by finding distancing and approach procedures through the priesthood might be said to be a defense. The sexual and aggressive drives would be controlled through the vows to the church, but behind this would be an uneasy peace. It would seem that this is not sublimation in a realistic sense but would still have many conflictive aspects which would break out in adulthood. The thing it lacks is an investment in the primary objects of religion, God, Christ, and even Mary. And one discovers that so far as Terry is concerned these concepts lack feeling tone, with the exception of Mary. There is, however, a redeeming side to Terry, part of which has been with him from childhood and part of which may be arising as a part of the adolescent identity crisis and that is his analytic, problem-solving side, with its emotional corollary of doubt. Right now he doubts his reasons for going into the priesthood and whether he has an authentic call. He wants to analyze religion and to ferret out the answers with his good, intact intelligence. He doubts authorities, at first parental and now those which have taught him through school. This doubt often is turned now toward himself— when the authority of the church seems so strong. And he phrases this in terms of whether he has an authentic call, one defined by the church. This is active coping with the vocational side of his life. If, in fact, he decides to go into the priesthood and through the high school years is able to get beyond intellectualizing and hiding the feelingful side of his nature, he may be able with his whole being to make an authentic commitment to God and the church. This, however, would be sorting out the "dated emotions" coming from his family triangle and doing this because it bears the hallmark of himself over against God's call. It may be asking too much of him. But it would mean a moving from his present vulnerable position to one of ego strength in maturity.

Without prejudging Terry's religious orientation, the reader will want to ask: How does Terry's religious stance differ from Helen's? Are there similarities between him and her in the way each established controls over their strong drive systems? Does Terry's religious identity (bandit priest—prodigal son) differ radically from Helen's? What are the healthy and what are the unhealthy aspects of this identity? Does Terry's desire to become a priest—now temporarily put aside—appear to have more or less faith commitment to it than Helen's private devotion toward God? The reader is not asked to take any prior interpretation as final but to wrestle out these questions for himself.

We shall now turn to the religious practices of the larger group of fifty. It should be noted that in this section of the United States the churches still hold a formidable place in the community. The families studied are typical of the middle-class group in Capital City. The questions of conventionality and conformity in the parents and their children can be studied with some hope of gaining some clarity about the problem. Terry is a religious activist, but Roddy, the boy we will discuss next, is a secular activist. It should be possible to ask then, what difference does the church make in the lives of these two boys? And what difference do "religious activities" make in the growth and development of the entire group?

6

Religious Practices

At the very beginning of this study, as well as at the end, each consultant made a statement which indicated that the youth who were involved with the study were not sincerely religious, but were simply conventional in the practice of the faith which their parents practiced. The first statement was by a psychiatrist who had interviewed more than forty of the young people in the Child Study group. He stated that the adolescents represented in the sample were institutionalists and conformists so far as religious and moral behavior is concerned. With one or two exceptions they have not experienced firsthand struggle with religious realities, by which he meant sin, guilt, forgiveness, redemption, faith, and commitment. They were living on values fed into them by their parents, such as "Don't stick your neck out," "Obey the rules while the boss is around," "Don't rat on a friend." But he felt that in terms of the transcendental they were oblivious. This is revealed in little concern about the soul after death, about a direct experience with God, or with the risk side of faith. He stated that the youth see the discrepancy between what parents say they believe and what they do. Therefore, they, the youth, pay lip service to the articles of belief but their real loyalties are the corporate values, namely what the group thinks and says and tells them to do. This is instrumentalism with a vengeance. What gives them importance is acceptance by the group, the security and material things which lend them security and momentary pleasures. There is fear of the bomb which gives rise to fear of death. There is insecurity represented by the draft. There is an awareness of the social revolution, represented by the Negro uprising in the south. But the fact that the churches by and large appear to be keeping their skirts clean of this, and that the teaching of the churches is irrelevant to social issues makes them see the difference between theology and life. The shocking thing is that many do not see such a difference between the preaching and practice of the church because they are attending the church, church school, and youth group for purely utilitarian reasons. The church is out of phase with society, but so are they. Therefore, there is a conventionality and superficiality about the young people betrayed by their practices.

The psychologist echoed this expression at the end of the study after doing some ratings on the conventionality of belief on the part of the thirty youth of the sample. He stated that he felt that by and large the young people were conventional in their beliefs and practices, that they attended church or church school or the youth group but did not have motivation in and for themselves. He felt that they knew the words but not the music of religion, that they were uninfluenced by it, and that they took their values from the peer group or from the corporate society, with tastes set by radio, television, movies, and teen magazines. He did not see the church as relevant to youth. Moreover, he felt that parents, being out of phase with both the adult group and the youth group, were unable to articulate their own values beyond that of conformity with what society demanded of them. Therefore, they did not serve as adequate teachers of their children. Most of the ministers, he felt, were not in touch with young people and therefore could not serve as religious and moral guides for the majority. There might be exceptions in this group, he felt, mainly because of the midwestern, semirural area which they came from, but more than likely they reflect the urban values and beliefs which are prevalent among the young people in and around large urban centers throughout the nation.

It is to test the reliability of these statements with a sample of forty-six to fifty young adolescents that this chapter is concerned. What are the participation patterns by Protestant and Catholic youth in a large midwestern state capital? What is the feeling toward the church by the adolescents and their parents? What attracts and detracts young people from church school, from parochial school religion classes, the youth fellowship, or similar Catholic clubs? What, in other words, can one say about their religious behavior measured against the behavior of their parents and the impressions and evaluation of their religious leaders? What is the religious activity in the home? That is, what are the practices of prayer, the observance of religious holidays, the religious sayings of the mother over against secular sayings, and how does religion influence their daily life, particularly in matters of morals? Finally, what is the role of personal religion summed up in the parent's life and in the youth's life, with examples of both drawn from the interviews? Conventionality or conformity patterns will become apparent as this kind of intensive study is completed.

To get answers to these and other questions, the interviewing psychologist, Mrs. Julie Fewster, went to the homes of over fifty of the youth and spent an hour and a half with the mother supplementing information received from the minister which she obtained in another interview. In most instances, using controlled probing type questions, showing interest in the youth for his own sake, the psychologist obtained the information needed. The fact that she was interested at the time in attending a school of theology and in going into religious education herself allowed her to gain rapport with the mothers and pastors. I have found in similar fashion that my religious role serves as a means of gaining rapport with the youth. In only two instances were the mothers so hostile to religion that the major questions could not be asked. In several instances, however, the mother's psychological needs were so great that she gave considerably more information about herself than the youth. However, the means employed in gaining information about religious practices can be termed successful in that we were able to gather the information needed.

113

1. INSTITUTIONAL PRACTICES

According to Gordon Allport, an individual's religious behavior can be either institutional or interiorized. By this he means the individual can conform to rigid in-group practices for social reasons, or he can practice his faith as a way of life for its own sake. More recently, he has called these two modes of religious behavior extrinsic and intrinsic. The extrinsic person (formerly the institutionalist) practices his religion for utilitarian self-serving reasons; his religious behavior "confers safety, status, comfort and talismanic favors upon the believer." An "intrinsic" religion is "larger than the self, wholly beyond the self, directed to what Rudolf Otto calls the 'numinosum'—or the Holy." [1]

Granting that all adolescents are a mixture of intrinsic and extrinsic motives, it serves our purpose to examine how well they conform or do not conform to their parents' and religious leaders' expectations of them as to institutional practices.

By far the largest group in our study is the conventional group (44.4 percent; 26.6 percent active against 24.4 percent inactive). The attitudes run along a spectrum from dependence through warmth, approval, and neutral to resistance. By dependence is meant that the youth or his family lean heavily upon the church for their support; by warmth is meant that the persons respond with strong emotion toward the church but more for the purpose of guidance and direction; by approval is meant that the persons approve generally of the church and its program, however, without strong commitment to it; by neutrality is meant that the persons do not fight the church, neither do they support it very strongly; by resistance is meant that there is a negative attitude toward the church which prevents attendance or support.

Church Participation

Conventional attendance means at least once a month; above that is rated regular attendance, below that is rated seldom attend or inactive.

[1] Gordon Allport, *Religion in the Developing Personality* (New York: Academy of Religion and Mental Health, University Press, 1960, p. 33.

For only 13.3 percent can religion be said to play a leading role in the home; i.e., where religion is practiced as a family group. [2]

Church Participation by Protestant and Catholic Youth[3]

Name	Attendance Pattern	Attitude Toward Church Parents	Youth
1. Lowell	Attend as a group	Warm	Dependence
2. Warren	Attend church school	Approval	Warm
3. Wayne	Attend as a group	Warm	Warm
4. Jordan	Attend as a group	Warm	Warm
5. Kendle	Attend as a group	Dependence	Dependence
6. Taylor	Attend as a group	Dependence	Approval
7. Gregory	Mother, youth attend, father less	Warm	Warm
8. Cooper, R & C	Mother, youth attend, father less	M Warm; F Neutral	R Neutral C Resistance
10. Coach	Mother, youth attend, father less	Warm	Approval
11. Dickinson	Mother, youth attend, father less	M Dependence; F Neutral	Approval
12. Howe, D & V	Mother, youth attend, father less	M Dependence; F Approval	V Warm D Approval
14. Holt	Mother, youth attend, father less	Approval	Approval
15. Scarf, N.	Conventional	Approval	Approval
16. Montbatten	Conventional	Approval	Warm
17. David	Conventional	Approval	Approval
18. Williams	Conventional	Approval	Warm
19. Rogers, S & M	Conventional	Approval	S Approval M Warm
21. Saunders	Conventional	Approval	Approval
22. Wolfe	Conventional	Approval	Warm
23. Boston	Conventional	F Warm; M Approval	Approval
24. Scarf, C.	Conventional	M Approval; F Neutral	Resistance
25. Caster, S.	Conventional	M Warm; F Neutral	Warm
26. Moffat	Conventional	M Approval; F Neutral	Approval
27. Wilkins	Conventional	M Warm; F Neutral	Resistance
28. Brown	Conventional	M Approval; F Neutral	Approval

[2] National statistics show about two thirds of the population belong to some church (here about 71 percent). There is no way to measure conventionality by statistics except that of total membership. Denominational groups in the U. S. report one third of their members attend church each Sunday.

[3] Ratings follow interview with both mother and minister and are checked by staff of the Normal Development Project.

Name	Attendance Pattern	Attitude Toward Church	
		Parents	Youth
29. Stevens	Conventional	M Approval; F Neutral	Approval
30. Brand	Conventional	M Approval; F Neutral	Resistance
31. Chase	Conventional	F Warm; M Approval	Neutral
32. Ramsey, Sh & St	Conventional	F Warm; M Approval	Sh Approval St Approval
34. Redding	Conventional	M Approval; F Neutral	Approval
35. Todd	Seldom	M Approval; F Neutral	Approval
36. Paulson	Seldom. Conventional before divorce	M Approval; F Neutral	Approval
37. Porter	Seldom	M Approval; F Neutral	Resistance
38. Timberlake	Inactive. Daughter active	M and F Neutral	Warm
39. Moore	Inactive	M and F Neutral	Resistance
40. Holloway	Inactive	M and F Neutral	Approval
41. Rust	Stepparents inactive	M and F Neutral	Warm
42. Wilson	Inactive	Resistance	Neutral
43. Trainor	Inactive	Resistance	Approval
44. West	Inactive	Resistance	Resistance
45. Spencer	Inactive	M Approval; F Resistance	Resistance

A second look at the preceding chart turns up another piece of evidence. By measuring the parents' attitude toward the church against the youths', one becomes aware of the conditioning effects of the parents' attitude, as well as the pattern of conformity handed down from one generation to another. In the group which attend as a total family the attitudes of dependence, warmth, and approval are transmitted with few exceptions. The parents' example of church attendance and participation in the religious community is caught—particularly from those parents who may teach youth in church school, youth group, or confirmation class. Among the families where the father's participation is less than the mother's, the girls tend to keep up the same level of interest as the mother, with one exception. Daryl who is backing off from being called a "Holy Joe" by her peers, now refuses to attend daily mass. The boys, however, tend to follow the father's participation pattern or attempt to gain some independence from weekly attendance. When the father attends less, the boys see this as a chink in the family's religious armor and use it as a reason for staying home. The Cooper boys are an example of this. Ray says, "Nobody likes church. I'm not going

116

when I'm big." The minister reports, "Chester will come and usually sit in the back seat and slump down showing little interest. In fact, he's very apathetic." Mrs. Cooper: "The girls haven't had a negative attitude toward religion as have the boys. This is probably because they have friends here." Generally speaking, one may conclude that where the father shows less interest, the mother's interest may be transmitted to the girls, but the boys, after puberty, may desire to stop attending church.

In conventional homes, where the parents attend church more irregularly and with an extrinsic motivation, the young people in all likelihood develop the same attitude. In four instances youth have a more positive attitude toward church than their parents. For Mark and Milly it is because of excellent parochial school training; for Milly the change from rebellion to warmth has come within the past year. For Julia and Stanley it is the influence of a Protestant pastor.

In the conventional families where one parent is less interested in church than the other, resistance toward church develops in three of the youths and neutrality in one. The young person goes a step beyond the parents and may for personal reasons or because friends have stopped going rebel against going himself. The conventional parent is at a loss as to how to handle this. For example, Jack says about going to church, "Oh, do I have to?" Sylvia says, "Jane doesn't go, so why should I?" Jennifer's mother: "She will attend, but she's not particularly eager to go." "Donald's older brother is no longer home to set a good example; his father lacks interest; the entire family has become more lax," says Mrs. Dickinson.

The majority attend with some regularity, but, as the religious interviewer discovered, with "approval" rather than with a consuming interest. This attitude is not neutrality but conformity and conventionality, one may conclude. The peer group attends and the young person goes because parents desire it and "it is the thing to do."

In the seldom attenders and inactive families one notices two phenomena of profoundly different nature. First, as one might expect, the youth whose parents do not attend refuse to attend themselves after they reach adolescence. The largest number of resisting

117

youth are in this group. One mother, Mrs. West, flatly refused to discuss religion with the interviewer. Her daughter behaved the same way; for her religion was a "bug-a-boo" and clearly off limits. However, in two inactive families the daughters display a warmth toward religion and follow the example of peers and siblings in getting to church. Furthermore, in four other families, though the parents do not attend, the youth show approval by attending with some regularity. Here one may allow for the faith filling a void in the young person's life not supplied by the family, or for the church fellowship providing a "larger family" for them. The opposite tendency can be explained in terms of the youths' inner desire for *faith* and for a social group.

Church School Attendance

The first crack in youth's religious behavior is shown in church school attendance. The decline of adult attendance at such classes, though not as strongly felt in the midwest, is still in evidence. If the parents do not attend but go to church instead, the young adolescent may pick up this pattern. The parents' stance toward church school attendance is a big factor in the youth's religious behavior; of equal importance is his own attitude.

Patterns of Church School Attendance and of Parochial School

Name	Parents' Attitude	Youth Attendance	Youth's Influence (+ Positive − Negative)
1. Gregory	Required	Yes	+ desire, parents
2. Lowell	Required	Yes	+ teacher, parents
3. Cooper, C.	Required	Yes	+ teacher, habit
4. Cooper, R.	Required	Yes	+ teacher, habit
5. Dickinson	Required	No	− baseball
6. Warren	Required	Yes	+ teacher, desire
7. Best	Required	Yes	+ teacher, desire
8. Brown	Required	No	− peers
9. Coach	Required	Yes	+ teacher, peers

Name	Parents' Attitude	Youth Attendance	Youth's Influence
10. Caster	Required	Yes	+ content
11. Ivy	Required	Yes	+ parents
12. Montbatten	Required	Yes	+ peers
13. Boston	Required	No	− leadership
14. Taylor	Required	Yes	+ peers, sibs
15. Stevens	Optional	No	− parents, subject
16. Charles	Optional	Yes	+ content
17. David	Optional	No	− sibs, teachers
18. Moore	Optional	Yes	+ peers
19. Moffat	Optional	Yes	+ teacher
20. Porter	Optional	No	− peers
21. Scarf, N.	Optional	Yes	+ parents, − peer
22. Watson	Optional	Yes	+ peer
23. Wolfe	Optional	No	− content, leadership
24. Ramsey, Sh	Not required	Yes	+ parents, habit
25. Ramsey, St	Not required	Yes	+ parents, habit
26. Todd	Not required	No	− peers
27. Timberlake	Not required	Yes	+ peers
28. Wilkins	Not required	No	− parent, teacher
29. Holloway	Not required	No	− parents
30. Scarf, C.	Not required	No	− parent
31. Paulson	Discouraged	No	− parents
32. Rust	Discouraged	Yes	+ sibling
33. Trainor	Non-church	No	− parent
34. Wilson	Non-church	No	− parent

An analysis of these data reveals that twenty-one of thirty-four Protestant youth regularly attend church school in early adolescence (61+ percent). Of those who do not attend, two are required by parents, four have an option, four are not required, and three are discouraged. The youths' behavior becomes more intelligible when one puts the attendance patterns directly parallel with the parents' attitude. When parents require attendance only two of twelve youth do not go. When parents give them an option, five attend and four do not; when not required, three attend and four do not; when

119

discouraged, one attends and three do not. Though the population represented is too small to allow us to generalize, we do notice the interest and requirement of parents is *no small part* in adolescents' attendance at church school.

When we look more directly at what influences the youths' attitude toward church school, we get a clearer picture of participation patterns:

Table 6-1

	Total Influenced	Positive	Negative
Parents	16	11	5
Teachers	15	6	9
Siblings	2	1	1
Peers	8	1	7
Youth's desire	4	4	0
Habit	5	5	0
Subject matter	5	1	4
Other (method)	2	1	1

Our previous conclusion of the parents' predominant influence on young people's attitude toward church school is underscored. In the Taylor, Warren, Jones, and Lowell families parents not only attend but also teach and the children show a good deal of interest. The teacher becomes the central issue for children who are required to attend, and, unfortunately, the larger group is negative. Lack of discipline and preparation of the lesson, repetition of lessons, and boredom by the teachers are mentioned.

As Helen said of church school in the city, "I just dreaded to go to the Sunday school. Boys shot beebees and paper wads. . . . I think if it had been quieter and more peaceful, I would have gotten more out of it." She finds her class in the country much more helpful because of better discipline and a more interested teacher. Roddy liked debate and open discussion where the teacher asked questions. "I thought that was fun because we could all give our views on it."

Young people's going out of habit and out of desire are of equal importance. However, when one looks at the negative influence of peers and siblings, one becomes aware that youth are conforming to peer standards. Sunday school is no longer an "in" kind of behavior, and they drop it to attend church, or, as we shall see, replace it with youth fellowship. Teddy sums up this attitude, "I figured I could get more out of church than I could out of Sunday school. It is more or less the same stuff over and over again, and secondly, there's not the dignity or reverence that you would find in church." One parent, actively involved in Christian education asked, "What can one hope to accomplish meeting only one hour a week and being taught by untrained teachers?" [4]

Youth Fellowship

The youth fellowship is an organization specifically designed for the social and religious needs of adolescents. It differs from the church school in that it is set up and run by the youth with adult advisors. Rather than having formal classes, it has less structure and a more varied and relaxed program of worship, study, and recreation. Recognizing the diminishing appeal of church school, we will find it instructive to see how this group responds to youth fellowship.

It is evident from the following chart that for thirty of the thirty-five Protestant youth a youth fellowship group is available. However, only fifteen, or about fifty percent, attend—considerably fewer

[4] The parochial school set-up is not comparable to Protestant church school. The data on the Roman Catholic children show that all but four of the families send their children. Two of these, however, are no longer communicants. In all instances but the latter, the youth have been subject to religious instruction of a more professional sort than Protestants. The level of catechetical learning is, with a few exception, much higher than the level of "Sunday school" learning.

Name	Parents' Attitude	Youth Attendance	Youth's Influence
35. Bowen	Required	Yes	+ Priest
36. Spencer	Non-church	No	— Parents
37. Rogers, V.	Required	Yes	+ Priest, Nuns
38. Howe, D.	Required	Yes	+ Nuns
39. Howe, V.	Required	Yes	+ Nuns
40. Hall, R.	Required	Yes	+ Nuns
41. Saunders	Not required	No	— Parents
42. Holt	Required	Yes	+ Priest
43. Kendle	Required	Yes	+ Priest
44. Rose	Required	Yes	+ Priest and Nuns
45. Rogers, M.	Required	Yes	+ Priest and Nuns
46. West	Non-church	No	— Parents
47. Wolfe	Required	Yes	+ Nuns

than attend church school. Although we do not have the data, it is highly probable that this is an optional activity so far as parents are concerned, and that the youth attends or does not attend out of his own desire or the influence of his peers. When the items which the young people gave as influencing their attitude toward youth fellowship are tabulated, this hypothesis gains more weight.

Youth Fellowship Attendance Patterns [5]

	Youth Fellowship		
Name	Available	Attend	Attitude
1. Ramsey, Sh	Yes	No	Transporation not available
2. Ramsey, St	Yes	No	Transporation not available
3. Stevens	Yes	No	— Content, leaders, minister
4. Gregory	Yes	Yes	+ Content, leaders
5. Lowell	Yes	Yes	+ Parents
6. Cooper, C.	Yes	Yes YFC	+ Peers, content
7. Cooper, R.	Yes	Yes	+ Peers
8. Todd	Yes	No	?
9. Timberlake, J.	Yes	No	— Peers
10. Dickinson	Yes	Yes	— Content, Baseball
11. Warren	Yes	Yes	+ Content, leaders
12. Best	Yes	No	(Accident)
13. Charles	Yes	No	— Content
14. Caster	Yes	Yes	+ Peers, content
15. Holloway	Yes	No	— Content
16. Ivy	Yes	Yes	+ Peers, parents, leaders
17. Jane	Yes	Yes	+ Peers

[5] Catholic youth, although they do not have a similar type of organization, do have Knights of the Altar for the boys. The participation pattern is as follows:

35. Bowen	Yes	Yes	Priest
36. Spencer	No church	No	— Parent
37. Rogers, V.	Yes	Yes	Priest
38. Howe, D.	No response	No response	No response
39. Howe, V.	No response	No response	No response
40. Hall	No response	No response	No response
41. Saunders	Yes	No	+ Peers
42. Holt	Yes	Yes	Priest
43. Kendle	Yes	Yes	Priest
44. Rose	Yes	No	— Parent
45. Rogers	Yes	Yes	Priest
46. West	No response	No response	No response
47. Wolfe	No response	No response	No response

	Youth Fellowship		
Name	Available	Attend	Attitude
18. Moore	Yes	No	— Content
19. Montbatten	Yes	Yes	+ Peers
20. Moffat	Yes	?	+ Peers, Grandparents
21. Porter	Yes	No	— Peers
22. Paulson	Yes	No	— Parents
23. Rust	Yes	Yes	+ Sib; — Transportation
24. Scarf, C.	Yes	No	(Horse)
25. Wilson	Yes	No	— Parents
26. Watson	Yes	Yes BB	+ Peers
27. Wolfe	Yes	No YC	— Content, leaders
28. Boston	Yes	No	— Leaders
29. Taylor	Yes	Yes	+ Peers
30. Brown	?	?	?
31. David	No	? CSB	?
32. Wilkins	No	No	— Parents, peers, content
33. Scarf, N.	No Church	No	— Leaders, minister
34. Trainor	No Church	No	— Parents

Table 6-2

Participation and/or attitude influenced by:		
Parents	+2	−2
Leaders	+3	−4
Siblings	+1	0
Minister	+1	−4
Peers	+7	−2
Content	+5	−10
Youth leadership	+1	−1
Transportation	0	−3
School activities	0	−1
Other activities	0	−5

Since this is a peer-oriented and peer-led group, the youth are influenced most highly by their contemporaries (nine). Being given responsibility calls out their desire to participate. Sylvia, for example, is reported to have spoken of the feeling of importance at serving on the cabinet and being challenged by those older than she. Bruce J., asked to serve on the Christian education committee, has taken a new interest in the church. Sylvia's mother says her daughter "enjoys the evening youth group for it is more social than Sunday school —the boys in the youth group are one of the main drawing factors." The social life with one's peers which is afforded by the organization is one of its chief attractions. Susan reports negatively that she didn't like the youth fellowship because the minister never let them do anything social. And Diane preferred the youth group at another church where social life is more prominent.

The adult leadership of the group is crucial, according to the data. It would appear that though youth desire responsibility they still need the guidance of their elders in order to organize and run their group. Twice the number reported negative attitudes toward adult leaders, when one adds ministers in the leadership role (—eight to +four). Mrs. Park says, "Attractive cue people are important as leaders." Her son, Greg, is not as interested in the group following the death of a Christian education director. Others criticized the group for failure of adult leadership. In a study of Kansas youth fellowships done in 1961, H. W. Lattimore discovered an adult leader's ability was not rated as very important, but strong emphasis was put on his faith (23 percent); enjoying and understanding youth (23 percent); giving some degree of guidance (23 percent); having interest in and some ideas about the functioning of a youth program (4 percent); and having good character (5 percent).[6] Youth want their adult leaders to "like, love, and understand high school age youth" and they "must enjoy young people without acting like one."

The final area of central importance appears to be the content of the youth fellowship program. Chester prefers "Youth for Christ" (over his disorganized youth group) because of its organized and interesting program. Greg complains that his group needs more service projects. "We always talk about doing something but never do anything." Diane reiterates, "They get up there, we sing a couple of songs and then someone gets up and gives a dull, boring lesson and we decide to have a party that we never do have." Teddy sums up in his solemn way: "I consider it (YF) more or less a supplement to the church. . . . The church meeting is the basis of teaching of

---

[6] "The Youth Fellowship," unpublished manuscript, Lawrence, Kansas, 1961.

the religion and all the supplement should have is perhaps a few more talks and less games than they have at our church." The purpose of the youth fellowship is for learning the faith and developing ways of practicing it within a committed group, the youth in Lattimore's study enunciated. The previous chapter indicated that youth not only wanted to discuss their religious ideas and convictions but "brimmed over" in an interview when given half a chance. The conventionality of most youth groups may be a product of poor organization and poor direction. Were adult leaders and youth to meet on a vital basis, the youth fellowship, now hit and miss, might be a dynamic organization within the church.

Relationship with the Pastor

The families' relationship with the pastor is, within both Protestant and Catholic churches, of tremendous importance in determining whether the family is "intrinsic" or "extrinsic" in their religious practices. The interviewer discovered discrepancies between the pastor's estimate of the religiosity of a family and the family's estimate of their own devotion. She hypothesized the following reasons:

(1) People are more "religious" around their ministers; (2) ministers tend to "accentuate the positive" for they are less critical of people; (3) ministers need to "accentuate the positive" to show their ministry is successful; (4) the minister has a higher concept of church membership than the layman who considers himself a strong member; and (5) the minister is not in active communication with the lay family. The relationship to pastors is both positive and negative in both faith groups as the following chart shows.

Families' Relationship with Minister [7]

	Rating	Member in Church Vocation	Counseling with Him
1. Ramsey, Sh.	+	Yes	Yes
2. Ramsey, St.	+	Yes	Yes

[7] "Member in church vocation" means a parent, uncle, aunt, or cousin is in the ministry; "counseling with him" means family has sought the minister's counsel.

	Rating	Member in Church Vocation	Counseling with Him
3. Timberlake	+	Yes	
4. Wilkins	+	No	Yes
5. Warren	+	No	Yes
6. Best	+	No	No
7. Coach	+	No	Yes
8. Jane	+	No	Yes
9. Paulson	+	No	Yes
10. Rust	+	No	Yes
11. Wolfe, B.	+	No	Yes
12. Taylor	+	No	Yes
13. Bowen	+	Yes	Yes
14. Rogers, V.	+	No	No
15. Rogers, M.	+	No	No
16. Howe, D.	+	No	Yes
17. Howe, V.	+	No	Yes
18. Howard	+	Yes	Yes
19. Kendle	+		Yes
20. Wolfe, A.	+	No	Yes
21. Lowell	Neutral	No	Yes
22. Holloway	Neutral		
23. Ivy	Neutral	Yes	
24. Scarf	Non-church		
25. Trainor	Non-church		
26. Spencer	Non-church	No	Yes
27. West	Non-church	No	No
28. Stevens	—	No	No
29. Caster, S.	—		
30. David	—		
31. Boston	—		Yes
32. Gregory	No answer		
33. Cooper, C.	No answer		Yes
34. Cooper, R.	No answer		Yes
35. Todd	No answer		
36. Dickinson	No answer		Yes
37. Brown	No answer		
38. Charles	No answer	Yes	
39. Moore	No answer		
40. Montbatten	No answer		
41. Moffat	No answer		

	Rating	Member in Church Vocation	Counseling with Him
42. Porter	No answer		
43. Scarf, C.	No answer		
44. Wilson	No answer		
45. Watson	No answer		Yes
46. Saunders	No answer		
47. Rose	No answer		
48. Holt, R.	No answer		

An analysis of the data shows that one third of the Protestants are positive and only one sixth are negative toward their pastors. However, the "no answer" or neutral comments make one wonder if this large number either are not acquainted with or only slightly known by him. On the basis of interview material we can safely say that pastors with large congregations simply did not know their youth personally. The Catholic group know their priest much better, with only three giving "no answer," and are predominantly positive toward him (eight positive and two negative). The parochial school experience has brought them into some relationship with the priest.

The quality of the relationship with pastor and priest is revealed by the counseling relationship with pastor and priest and the number of those families with members in a Christian vocation. Only one seventh of the Protestant families boast a minister as grandparent or uncle, but one fourth of the Roman Catholic families do. Almost half of the Protestant families had sought out their pastor for counseling; however, we note that more than two thirds of the Roman Catholic families had. This probably demonstrates the easy movement from the confessional to counseling room by Catholic young people.

The authority of the priest comes from his office, and the youth appear to respect him for his knowledge and priestly function. Most of the Catholic boys have known him by serving as altar boys. Those who are negative toward him are so because he is not acquainted with them. The authority of the Protestant pastor appears to come more from his personality. The large group of

127

neutrals or conventionals appear not to know him; the negatives, such as Diane, are put off by hypocrisy and judgmental attitudes. Those who are positive have gotten to know him as a friend. Greg, Lenny, and Maurice, all have made personal friendships with the pastor, and Helen looks up to him as an ideal, so much so that she quotes him continually as the authority for her own faith statements. We shall investigate the pastor-youth relationship further in the chapter on confirmation. Enough data are in evidence here to show its seminal importance.

2. RELIGIOUS ACTIVITY IN THE HOME

The second place where one may measure "conformity" is within the homes of the youth. Here one gets a little closer to *intrinsic faith,* as the prayer practices, religious holiday observances, and religious sayings or mottoes come under scrutiny. If, as Randolph C. Miller [8] and others claim, parents are the real teachers of religion, can we discover it within this normal group? Does the Christian faith as expressed through the institutional church have any influence in the lives of these parents and these adolescents? Is it meaningful to the parent and not to the child, or to the child and not to the parent? By adolescence has the peer group become of such importance to the child that neither ministers nor parents wield much influence with him? Has he become a *solid conformist* to what his contemporaries think and feel and value?

Upon entering the home the interviewer noted such things as the prominence of the Bible, of religious pictures, mottoes, and statues within the rooms. However, she found that by talking about when and how often the family prayed and the manner of its practice she was able to get the clearest picture of religious training. She asked about the early teaching of prayers such as "Now I Lay Me" or the "Rosary" and from this led the mother up to the current practice of prayer by the young person. We were interested in the family's reliance on prayer in crisis, as well as its everyday use at bedtime and mealtime.

[8] *Education for Christian Living* (Englewood Cliffs: Prentice-Hall, 1956).

Prayer Practice in the Home

		Crisis	Bedtime	Mealtime
1.	Ramsey, Sh	Yes	Prays constantly	When father is gone
2.	Ramsey, St	Yes	Prays constantly	When father is gone
3.	Gregory	Yes	Until 10	Don't know
4.	Lowell	Yes	30-40 minutes at time	Take turns
5.	Cooper, C.	Yes	Until 9: don't know	Father, children
6.	Cooper, R.	Yes	Until 9: don't know	Father, children
7.	Todd	Yes	Until 8: reminds her	Yes
8.	Wilkins	Yes	Yes: Mother reminds	Yes
9.	Warren	Yes	Yes: always	Yes
10.	Brown	Yes	Yes	Usually
11.	Ivy	Yes	Until 10	Yes
12.	Porter	Yes	When little: Uncertain	Yes
13.	Boston	Yes	No	Yes
14.	Taylor	Yes	Yes	Yes
15.	Nash	Yes	Uncertain	No
16.	Bowen	Yes	Yes	Yes
17.	Howard	Yes	Morning and Evening	Yes
18.	Holt	Yes	Yes	Yes
19.	Charles	Yes	No	Usually
20.	Timberlake	At operation	Until 8	No
21.	Moore	At accident	Until Jr. High, Uncertain	Yes
22.	Montbatten	At accident	When little: Uncertain	No
23.	Wolfe, B.	At operation	Until 8: Uncertain	Yes
24.	Howe, D.	In illness, Test	Yes, in bed	Sign of cross
25.	Howe, V.	In illness, Test	Yes, in bed	Sign of cross
26.	Holloway	At death	Until 11, Uncertain	Yes
27.	Jane	At death	Until 8	Yes
28.	Wolfe, A.	At death	Yes	Yes

	Crisis	Bedtime	Mealtime
29. Coach	No	Yes	At noon
30. Moffat	No	Until Jr. High, Uncertain	No
31. Scarf, N.	No	Now	At noon
32. Spencer	No	No	No
33. Wilson	Not necessary	No	Holy seasons
34. Dickinson	No answer	Don't know	Occasionally
35. Best	No answer	No	No
36. Caster	No answer	Until 9: Uncertain	Yes
37. David	No answer	No	No
38. Paulson	No answer	No	No
39. Rust	No answer	Uncertain	Yes
40. Scarf, C.	No answer	Thought at bedtime	No
41. Trainor	No answer	No	No
42. Howard	No answer	Yes	No
43. Rogers, V.	No answer	When a child: Uncertain	Yes
44. Saunders	No answer	When a child: Uncertain	Yes
45. Rose	No answer	When a child: Uncertain	No
46. Rogers, M.	No answer	When a child: Uncertain	Yes
47. Stevens	No answer	Never	At supper
48. West	No answer	No	No
49. Watson	No answer	No	No

We were fortunate to be able to draw on material gathered by the Normal Development Project immediately following John F. Kennedy's assassination and have pointed to this as an example of the youth's recourse to prayer in national crisis. See table 6-3.

The individual responses are both interesting and significant: the two Howe sisters, both Catholics, said they wanted to go to church and offer sacrifice; Mike Saunders, another Catholic said he thought the only thing he could do was pray; Greg, whom we met in chapter 1, said he felt he must pray; Darlene Lowell, a fundamentalist girl, said "God said in the Bible we must pray for

Table 6-3

Youth's Response to Kennedy Assassination

Those who offered individual prayers	5	10%
Those who attended mass as a group	5	10%
Those who did not mention prayer as a response	40	80%
	50	100%

our enemies"; Diane Taylor prayed and hoped he would live; and Helen prayed and wanted to comfort Mrs. Kennedy. [9]

Several facts are immediately apparent upon a survey of the data: (1) More families pray at times of crisis, such as the death of a relative, sickness, an accident or when a member is in danger than pray every day (50 percent). (2) Parents generally teach their children certain "memory prayers" such as "Now I Lay Me," "Our Father," or the "Rosary" and hear these prayers until the child is old enough to go to bed alone. Almost half the total number are uncertain about whether the child prays as an adolescent. (3) Prayers are generally said at mealtime—a "rote" prayer often repeated by the child, according to the majority (66.6 percent). For those who gave no answer, one may guess the child does not pray. This makes up just fourteen or a little less than 40 percent of the cases.

In only four families was there evidence of family devotions or prayers except for grace at meals. Prayer was thought of as a "solitary relationship with God" and therefore private to the parents. As it turned out, after the parents did their initial teaching of formal prayers to their children, they were left to "go it alone." At a time of national emergency, such as John F. Kennedy's death, it is not surprising that there is evidence that only ten youth prayed

[9] For a detailed report by the Child Study investigators of this matter see "Young Teenagers' Responses to the Assassination of President Kennedy," Sylvia Ginsparg, Alice Moriarty, and Lois Murphy, in Children and the Death of a President, Martha Wolfenstein and G. W. Kliman, eds. (Garden City: Doubleday & Company, 1965).

as an immediate response. The spontaneous prayer, or prayer by the family involving its own needs for dependence, guidance, and support, appears to be lacking. Prayer is, for the majority, a "convention" used in church and formally said at home but without a great deal of personal meaning except, as one mother said, a *thought,* perhaps merely a "habit" at mealtime and bedtime.

For a few the practice of prayer has value, and it might be well to look at these to discover what it is. For several it was for *help in times of crises.* The Howe sisters pray hard when "they have tests and other such things." Rachel was taught a song and a prayer about Mary when she was seriously ill and developed a feeling of closeness to the Virgin. Several young people were able to move prayer from formality to spontaneity of expression. Bertha wrote and memorized a prayer which she gave at a church meeting. Mrs. Jane reported that Maurice gave the prayer at a boy's camp during the summer. Helen prayed when she first moved to the country to overcome her loneliness and was evidently *strengthened* to face a new situation. And for Diane and Teddy prayer has become meditative. Diane had formerly prayed for a victory in a basketball game but has come to see God's concern as bigger than she or her group. Teddy has concluded rather maturely, "If he wills, it will come; but it's up to him." And several mothers such as Mrs. Howard have taught their youth: "Our prayers are always answered even though it is not always the way we want them answered." The values of support, strength, problem solving, and acceptance of difficulty are present with those to whom prayer is meaningful.

A very good means of tapping the mother's religious teaching of youth was to ask them their favorite scriptural or religious teaching alongside a family saying. When crises arise—large or small—what does the family live by, and is there any way of discovering if the faith taught in the church has direct bearing on their lives? Only twenty of the fifty families reported such saying, which may indicate that either a small group operates this way, or that most families have a faith which is not clearly articulated. (I would judge on the basis of the interviews that the latter is the case.) However, it is interesting to see the similarities and differences in the religious and secular sayings.

Sayings in Difficulty [10]

		Religious Saying	Secular Saying
1. Gregory	M:	"The good Lord must have been with us"	"If we just have patience, things will work out"
2. Lowell	M:	"God is our answer to our problem"	
3. Coopers	M:	"We have to take our time and pray about that"	M: "There's always another day"
4. Timberlake	M:	"In quietness and confidence shall be our strength"	M: "Whatever is worth doing is worth doing well"
5. Wilkins			M: "Let's not judge until we know how we feel." "We always have to hope for the best"
6. Dickinson		No sayings; reality is more important	
7. Warren			M: "All things happen at once. Trouble never comes singly; they come married with big families"
8. Caster, S.			"Tomorrow's another day." "Things can't get any worse than they are"
9. David			"Think positive. Put your best foot forward"
10. Jane		"All things work together for good to those who love the Lord"	
11. Moore			"No matter how bad something is something good will come out of it"
12. Moffat			"When you're on the bottom, there's only one way and that's up." "When you're on the top the only other way is down"
13. Scarf		"God guides in every decision"	
14. Watson		"All things work together for good of them that love God"	
15. Wolfe			"Hitch to the stars, reach for the highest and the best." "Material things are not the most important things in life"

[10] Only those who told the interviewer of a saying, either religious or secular, are reported.

	Religious Saying	Secular Saying
16. Boston	"We'll do this next week, God willing"	"Do all you can, and if you've done all you can then that's it."
17. Rogers, V. & M.		"Well, it can't get any worse."
18. Howard	"We can pray about it"	"There's always hope."
19. Holt	"The Lord helps those who help themselves"	
20. Kendle	"We will always have to have faith in God. He will help us you know"	

The religious sayings are in most cases from the Bible and reflect a dependence upon God for support, strength, and guidance. Prayer is the chief means encouraged to find this support. One would imagine that youth who heard such statements made by their parents in existential situations would learn to rely upon the strength of God for their strength. The secular sayings, however, teach other virtues and other values which, except in one or two instances, enjoin self-reliance and an independent spirit. These come from "pioneer America," still a part of the folkways of the midwest. Time is on our side; if we have patience, work hard, and think positively things will come out successfully for us. One can even, on the basis of this small bit of evidence, point up the conflict of values between what the church teaches and what parents live by. One imagines that the youth becomes aware of the conflict and generally understands the greater importance of the pragmatic, "success-oriented" secular teachings. And he learns by indirection to conform to the values which may make him a success in his social group. God may then be thought of as the "man in the wings"—never in the center of the stage where the action is—but important to have around to prompt us to say the right words. This remains to be discussed in later chapters.

Role of Personal Religion

It is now possible to draw all the data together from parents' and pastors' interviews and evaluate the role of personal religion in the mother's life, the father's life, and the youth's life.

Role of Religion

M=Mother
F=Father

Definitions of terms as used here:

1. *Controlling:* Religion is central to one so that all his behavior, thought, and attitudes are brought under its domination.

2. *Guiding:* Religion is important as a directive to one's daily life, being looked to for help in decision making and coping with problems.

3. *Supportive:* Religion is important in providing one with strength to face crisis situations such as death and illness, which cannot be changed but which can be met with equanimity.

4. *Social Satisfaction:* Religion provides one with the security and support of a social fellowship.

5. *Conventional:* Religion is a set of customs in which one takes part for pragmatic reasons of status, prestige, etc.

6. *Indifferent:* Religion makes little difference in-so-far as one thinks, feels, or behaves in society.

7. *Hostile:* Religion is reacted to by negative attitude, speech, or behavior reflecting hostility and/or rejection.

Youth

1. Controlling—M
   Controlling—F
   Darlene—Controlling

2. Controlling—M
   Conventional—F
   Chester—Social
   Satisfaction (Indifferent)
   Ray—Social Satisfaction

3. Dominant—M
   Guiding—F
   Diane—Guiding

4. Dominant—M
   Indifferent—F
   Janice—Guiding

5. Dominant—M
   Indifferent—F
   Donald—Conventional

6. Guiding—M
   Conventional—F
   Susan—Conventional

135

Youth

7. Guiding—M Guiding—F	Greg—Guiding
8. Guiding—M Guiding—F	Helen—Guiding
9. Guiding—M Guiding—F	Sylvia—Guiding
10. Guiding—M Guiding—F	Bertha—Indifferent

11. Guiding—M
    Guiding—F
	Maurice—Guiding
	   or Conventional

12. Guiding—M Guiding—F	Julia—Guiding
13. Guiding—M Guiding—F	Norma—Guiding
14. Guiding—M Guiding—F	Kitty—Guiding
15. Guiding—M Guiding—F	Stewart—Guiding
16. Guiding—M Indifferent—F	Lenny—Guiding
17. Guiding—M Indifferent—F	Jack—Indifferent

18. Guiding—M
    Indifferent—F
	Patricia—Social
	   Satisfaction

19. Indifferent—M Guiding—F	Brenda—Supportive
20. Guiding—M Indifferent—F	Gordon—Hostile
21. Guiding—M Indifferent—F	Rachel—Supportive
22. Supportive—M Dominant—F	Sheila—Guiding Steve—Conventional

Youth

23. Supportive—M
    Indifferent—F
    Susan—Conventional

24. Supportive—M
    Indifferent—F
    Jennifer—Indifferent

25. Supportive—M
    Indifferent—F
    Silas—Social
       Satisfaction

26. Social Satisfaction—M
    Conventional—F
    Paula—Indifferent

27. Conventional—M
    Supportive—F
    Richard—Indifferent

28. Conventional—M
    Guiding—F
    Dennis—Indifferent

29. Conventional—M
    Conventional—F
    Simon—Conventional

30. Conventional—M
    Conventional—F
    Tony—Social
       Satisfaction

31. Conventional—M
    Conventional—F
    Cassy—Conventional

32. Conventional—M
    Conventional—F
    Vernon—Conventional

33. Conventional—M
    Conventional—F
    Martin—Conventional

34. Conventional—M
    Conventional—F
    Ronald—Conventional

35. Conventional—M
    Indifferent—F
    Delbert—Conventional

36. Conventional—M
    Conventional—F
    Mark R—Conventional

37. Conventional—M
    Conventional—F
    Millie—Supportive

38. Indifferent—M
    Indifferent—F
    Sherry—Supportive

137

Youth

39. Indifferent—M   Claudia—Conventional
    Soc. Satisfaction—F

40. Indifferent—M   Adele—Supportive
    Hostile—F

41. Indifferent—M   Jack—Indifferent
    Indifferent—F

42. Hostile—M   Corliss—Hostile
    Hostile—F

43. Guiding—M   Daryl—Conventional
    Conventional—F   Vivian—Guiding

44. Guiding—M   Vernon—Conventional
    Conventional—F

Table 6-4

Nature of Religious Orientation

		Controlling	Guiding	Supportive	Social Satisfaction	Conventional	Indifferent	Hostile
Mother	Number	4	17	4	1	10	5	1
	Percent	8.5	36	8.5	2	21.3	11	2
Father	Number	2	11	1	1	11	13	2
	Percent	4.3	23.4	2	2	23.4	28	4.3
Youth	Number	1	12	4	6	11	10	2
	Percent	2	25.5	8.5	12.3	23.4	21.3	4.3

We may find examples of each of these religious orientations among the interviews. In the *controlling* group are several fundamentalist families who are obsessive in their preoccupation with religion. Particularly in the area of moral behavior is this so. Mrs. Cooper says that Chester's faith means he cannot play baseball on Sunday. Mrs. Lowell taught Darlene that it is wrong to dance and requested that she be excused from rhythmic dancing in junior high school, causing some difficulty. Mrs. Dickinson has told her children they will be punished for lying. "Breaking a law is wrong in itself. If you can keep the laws of the Lord, it will be easier to obey the laws of the land."

The *guiding* families have sought more directly to know "the will of God" in various problems they have confronted. Perhaps the youth who have considered the ministry or a church vocation best illustrate this. Stewart has been eager to be a priest as long as his parents remember. They tried to discourage him but sought guidance in prayer and from priests before letting him go to minor seminary. Terry, on the other hand, sought similar guidance and discovered, "Well, I know it involves vows as well as a lot more self than I thought it did or something. I just don't want to now." Without realizing it, Teddy displays guidance even when discussing a church vocation. He says, "I mean, you don't have to become a minister to serve God in the church, and they say if everyone was a minister, the ministers wouldn't have anyone to preach to."

The *supportive* group have generally had more tragedy in their lives; however, for some there is generally just a more dependent attitude toward God. Adele for example, desires baptism for the reason that she would be closer to Christ. Following the loss of a sixteen-year-old brother, both Helen and her mother relied heavily upon their church and the faith for support through the grief. Mrs. Ramsey says their faith helps them accept the fact they have less than others in the neighborhood. Mrs. Wilson said she did not feel one had the "right" to pray during a crisis if one didn't pray the rest of the time. When she prays she does not ask for selfish things but asks for strength and guidance.

The *conventional* and *socially satisfied* group saw little connection between their faith and moral life. Mrs. Pyle said she separated ethics from religion a long time ago. Mrs. David, too, failed to see the connection between Paula's religious beliefs and her ideals. For Daryl Howe the conformity of the peer group held the upper hand. She wants to be popular, her mother says, and follows what her social clique says and does.

The *indifferent* group are a little further removed from the influence of the faith. Although there are no statements for this group, the interviewer did give as reasons: (1) the indifference or negative attitude of the parents (six) ; (2) the fact the religion was not socially satisfying to youth (two) ; and (3) rebellion where the parents were too strict earlier. She felt the parents conveyed these attitudes by their actions, by not attending church themselves, and by their negative statements about religion.

The *hostile* group made up of one father and one total family appears to be those for whom religion has been a completely negative experience. As indicated earlier with Mrs. West and her daughter, religion was such a painful area that they both refused to discuss it at all with the interviewer. The father of the other family, since he had alcohol problems and his wife was severely ill, was filled with guilt and unable to speak about it at all.

One may draw some general conclusions from this last chart and from table 6-3 which may bring us to a summary of the study of religious practices. First, there are fewer youth compared to parents in the extreme categories (controlling or hostile). In fact, there are fewer in the guiding and sustaining categories, although percentage-wise there are as many in the guiding (25.5 percent) as the fathers in this category and as many in the sustaining as mothers (8.5 percent). There is a considerably larger group of youth than parents in the socially satisfying area (12.3 percent—compared with 2 percent). Moreover, if one adds this group to the conventional group it makes up the highest percentage for the youth (36.7 percent). The indifferent group again is higher than that of the mothers and about equal to the group of indifferent fathers.

Looking at the relation of individual ratings of mother's and father's concern for religion with their youth, one discovers other items of note. For twenty of the families the youth felt religion fulfilled the same personal role for them as for their parents. However, thirteen youth displayed *less interest* and zeal for religion and, where the family was divided in interest, the tendency for the youth was to show *less interest* than the strongest member. For four there was more interest, but this appears to be a kind of "reverse rebellion" or, as in the instance of church attendance, seeking for satisfaction of emotional needs from a larger family, the church. Although the mother was the one interviewed and in most interviews appeared as the teacher of formal religion, in those cases where the youth had a choice, a majority of both sexes chose their father's practice of religion for themselves. (Boys: seven—father, three—mother. Girls: six—father, four—mother.) One might guess that both boys and girls are rebelling somewhat against mother's control and dominance and find the father a support and defense in a vital area. The most outstanding feature of all this is the "three generation phenomenon" which is in operation: "If parents have a firsthand experience with the 'faith,' their children practice the faith but for socially satisfying or conventional motives. And *their children*, represented by the majority of this group, are either indifferent or irreligious and must somehow come into a firsthand experience again." And in a prophecy-fulfilling way a small number of "needy" adolescents are doing just that!

3. CONCLUSIONS

We may well ask now how accurate the psychiatrist and psychologist were with regard to the conventionality or conformity patterns of this group. When we review the analysis of the data, we become aware of the fact that they are correct with regard to the majority of the youth concerning their level of participation in the institutional church, their feelings toward the church, their participation in and attitudes toward the church school and youth fellowship. They are not accurate with respect to a minority of the group who could be called "intrinsically religious," using Allport's term. There are a number of youth, both young men and young women, who practice prayer, who attend church and church school, and who are highly involved in the youth groups in the churches for whom religion is an intensely meaningful thing. From the interviews regarding their beliefs, it will be remembered that there was a struggle to make meaning out of the tradition which they received from their parents. There was an attempt to cope with the difficulties in their lives and, although the majority represented in this sample are apparently in the grips of conformity to the peer group, there is a minority which finds religion dominant, supportive, or guiding.

The other conclusion to which we must come as a result of this chapter is that the parents up until the period of early adolescence have been the teachers of their children in matters religious.

141

They have been poorly prepared as teachers and, in general, have taught moralisms or have not been able to comprehend the conflicts between the tradition and the conventionalities which come to them from society. It will be noted that the Roman Catholic Church has, by and large, done a better job of enlisting their youth to practice their faith. On the other hand, the Protestant young people have had perhaps greater freedom to doubt and to question and to stay away from church services, church school, and youth fellowship during the period of doubt and testing. The role of the church and the role of the parents in the preparation of youth for confirmation and church membership is, therefore, a crucial one and one which we shall discuss in chapter 8 on confirmation.

7

Roddy
the Study of a Conformist Boy

Roddy may well be studied at this juncture between our discussion of religious practices and confirmation. For in a very real sense he is the result of our highly mobile civilization, a church "drop out." His parents at the time of the study had moved from one job to another and were temporarily in this city and not yet located as to church and church school. Roddy appears to be a young man who can think religiously but who is totally lacking in the facts of the faith. Nor does he have much guidance as to where he could commit himself religiously.

The questions we want to ask of him, therefore, are perhaps out of focus, but we hope by the end of the study to get them into a larger perspective. (1) Has religion played any part in his development? (2) What is the source of his impulse control? (3) Where does he get his sense of identity? (4) Whence comes his motivation to become a missionary doctor?

The balance between conformity and creativity is a delicate one in Roddy. The reader, therefore, will want to be sensitive to the relationship between Roddy and his parents over against his relationship to his peers. The use of vocation to distance oneself from parental controls is a dynamic that the reader will want to be aware of. Finally, the question of conformity which loomed so prominently in the last chapter will need to be examined carefully in Roddy's life story, i.e., how does it develop, what end does it serve, and what does it do to the religious motive?

Roddy Nash is a wiry, effervescent, athletic boy of fourteen years six months. He has dark hair, an olive complexion, agate-blue eyes, and resembles his brunette mother rather than his blonde father. When seen, just after Christmas, he wore a new blaze-red shirt, black trousers, and black shoes, which were obviously bought for their orthopedic usefulness rather than their style. He gestures dramatically when talking, and his face is highly mobile in conversation. However, his voice at times is dull and monotone, and his earlier speech difficulty occurs when he is under stress or attempting to explain an idea too big for him. His complexion is clear, though he recently entered puberty. He is extroverted at first meeting and appears to want to help the interviewer in whatever project he is involved. Though he may not be practicing his religion, he wants the interviewer to know that "religion is really a big thing at his school" as though to encourage him for any lacks in the material.

Roddy is now in the second year of junior high school in a large midwestern city. He excels in his studies, is a high scorer on the basketball team, and has served as president of his class. This has been accomplished even though he moved to this city just a year and a half ago, when his father took a position with a large loan company. He has one sibling, a sister, Betty Lee aged nine, who is also a brunette. The family lives in a rented home in a new section of the city, near a newly built Presbyterian church. None of the family attend church or church school here, however, the feeling being that they are here only on a temporary basis. The mother works as a secretary in a city office, since she is at a distance from any of her family, and she feels it necessary to supplement the family budget. She would very much like to move to a permanent

144

home, which they could own, preferably in a smaller town. Roddy, however, very much likes this location and feels as much at home here as at any of the five locations in which they have lived.

1. RELIGIOUS PRACTICES

The Nash family might be described as nominal Protestant. The mother and father were married in a Protestant church in her hometown in 1943, and after Roddy's birth in 1948 they journeyed back to the church for his baptism at age two. "His early illnesses prevented his having it done any sooner (GH, 1950)," said Mrs. Nash. He started into Sunday school in a neighborhood church at the beginners' level, and he and his sister attended here with regularity until they started moving around, when the father was transferred in his jobs. Roddy says with some pride that he attended without missing for two years, from age seven to eight, and won a Bible, which he has read as a part of other church school classes. (CWS, 1962)

The mobility of the family at first did not affect church attendance, i.e., when they moved to another state for two years, they became a part of the local church, a friendly one, reports the mother. And when they moved to a large city in another state, they even went to the "cathedrally church," too large to get to know anyone at worship. The entire family went to Bible school there, and mother and Roddy both report enjoying the discussions. They even discussed some of the issues around the table at that time.

But the most recent move has militated against church attendance, and the mother reports that they have not entered any community activities but the recreation association for the two children and work. Mrs. Nash took a job shortly after the move and has not even grown acquainted with the neighbors except to say "Hello." Mr. Nash spends his spare time hunting, fishing, and golfing, taking Roddy when he can. The family knows the location of the Presbyterian church and knows that they have completed a new building, but Mrs. Nash hopes that they will move this time to a permanent location and is not putting down roots. The family does not even attend church now at Christmas or Easter, and, though the mother feels guilty about it, she is not making any moves toward putting the children in church school, or attending church herself. Meanwhile, Roddy says he misses church and wished that he could become a part of a church group.

2. RELIGIOUS BELIEFS

Roddy's belief system is not orthodox, although it has some of the elements of ideas which he has heard from church and church school in earlier years. It is perhaps the most idiosyncratic of those we studied, with more fantasy, "privatistic" elements, and elaboration. We shall return to the imaginative side when we report his attitudes. This is perhaps enough to prepare the reader for what follows.

"I believe in God and that he sent his son down to earth, and that when he was killed, he sacrificed his life for us." This is what Roddy first reports about his beliefs. But when questioned further about God as creator, he begins to see the conflict between the scientific and the Genesis account. God has the power to create *ex nihilo*, "Pooie and there it was," or the earth could have been created following an explosion off the sun over a long period of time. (CWS, 1962) But it had to be God who did it. Regarding God's nature, Roddy is troubled by the invisibility of deity. If one could only see him, it would settle a million and one questions. Since he created man in his image, it must mean he has a body, but what that body might look like is unknown. He wishes the scientists and theologians would get together and figure this thing out. God is good, so that hurricanes and illnesses are probably punishments for man's sins, or they might not seem evil from God's perspective.

Jesus' divinity is not linked to his incarnation but to his miraculous power to heal diseases and to his leadership of men. This must mean he is related to a higher power. His teachings are little known to Roddy, except that he lived a life of sacrifice and taught his disciples to do likewise. It was Jesus' death on the cross which epitomized his teachings, and it was his resurrection which convinced his disciples that this was the way to go to heaven. How Jesus' death saves people from their sins was an unexplored topic for Roddy, but he applied a scientific mind to it and said the only way to know would be to devise an experiment: (1) have him live

146

to old age and die and see what happens, (2) have him die a young man on the cross. He could see that the second alternative was followed but wondered what would have happened if there had been no cross. (CWS, 1962)

To the questions about beliefs in heaven and hell he at first replied flippantly that he did not know about them, he had never been there. But when pushed further, he replied that he hoped there was an eternal life, but he did not know how extreme it got. By this he meant he did not know the character of the existence, whether it would be like life on earth or different. He felt that heaven was a reward for the good life, and that hell was a punishment for stealing, cheating, killing, or not working. With regard to attitudes, he felt that one could believe in America and not believe in Russia and go to heaven; as a Russian one could believe in Russia and not believe in America and go to heaven; but if one did not believe in anything, believed that the world should not have been created and that everyone was nuts, he would probably go to hell. Here he got into his most philosophical mood and tried to liken heaven to preexistence and felt he could have lived previously and forgotten this life. So, too, he could exist in heaven and forget his life on earth. It all got pretty involved here, when he said he would like to find that pinpoint which separates the past from the future—it could be nothing or it could be infinity. It left his head spinning.

He began to fantasy how God controlled the universe and thought it might be set up on a democratic system, with angels for each planet and with Jesus as our representative on earth. Then God could send him here on Christmas and someone else to Mars on the fourth of July.

When he got to the point of discussing right and wrong and how one determined this, he picked out the tape recorder as an example in the room and elaborated on this without knowing where he was going at the beginning. Desire is a thin line which flows at the top of the tape, and a thin line below says, Should I? or Shouldn't I? What one does comes from other people's actions and whether these actions were rewarded or punished. He did not come to his parents' part in helping him determine right or wrong until asked directly about it, the peer group seeming to him the more important. On smoking and drinking, however, it became apparent that his parents had been the determining force, along with his interest in health. "One might just as well drink acid, if he wants his stomach eaten out, as drink liquor," said Roddy. Concerning boy-girl relations, he reported that there was no necking in WRAP, the recreational group to which he belongs. When queried about sex relations he used a relative yardstick, so that if a couple were teenagers they should not have sex relations before marriage. But if they were seventy years old and were not married it should be allowed them. When told of the meaning of the sixth commandment, he said he would go wholeheartedly with that but then went back to his original position. The absence of parental teaching, as well as church school teaching, at this point was most apparent.

He believes that prayer is a good thing and thinks of it mainly as a way to seek forgiveness. He has never prayed in a crisis, saying that he has never been in that much trouble. He does not think God will magically answer prayers for money, but he would answer prayers for small things such as if one's mother were sick with cancer or polio. He seems particularly interested in the relation of prayer and health and queried the interviewer about Oral Roberts and Christian Science. Again there was obviously no criterion from church teaching against which to measure these movements about which he had read or heard on television.

In general I got the impression that Roddy's answers to the questions about his beliefs were like answers to a test for which he had not studied. He is an extremely intelligent boy who has not been exposed to much current religious thinking and discussion. He has not been a part of a membership or confirmation class, and the closest to religious discussion he has come recently has been in a social studies class where the teacher has exposed them to debate between evolution and the biblical doctrine of creation. Roddy has the interest and intelligence to deal with questions of this sort, but the content of the discussion has simply not been provided. What one gets is the product of an active imagination and the idiosyncratic pattern of his own needs putting their mark on his answers. He is a boy adrift in a religious sea.

3. RELIGIOUS ATTITUDES

When one investigates Roddy's religious attitudes, it is necessary to use inference and projection from the interview and from the tests. There is not much information regarding religious attitudes in the historical material.

First, one is struck by Roddy's need for structure and his desire to conform to adult expectations. This attitude when set within a church group might make of him a religious conformist who believes what is taught him and who conforms to the teachings of the particular church which he attends. When one sees him outside the church, one sees him searching avidly for structure within the social groups which he attends and conforming to expectations of that group, whether it be his teachers in junior high school or his peers who make up his class or athletic team. The "hidden persuaders" would find a fertile mind here, were it not for his mother's strong convictions. One finds Roddy, therefore, parroting his mother's convictions and what he feels is expected of him in the social groups which he attends.

Second, there is an egocentric concern throughout Roddy's Religious Projective Pictures. He is concerned about his body and its injury, about disease and its impress upon his family, about death and the crises it brings to children of families. (Godin pictures 7, 8, 12) In one (picture 3) he sees a family caught behind the Berlin Wall and their successful breakthrough from behind the wall. On the TAT he sees one person with the alternative of shooting a man or becoming a doctor. (AM, 1957) One becomes aware of the conflictual elements in Roddy's personality, but these keep him from seeing other individuals as individuals. He sees them as objects to manipulate, to satisfy his needs, or to perform before whether as an athlete or as a leader. He does this in a likeable fashion but with little empathy for the other fellow's position. His own needs are too great for that. He is rather involved in himself, his own ambitions, and what he would make of himself.

Third, there is a need to sacrifice himself and these individualistic needs to the group and its service. This combines the conformity trend with the narcissistic need. It is as though he knows the group will not stand for too much showing off or too much towering above them, and he wants to put what abilities and talents he has at their service. He has a heroic desire to commit himself to some great cause. As we explore his vocational commitment later on, we shall try to uncover why he sees medicine as the avenue for doing this, and why he should want to go to Africa to practice medicine, or to practice brain surgery as a specialty. But without the church sounding the call to commitment and service, here is a boy who has, within his own dynamics, heard such a call. His call might even preclude marriage. As he says, he does not think you should ask a girl to share a life in the jungle with you, that she would be crazy to do that. So one finally has a priestly kind of dedication in a boy who has not had the model of a priest to inspire it.

Fourth, one must add the element of imagination and of wonder, in a boy given to limiting his fantasy within a structure and limiting the expression of his vital urges to the expectations of parents and his peer group. When the opportunity arises in the religious interview to let his imagination go, Roddy has the ability to speculate in a highly idiosyncratic way and to pose alternatives, none of which appear to come from his immediate environment. His mind is given to concrete thinking, and at first he would appear to depend on the tester to give him cues as to what to give on the Religious Projective. But upon further talk he begins to "loop the loops" (LBM, 1963) in his fantasy and can with whimsy and tremendous elaboration talk of things way beyond his ken. This kind of mind appears to be more that of the science-fiction writer than the scientist, and the religious novelist than the theologian. But at least there are possibilities of "wonder about God" and religious imagination which his religious training has not as yet tapped.

4. QUESTIONS

We shall now look into the longitudinal material, having this cross-sectional impression of Roddy at fourteen, to ask certain questions regarding his religious development. We should say at the outset that Roddy is one of the children whom Grace Heider rated as highly vulnerable at infancy and preschool, but who the other psychologists think has made tremendous strides by time of adolescence. He has, as one indication of his change in vulnerability, moved in IQ scores from 100 on the Binet at preschool to 123 on the Wechsler at latency and 127 at prepuberty. (AM, 1960)

1. Has religion or a substitute for religion played any part in his shift in vulnerability or ability to cope with his problems? It is well to add "substitute for religion," in that he may have learned something from his parents or other teachers which is not classically religious which has enabled him to handle his initial vulnerability. Nevertheless, this philosophy or ethic may have sustained him in his shift in vulnerability.

2. What is the source of impulse control? In a family only nominally religious what is the basis of the discipline which is taught the children, and from whence come the concepts which teach them about right and wrong?

3. Where does Roddy get his sense of identity? Who are his identification figures? Do they come from the religious realm or from some other source? Has he solved the identity crisis? And if so, has religion played any part in it, or is it playing any part in it?

4. Whence came his motivation to become a missionary doctor? We have indicated earlier that he has an almost priestly motivation to renounce marriage and to go to the jungles of Africa to practice medicine among the natives? What are the dynamic sources of this motivation? Are there any religious springs at all to this motivation? And if not, where does he get the idea and the inspiration to make this sacrifice?

5. DEVELOPMENT OF RODDY'S RELIGIOUS ORIENTATION

What kind of world did Roddy come into? And what kind of baby was he at birth? He was born to a high-school-educated couple who married in 1943 before Mr. Nash was called to service. They lived in a three-room apartment on a dead-end street. After the war, and after long waiting, Roddy arrived. The mother's parents had died in her infancy, and she was reared by a couple who took her in after rearing two other orphans who were Mrs. Nash's only relatives. She intensely looked forward to Roddy's coming; in fact, she told one investigator, "He is the first person of my own flesh and blood I've ever had. Even my husband doesn't belong to me that way. I've never had anybody. Maybe I've gone overboard for him but I just want everything to be right for him." (GH, 1953) The father had been a victim of allergies and was hypersensitive to skin diseases, and this constitution Roddy inherited; in physique, however, he resembles his mother, an ectomesomorph (Sheldon's ratings).

He was born full term, weighing six pounds thirteen ounces, rather long and not heavy. His mother could not nurse him. But he took to formula, suffering some minor stomach pains after eating. He was first observed in the Infancy Study at twenty weeks, at which time the most striking things about him were his perceptual sensitivity and the intensity of his response to stimuli. He was highly vocal and would smile easily upon the approach of an investigator. In fact, he would chuckle and even laugh out loud. He would show tension by extending his arms and legs and quivering in excitement. [1]

The mother was warm and affectionate, even mildly stimulating toward the baby. She was aware of his needs for the bottle or to be changed. But she seemed to want him to adapt to her predetermined standards and would take the nipple out of his mouth when she thought he should not have it. She was careful about his cleanliness and would talk to him when he was "naughty" and soiled himself. She would show abruptness in moving him or changing his position to suit her own needs. Her ideas of child care she summarized as, "I go by the baby and not by the book." However, she had read widely in child-care books, but she selected what she agreed with and ignored what she did not. As he grew, she told Dr. Heider (1953), she kept him awake forcefully when he threatened to shift his bedtime, and she reduced his intake by degrees in order to eliminate one of his feedings. On the whole she seemed to take her task as one of "molding him from without rather than of watching his development and taking her cues from him." (GH, 1953) Along with this interrupting, controlling behavior, she acted as though he were an extension of herself and needed discipline as her arm would need it. Dr. Heider based her high vulnerability rating, therefore, on the combination of organic weaknesses—

[1] Sylvia Brody, *Patterns of Mothering* (New York: International Universities Press, 1956), p. 197.

apparent in his infections and hypersensitivities—shown at birth coupled with this kind of mother who would not be sensitive to these weaknesses but would try to mold him after her own image.

Vulnerability. The fact that he remained highly vulnerable at age five was the result of a heightening of these tendencies. The mother went to work when Roddy was seven and a half months, but she herself had to be hospitalized with tuberculosis when he was approximately one year. Her illness, she states, left her highly nervous, but she returned to work, stopping only long enough to have the second sibling when Roddy was five. Roddy liked his grandmother to baby-sit with him, when they lived in his native city, but has not liked the housekeepers who have been in the home since. He developed into one of the most active and highly excitable five-year-olds in the study. He is described at this period as resembling a little monkey, running about, distractible by anything in the room, finding it difficult to concentrate on one task, but following many lines of interest.

His illnesses had been the common childhood ones, with an accident at one and a half requiring head stitches and his allergies causing difficulties. The mother stated at this time she thought her son to be "accident prone." It is easy to see how he would tend to break things before he developed neuromuscular skills. He was, according to the observer at the preschool party, "brimming over with a certain self-conscious, over-excited, over-wound-up animation." (WM, 1954) He learned to climb, run, and jump on a new apparatus, ran a close second in the peanut hunt, and was adept at outrunning many of the other boys. He knew he was being observed and stated, "I wish you'd quit watching us."

In the play sessions the woman psychologist appeared to make him guilty in setting limits on his breaking crayons, whereas the male psychiatrist faded into the background, and Roddy became much more aggressive toward the inflated clown, Bobo. He appeared to want contact with adults and to have them control his aggressive energy, but after expending himself totally on a test or a session he might sink in exhaustion into a car seat and become quiet on the way home. (PT, 1953)

He was afraid of the dark at this stage and of a policeman friend who came to the house. His hero was Hopalong Cassidy, rather than

Howdy Doody, and he reports wanting to be a soldier like his dad. The birth of Betty Lee made several changes in his life style. He regressed in his ability to dress himself, when he saw the baby being dressed and undressed. His mother told him if he were not old enough to dress he was not old enough to go out.

He did not like to play alone but must involve another adult, either mother or grandmother. When he would play on a swing, he would not take his turn but would come in to complain to his mother. Then he would return to play and tell the kids to play "good" because his mother said so. He knew how to get off his feet if he got tired; then he would go back and start up again.

The vulnerability in the child still showed in the combination of tension shown in his thin skin and his speech. He stammered in a "push-of-speech" fashion and found articulation and consonant substitution difficult. At puberty there may have been a neurological basis for this which had healed over, the speech pathologist said, but there was no firm evidence for this. (CR, 1962) Dr. Murphy found him a tense child, concerned with not breaking and with living up to expectations. He seemed to be involved in "pseudo-coping" (LBM, 1953), going through the motions but not actively involved in meeting the challenges of his environment. His Rorschach seemed overly concrete, with few W's (whole responses) and with a latching onto the known and looking to the adult for cues as to what he should see. (WK, 1953) His average IQ showed that he was just at the normal level and not using all his potentiality, so much of his time being spent in spinning his wheels in hyperactivity. We shall pick up the shift in vulnerability later, but let us turn now to look at the development of controls in Roddy.

Controls. In the development of controls in Roddy, one finds one of the central dynamics of his personality and perhaps the substitute for religion in his life. We have already discovered how the mother began his discipline as soon as he was born. Lois Murphy described her training methods as combining "enormous support plus unhesitating discipline and curbing of impetuousness." One wonders, however, if his mother ever allowed herself to express her love and the feeling she had for the child, for Roddy spoke to the psychiatrist (PT, 1953) at the preschool exam that talk of love "hurt his ears." The mother began as soon as she nursed the child to treat him like a "little gentleman," as her firstborn and her first "flesh-and-blood" relation, and to invest herself in turning him out right. Her discipline and training methods were a combination of what she had read in the baby books, what she had picked up from her adopting father about right and wrong, and her own good sense.

Roddy matured on the schedule he set along with his mother. Mother did not hurry him but was "in phase" with his maturation. He used a pacifier for the first six months, even though mother knew the books decried their use. However, following weaning at fourteen months, he did not suck his thumb. He began walking at eleven months. Mother began toilet training him at sixteen months and he was trained in a week according to her reports. No "catch the baby" type of training for her, she stated. He was dry day and night after this time. She was verbally aggressive to him but allowed him latitude in his behavior. For example, she would upbraid him about his "messiness" in eating but would tolerate freedom of movement and never go so far in disciplining him as she would say she was going to. But the threat was always, even as a baby, "If you are going to be so messy, you won't get any more." And she might interrupt some activity because it interfered with her own schedule, rather than being entirely sensitive to his own needs.

Though we do not have complete records of the childhood stage, it might be important to determine the mother's standards and see how these were imparted to Roddy at this time leading to their incorporation in his superego. Her adopting father appears to have been a highly disciplined person who set her to accept and to develop responsibility. Mrs. Nash stated to the home visitor,

His principal responsibility is to himself. I try to present a way of living. This is the way my father taught me and I think it's important. I preach (sic) year after year that his responsibility is to himself and I don't say that he has to do anything. I just don't believe in chores. I remember from my own childhood that my mother was always saying, Do this, Do that, and I resented it. And on the other hand, my father taught the philosophy of responsibility to oneself and you see which way I chose. I just don't like being told what to do and I don't think anyone else does.

This idea of responsibility also covers relations with others, as she states, "This is another idea I got from my father, . . . not only responsibility and respect to one's self but respect and responsibility to others." Truth telling appears to be the cardinal principle of her code. She expected to tell the children the truth and expected the same treatment from them. She stated: "That's my whole theory in raising kids. If they cannot tell me the truth I'm not going to have any faith in them." (GH, 1960)

An instance of teaching responsibility came at the point of Roddy's wanting an allowance. She let him have a dollar at age six. After this when he wanted his supper, she charged him ten cents for the service and ten cents per item served. He reacted, saying, "Aw ma, if that's what you are going to do, I don't want no allowance" (MF, 1961). Again, she allowed him rope at the time he wanted to stay up to 11:30 to watch a horror movie, but just enough to hang himself. He got tired of waiting at 9:30 P.M., when the mother said she would not stay up with him and made the conditions anything but palatable for the child. He went to bed rather than displeasing her any more. The mother appears to have taught him that adults know better than children what is good for them. Concerning behavior of which she did not approve, she subtly coerced Roddy into seeing her side.

When Roddy was naughty—for instance, in maneuvering a little cousin into getting a spanking—the mother handled it by spanking Roddy. It only took one spanking to teach him not to repeat a certain type of behavior. He had a lot of seemingly uncontrolled energy, but he would not pick a fight. Nor would he stand up for himself if a playmate would take one of his possessions. He would come into his mother to straighten things out. The mother at this time wished he had more backbone and stood up for his own things in a more manly fashion. Her method apparently made him alert to the faults of others, and upon catching them in misbehavior he would moralize to them, much in the same tone as his mother used. He took discipline hard, she said, and he had a time getting over a spanking. He would try to smooth things over with the mother, saying he was sorry, and try to get back into her good graces. (GH, 1953) The mother reported at this time her ideal was for him "to be good," and she applied external coercion in a persistent and highly selective fashion to gain her ends.

At age five Roddy's superego was fashioned almost entirely by his mother. He had introjected her standards for him, and her voice of authority spoke to him with all the force of law. He did not resolve the oedipal struggle by turning toward the father except only superficially. His father took him fishing and taught him to swim with a life jacket. He adopted some of his father's manly swagger, but inwardly he felt his mother's standards and ideals were the ones to live by. The mother taught him to channel his aggression—remember that at the time of entering kindergarten he was highly motoric. At kindergarten and at the Project Center, when the limits were not provided, there was a lot of undirected chattering, banging, jumping and grabbing. (GH, 1953) He was irritated by inactivity, yet bounded back to the tests at the slightest suggestion of the examiner. AM reports that he was aggressive in his handling of toys but quite gentle toward a woman psychologist. He was upset when he colored outside the lines but was able to show a "drunkenness of aggression" toward a male examiner. The whole picture was one of tight limits set upon a highly active child, who had accepted these limits as the rules of the game.

How did this high discipline affect Roddy through latency? It appears to have helped him sublimate his aggression toward his parents into coordinated and directed activity. He became highly competitive with his peers and behaved always in a conforming fashion with his elders. At age eight he was observed to "be able to channel his energies into more direct and steady problem-solving efforts and to set effective and realistic limits for himself." (AM, 1956) His IQ, as was indicated earlier, climbed eighteen points, and the psychologist reported that by age twelve he could temper his reactivity and intensity somewhat and that his vigor was now expressed by visual and verbal exploring, whereas in preschool it was entirely motoric.

It was during latency that he began to move around with his parents from place to place, his present school being his fourth. Rather than being disrupted, he learned to cope with the changing environments by adapting to the various teachers' authority and to challenge his peers only in sports and in school subjects. He was able, with his mother's philosophy of "Do your best" and "Do what is asked of you," to excel in grades and to become by the sixth grade a high scorer on the basketball team. Upon moving to a new city in the fall and being placed with other new residents in one class, his ability was recognized immediately, so that his peers elected him president of his class.

The question becomes one of the strength of his controls and the integrity of his superego. It would appear that he has adapted to the demands made upon him and conformed with adult expectations so well that he should not be in any trouble with his environment. In fact, in a city with a highly mobile culture of rootless people, he is one who has not invested himself in any values but success in immediate tasks and conformity to what he senses are the demands put upon him by his parents and teachers. He reports that what he likes of church when he goes is the preacher making hard demands of him that he would have to live up to. This sounds much like the hard demands which his mother has continuously made of him and the reality which she has always brought to challenge his fantasy and imagination.

He impresses the examiners at puberty with his "masculine competence" and his surface feeling of being important. The psychiatrist, however, feels that "he is almost afraid to look into himself, and that he tends to worry about performance in subjects in which he is best." (PT, 1960) He says, "One can see that Roddy is struggling toward very high ethical standards and this is particularly encouraged by the wish to suppress angry, frustrated feelings as well as sexual impulses within himself. Male aggressiveness is not acceptable except in a highly sublimated fashion and even then it must be elaborately tied down by major responsibilities of a professional nature." (PT, 1960)

He accepts authority and power unquestioningly and apparently feels he cannot fight back. His mother has taught him well, perhaps overtaught him, a religion of law and obedience. His superego is well trained, but whether it will break down in adolescence, with the stronger sex drive, and when he begins to see varying modes of behavior in high school is another question. He appears to conform mainly to the word of adults at the present time. However, as appears from the material on right and wrong, he speculates on adultery and, would apply a standard which would be amenable to his age group. Conformity to the standards of the peer group might be tempting to him when he gets outside the tight orbit of his mother. The church as an arbiter of morals is not a force in his life at present, nor is it a releasing power from his primary loyalty to his family. The family, particularly the mother, is *all* right now. One gets the impression that if there is a vacuum this boy will not have developed his own principles or standards to the point that he will be self-regulating in his behavior. When he was six, he took his mother's hand to cross the street, not to guide him, but to keep him back from darting in the path of an auto (MM, 1962). Perhaps this has served to discipline this high-spirited boy during childhood and adolescence but has militated against the formation of an integrated conscience.

Identity. It now becomes possible to deal with Roddy's identity crises and to raise the question of the religious aspects of his identification. Let it be said at the outset that he resembles the adolescent with an orestes complex described by Rollo May [2] as someone who must struggle against mother's domination for his own identity. Both psychiatrist and psychologist interviewing him and studying his life materials point out the overemphasis on mother in the oedipal triangle. (PT, VG, 1960) The mother is seen as more threatening to him at age five than the father. On the CAT (Children's Apperception Test) the psychologist points out that he often reverses roles and reverses feelings of omnipotence from adults to children. Children are usually seen as depriving the adults. The question he seems to be asking is, "Am I a capable boy or am I a helpless baby?" The emphasis on striving and mastery with the fears and anxieties of failure can be more closely related to the disciplining and controlling mother than the father. Says Vilma Gupta,

It is evident that the oedipal theme seems connected with infantile dependency upon the mother. The mother generally is perceived as giving security, succoring and supportive but also the disciplinarian. Perhaps this gives rise to a certain ambivalence toward her and the close and prolonged contact with her may give rise to some confusion in

[2] *Man's Search for Himself* (New York: W. W. Norton & Company, 1953), p. 125 ff.

sexual roles. Growing up into a male adult appears quite stressful because it deals with struggling through aggression toward others and also maintaining constructive striving. (1962)

Roddy attempted to identify with father prematurely, as stated above, but the identification was superficial in adopting a male swagger and male activities. The father was close to him at this period, as he still is as much as he can. He taught him to swim and to play ball, holding up the near success he had in professional baseball as an ideal. He took him fishing and hunting as well. However, Roddy must have been aware through latency of how this made the mother jealous, and the talks with mother and her moralism continued to give him whatever centering values he held. He never took his father as an ideal, as we shall see further when we discuss his vocational aspiration. In fact, the father failed in business at this period, when Roddy was six. Mother emphasized this by going back to work and becoming preoccupied with finances.

Roddy's early self-image was being a leader or a "big shot." A story that comes from his preschool period relates how a group of bigger boys stopped on bicycles to ask him directions to a certain place. Rather than admit his ignorance, Roddy directed them to take this street, then that, literally leading them on a wild goose chase. He reports to the psychiatrist that he wants to grow up so that he can beat up bigger kids in the grades above him. He literally wants to be a "big shot" and make an impression. Dr. Mayman sees the boy, as he develops, linking ambition, learned from mother, with compulsion, a tendency to see wholes. The drive to get ahead becomes the channel for his aggression, and he learns from mother that to do this he must help himself. (MM, 1962)

His identification becomes one of the leader by adolescence. He is preoccupied at puberty with the questions of identity: "Who am I? What am I? Where am I going?" He can't let go enough to get involved with things. (AM, 1962) He knows that mother expects certain things of him, he wants to please her, and he has been supported and reinforced in his strivings so that he feels capable of success if he can just be sure what she wants of him. The things he has turned his hand to, in competition with his peers, have succeeded. In fact, the mother is quite surprised at his budding abilities, in sports and in leadership in a class to which he has just come. But she is also liable to throw cold water on him when he pushes too far. When he tells her how smart he is or that he plans to be a six footer, she will cut him down to size. She points to the husband and shows how he is not tall nor is she, and how can he outwit heredity? Or she will put her high heels on and by so doing be taller than he and outwit him. Or she will in some other way let him know he still is just a "kid." (CWS, 1962)

He has turned outside the home to the peer group as a means of finding himself; there, having stood out as having abilities, he has had leadership thrust on him. He now finds conflict between satisfying his own egocentric needs and the need to blend his efforts with those of a group. He is also puzzled (as a reflection of his mother's opinion) by his own popularity. In humility he says, "I just don't want to judge myself. I want others . . . somebody to judge myself." This shows self-doubt, says the psychiatrist. (PT, 1960) It appears that Roddy's identity is loose and not well integrated, and that, for the present, he is operating in terms of other-direction. (Riesman) He feels he should achieve within a social structure, but he is troubled by the group's opinion of him, and whether their choice of him is actually deserved.

Yet this leader image is one which is becoming a controlling identification with little else to turn to for an identity-figure. He speaks, as we shall see, of Albert Schweitzer and Tom Dooley as men whom he admires through reading their autobiographies. The qualities he admires in Schweitzer are those of leadership and organizational ability—the fact that he could go into a jungle and carve out a hospital and get ignorant natives to help him in the task.

Religious Identification. In terms of religious identification, if he identifies with Jesus at all, it is a leader. He fails yet to see Jesus' Messiahship as based on his incarnation of God's love, but sees it rather in terms of impressing men with his message and performing miraculous acts which astound people into accepting him. For Roddy this is the way of leadership, of being a "molder of men" by being stronger than they are and using one's individual superiority to make them do his will. The ambivalence with the group is still there, and the use of his mother's control and extending her controlling ways to gain superiority with the group. The question here is whether Roddy will see the ideal of service or whether he will get to the point of operating out of a dynamic of love in his relation to a group. At present he runs the danger of "running out of gas"—his early enthusiasm—and having his mother's ambition fail him when his own weaknesses or vulnerabilities show themselves in later adolescence.

The feminine sexual identity, says the psychiatrist, underlies his superficial masculinity. The possibilities of working through the identity crisis are there, thinks the psychologist. As one summarizes, "this is a child in an unusual degree of uncrystallized integration, an unusual state of busy equilibration. . . . This is a child who is changing and who is going somewhere structurally but he is not there yet." (RG, 1962) One wonders if the identity of leader might be understood within Christian context, if he were exposed to this teaching and emotional learning. But with this lacking, one can suspect that the leadership will be other-directed, growing up in the adolescent culture of America.

All of this leads up to the question of where Roddy got his sense of vocation, and whether there are any religious aspects to it. In discussing the identity crises which Roddy went through we concluded that Roddy has tended to identify more with his mother than his father. The same can be seen in tracing his ideas about what he wants to do vocationally. When he was five he wanted to be a big league ball player as his father had tried to be. Shortly after that he talked about being a soldier, again like his father. But when Betty Lee, his sister, was born, he learned that mother went to a hospital and that a doctor attended her. The idea of being a doctor may have come into his mind then. When examined at the Project Center, he expressed interest in the stethoscope and blood pressure instrument of the examining physician and first expressed his desire to become a doctor. It should be said that the mother reinforced his desire almost from the start. Her brother-in-law, Dr. Rowe, whom they visited frequently in a neighboring state, was a country doctor. And she had started nurse's training which she had given up when she could not stand the sight of blood.

In attempting to trace the early dynamics of vocation Vilma Gupta sees it as a "certain assimilation of needs to succor others as well as to sublimate his aggression." This may be another way of speaking of a resolution of the orestes complex. Mother has appeared as the controlling and disciplining one in the family. She pointed out father's weaknesses and inadequacies by returning to work when father's business failed. Roddy had the burgeoning desire for autonomy and mastery shown in his tendencies to act the "big shot." He succeeded in expressing the desire to become a doctor in pleasing the mother and in channeling his aggressive urges in vocational ambition. This was not so much from empathy for suffering, unless it be his own, but a desire to find an identity beyond mother's control which still incorporated her values. She has kept bringing "reality" in to him in stressing the sacrifices which will be necessary to become a doctor, the long schooling, the hard financial road, the giving up of pleasures, but this simply whetted his ambition through latency. As discussed above, the ambition of his mother which he resonated helped him control his high energy and activity and by prepuberty showed in his increased IQ and leadership in his peer group.

With the onset of puberty, however, there came the ambition to become a missionary doctor like Albert Schweitzer. The question here is how much religion plays a part in this, and how much of it comes from his internal needs? Upon questioning, Roddy states that he first got the idea from reading a book on Schweitzer's life. Then he read another and saw a film about him, and he thought this is something he would like to do. When he spoke to his mother about this when he was twelve, she tried to humor him out of it, telling him how he would have to work for a while as a doctor in this country to get money enough to do it. She also told him no woman would go over to Africa with him, but this did not deter him. As she says, he sticks to it, no matter what they have said. At the outset the church appears to have little to do with this side of his vocational ambition. In fact, the interviewer told him for the first time of mission boards who could sponsor someone who wanted to do this, that a doctor no longer had to hew a mission out of the jungle as did Schweitzer.

The dynamics behind Roddy's missionary ambition appear similar to those behind his desire to be a doctor, perhaps exaggerated. With the outbreak of adolescent sexuality (about which Roddy

163

does not speak at all but, as in the questions about girls, tends to avoid) Roddy feels his mother's domination intensely. He seems to want to put distance between himself and his mother, and so he seizes on Africa as a distant spot where he could go to be a doctor. This is a way of handling the normal sexual drive by not getting married, too, for he figures no girl would want to go there with him. As he told me, "No girl in her right mind would want to go over there with all those natives." (CWS, 1962) He does mother one better in a kind of "one-upmanship" much like the showing off he did when he was five and six in talking of this.

The psychiatrist thinks that there is a lack of genuine commitment to medicine or the ideas of Schweitzer in Roddy at present. (PT, 1960) This would tend to substantiate interpreting Roddy's vocational ambitions as attempts to solve the conflict regarding dependency upon his mother by distancing and asceticism. (Anna Freud sees asceticism in adolescence as a means of handling instinctual anxiety.[3]) However, there is a search for meaning in Roddy's vocational search as indicated in his auxiliary interest in brain surgery. His enthusiastic curiosity pushes him to want to know first about the body, but now to know about the brain. He says about a surgical incision in the brain, "You don't know what you're hunting for, but it's there whatever it is." He said again, "I want to find out what makes the brain tick, what makes you nutty, where the memory is at." (CWS, 1962) There is something heroic in his desires, and something of the inquisitive curiosity of the boy interested in science, at this stage. Whether he becomes a missionary doctor is an open question. It may be the first part of his vocational interest to fall away, as he goes ahead in his schooling, because of the lack of religious motivation.

The question of how vulnerable Roddy is, is an open one. One might conclude with the rise in IQ, the successful accommodation to his teen-age culture of sports and school and teen club, that he has moved from high vulnerability to low vulnerability. But the looseness of integration, the conformity and echoing of mother's values, the diffuse sexual identity, and the use of vocation to resolve the mother-domination, and the tentativeness of the parents' situa-

---

[3] *The Ego and the Mechanisms of Defense* (New York: International Universities Press, 1964) , p. 167.

tion in the community would suggest that he is at best moderately vulnerable. There has been some movement away from his earlier weaknesses, particularly in speech and in the assumption of controls over his hyperactivity. Religion has not been the primary factor, but rather his mother's discipline and the stimulus of her values. In fact, there appears a danger of symbiosis if Roddy does go into medicine, with the mother turning away from the father, who in her eyes has not succeeded in business because of his own weakness, and turning to Roddy and working to satisfy her own ambitions. Were the father to become the head of a business and the family to secure a permanent home, there might not be so great a possibility of symbiotic relationship through Roddy's medical training.

There is a bright spot so far as religion is concerned, too, in Roddy's picture. He shows spotty training, as indicated, and does not know any hymns but Christmas carols. Furthermore he confuses the Lord's Prayer with "Now I Lay Me," and is not sure of his ground so far as the Ten Commandments are concerned. However, even with such little formal training, he possesses a sense of wonder about life, a genuine curiosity, and a heightened imagination which would leave him open to genuine religious experience. The only such experience he reports now comes not in prayer but in listening to the hard demands of a sermon and feeling the challenge of it. In responding to what he finds of struggle in life, he has found satisfaction in mastery and thrill in the midst of God's world. When asked by the psychiatrist what was the happiest experience of his life, he could recall no one experience but his genuine appreciation was of just living. There is in him—despite the rigid controls he has experienced—a sense of being in love with life. He likes its complexity and its surprise, and he wants to absorb as much of it as he can. This may be further developed as he continues to mature. It would appear to be the seed of genuine religious experience in him.

The appearance of some of the same dynamics in Roddy's life story as appeared in Terry's should make us ask ourselves some searching questions about the nature of church teaching and church practice. What is religious and what is a substitute for religion in both Terry's and Roddy's lives? Does the reader see similarities or differences between the two boys' desires to undertake a religious vocation? As we shall discuss in chapter 10, both boys were highly vulnerable in infancy and childhood. In what way has Terry used religion to gain control over his drives which Roddy has not? Helen was also ranked highly vulnerable in early life but her vulnerability rating dropped by adolescence. Is there a similarity in her gaining control and finding a sense of identity to what one observes in Roddy's life?

We shall now turn to questions about confirmation and the crises of adolescence. The biographies thus far have included a girl confirmed at age thirteen, a boy confirmed at age seven, and one who has not been confirmed at all. In examining the material on confirmation for the total group of fifty, the reader should look back at the biographies from time to time to discover what was happening to these youth at the time the church confronted them with the vows of membership. "What age is the proper age for confirmation?" is the question which may then come into focus.

8

Confirmation and the Crises of Adolescence

"How will the church give them faith?" is a question that both clergy and parents ask when confronting their youth. Particularly in today's industrialized, impersonal society how can adults help young people find their basic identity, life purpose, and motives for action? Earlier psychological studies made much of the storm-and-stress quality of adolescence and linked faith in Christ and individualized conversion with youth finding a steady and traditional role in a stable and well-defined church. But that was before today's social revolution had much impetus. Contemporary studies (Erikson, Friedenberg, Goodman, etc.) question the conformist character of both society and the church, as well as the attempt to pattern youth after traditional values when the whole drive of youth is toward change and coping with the new world coming to birth. These studies make a great deal of the fact that adolescence as a "passageway" between childhood and adulthood appears to be vanishing. Witness the preadolescent dating patterns and the earlier and earlier attempts to imitate the adult world.

Conformity to the peer group means that the "passageway"

aspects of confirmation may not be appropriate. If one "belongs" to the church as he does to the dance class and the scout group, how does this help him find justification? It may instead block him from real grappling with the issues of his life and from experiencing the world as it actually exists.

The empirical study thus far has demonstrated several things: (1) that young adolescents are at various levels in their thinking about religious beliefs; (2) that they are practicing their faith with tremendously varying patterns; (3) that church school and youth fellowship are being met with differing responses by young adolescents; (4) that personal religion is playing a widely different role in the lives of young people. We may well ask: What are the crises of young adolescents, and how is the church preparing youth for these crises? What are the patterns of church membership represented in this group, and what is the response of the adolescent to the church's initiation rites? Is there a best age for confirmation and for the teaching of the faith and helping youth enter the adult community of the faithful?

1. THE CRISES OF ADOLESCENCE

Adolescence we have defined as the shaky bridge between childhood and adulthood. As Erik Erikson points out, it is a crisis and not an affliction. By that we mean, "A normal phase of increased conflict characterized by a seeming fluctuation in ego strength and yet also by a high growth potential." [1] The crises of adolescence are brought on fundamentally by the physiological changes through which one has gone in his way toward manhood or womanhood. The crisis is more than physiological, however, in that at this stage certain expectations are put upon him by the community relative to his increased growth and capacity for work and social relations. Furthermore, these two aspects of crisis meet within the psyche of the adolescent as he comes to grips with his changing

[1] Erik Erikson, *Identity and the Life Cycle* (New York: International Universities Press, 1959), p. 116. Erikson uses the epi-genetic principle to explain growth. That is, "Anything that grows has a *ground plan* and out of this ground plan the *parts* arise, each part having its time of special ascendency, until all parts have arisen to form a *functioning whole*." p. 52.

organism and the changing expectations of the community. The community has in times past considered adolescence to be a period in which the youth moved from childhood to adulthood and was recognized in the school by a baccalaureate, in the sexual community by marriage, in the religious and political community by initiation rites. What we are attempting to do here is to look at contemporary youth, in particular the young people in this sample, to discover if the church's response to the young people is in phase with their psychological and sociological growth. [2]

Three phases of the crisis of adolescence have bearing upon the church's practice of confirmation. They are: the youth's change from concrete to abstract thinking, his search for identity, and his orientation toward and practice of future social roles. Let us look at each phase in turn.

a. Capacity for abstraction. In an experimental study of over fifteen hundred young adolescents, Professors Jean Piaget and Barbel Imhelder investigated and analyzed the changes in thinking in children from age eleven to fifteen. They discovered that this age group moves from concrete to what they call "formal" or logical operations. The latency (preadolescent) child thinks concretely and directly. He manipulates objects which he sees and feels first hand. So for him God may be a *man,* God may be mixed up with "Jesus," heaven may be a geographical place, and right and wrong may be specifically concrete acts.

The capacity to think logically is associated with the maturation of the nervous system and the completion of the "operational development of intelligence." This proceeds at differing rates, but during early adolescence (eleven to fifteen) the youth should develop this capacity for abstract thinking. Piaget defines this as "an ability to manipulate ideas, isolate variables and deduce potential relationships which can later be verified by experiment." [3] Piaget suggests that the preadolescent, eleven/twelve to thirteen/fourteen, can handle certain formal operations (implication, exclu-

[2] *Ibid.,* p. 155. "Only by maintaining in its institutionalized values meaningful correspondences to the main crises of ego development does a society manage to have at the disposal of its particular group identity a maximum of the conflict-free energy accrued from the childhood crises of a majority of its young members."

[3] *The Growth of Logical Thinking* (New York: Basic Books, 1958), p. viii, translator's note.

sion) successfully, but he is not able to set up an exhaustive method of proof. But the fourteen/fifteen-year-old adolescent does succeed in setting up proofs. "He systematically uses methods of control which require the combinatorial system, i.e., he varies a single factor at a time and excludes the others." [4] The adolescent thus is able first to think deductively and then inductively.

What are the implications for his religious thought? There should be a shift from concrete personalizing of God and concretizing of heaven and hell to more abstract speculation and reflection about the items of faith. He should be able to think about the idea of God, the ideals of right and wrong, and the rituals of his group. He should also be able through "reversal" to work with the discrepancies and disparities between the ideal and the actual. It is the "metaphysical age" par excellence, as Piaget says.

Whether a young adolescent does begin to think abstractly, and how he does, depends on several circumstances: (1) the growth of his logical capacities, (2) the permission of his parents and religious leaders to engage in such thinking, questioning, and doubting, and (3) the development of an outlook or viewpoint around which he can cluster his thoughts. We hesitate to call the latter a philosophy or world view, but it functions in just such a way, for it enables him to synthesize his past experience with his thinking and planning for the future. [5] Such activity takes him beyond the merely intellectual and rational and puts him right into the middle of *religion* which demands commitment, participation, and involvement. Whether and how these adolescents change from concrete to abstract thinking we shall investigate in the next section.

b. Search for identity. What Erik Erikson has called the "identity crisis" is usually experienced at mid-adolescence (age sixteen). Early adolescence is the preparation for the "crisis of identity" as prior stages of development have been the preparation for puberty. The ego of the child first develops about age two through the capacity to introject and project "appraisals" of himself by the significant adult

[4] *Ibid.*, p. 347 ff.
[5] E. Jacobson points out, "for long periods an adolescent's philosophy of life may vacillate in an almost preposterous way between opposite trends, depending on the predominant influence of either super-ego or id on his thinking." "Adolescent Moods and the Remodeling of Psychic Structures," *Psycho-Analytic Study of the Child*, XVI (1961), 164-83.

(the mother). ("I am a good boy"; "I love Mommy.") He separates himself from mother as a "me" but binds himself to her again as a "loved-one." The ego further develops about age six through the capacity to identify with the significant adult of the same sex—first by imitation, later by "role-play." ("Daddy likes to fish, so do I.") Introjection and identification, however, are only the primary processes, and with the onset of puberty their usefulness is over. The youth must discover *who he is anew* both as he experiences himself organically—with his growing body, his changing voice, his new sexual urges—and as he perceives how others experience him— pretty or awkward, smart or dumb, "in" or "out." Erikson says, "The sense of ego-identity . . . is the accrued confidence that one's ability to maintain inner sameness and continuity (one's ego in the psychological sense) is matched by the sameness and continuity of one's meaning for others." [6] Ego identity represents a gradual integration of all prior identifications, but it is also a new whole different from earlier unities.

The crisis of mid-adolescence hinges on finding one's identity or losing it in diffusion, self-doubt, and uncertainty about one's role in society. In latency the child felt, "I am what I know or what I can make." After puberty and the "inwardness" of thirteen or fourteen which it generates, the youth must put together the kaleidoscope of feelings, impressions, and thoughts about himself and "feedback" images from others, particularly his peers and significant adults, into a *coherent core of selfhood*. ("I am what I experience myself to be in conjunction with what others tell me I am.") The *meanings* he gives himself may be in conflict with the *meanings* others give to him. But the crucial function of mid-adolescence is to work out some resolution of this conflict.

What does this identity crisis say to the religious problem of adolescence? Erikson has phrased the crisis in other terms which speak more cogently to the religious area: The identity crisis may be further described as a crisis between fidelity and diversity. By fidelity, he means the "search for something or somebody to be true to" in the midst of shifting changes in social relations and the

[6] *Identity and the Life Cycle*, p. 89.

culture itself. [7] Fidelity is the root of youth's "disciplined devotion" and can be well placed or poorly placed. This depends upon the religious heritage of his parents, his own reactions to their authority and that of other authority-persons and of the ideological forces abroad (the civil-rights movement, the Peace Corps, radical right groups, religious sects, etc.). As Parsons and others have pointed out, in our rapidly changing society it is difficult for a youth to find his identity, particularly when his parents and pastor "cannot provide direct guidance and role models that would provide him with a reality structured definition of the situation." [8] Later we want to investigate several youths' identity crises and the relationship to their faith.

c. Orientation toward and practice of future social roles. The third crisis which young adolescents confront is the transition from childhood roles to adult roles. This transition has been traditionally handled by "rites of passage" as Van Gennerp and several anthropologists have discussed. There are ceremonial patterns which accompany a passage from one situation to another or from one cosmic or social world to another. For instance, a funeral ceremony can be called a "rite of separation" of family and friends from a loved one, a marriage ceremony a "rite of incorporation" of two single persons into the married community. And a confirmation ceremony is a "transition rite" in which the individual passes from one age to another. Van Gennerp cites the eleventh-century church membership rites as an example in which the catechumen was separated from the outside group, and during the transition period was exorcised and instructed, and then during the rites incorporated into the body of adult members. [9]

Puberty has traditionally been the period for these initiation and membership rites. In some cultures the rite involves the adolescent living separate from the community, and the boys having to prove themselves men by some feat of hunting or warfare. Circumcision, preparatory to fulfillment of the sexual role, has sometimes been performed. For the girls it has been separation until they became

[7] "Youth—Fidelity and Diversity," pp. 3 ff.

[8] T. Parsons, "Youth in the Context of American Society," in Erikson, *Youth: Change and Challenge,* pp. 115 ff.

[9] Arnold van Gennerp, *Rites of Passage* (Chicago: University of Chicago Press, 1960), pp. 93-95.

eligible for engagement and becoming sexual partners. The rites thus served unconscious purposes. Says Arlow, "The initiation rites solemnize the granting of such sexual and other privileges which accrue to mature men of the community. . . . Through these ceremonies a resolution of the hostility between the generations is facilitated and identification with the taboos and values of the group is effected." [10]

Does confirmation have any connection with "rites of passage"? The consensus of several writers—Arlow, Eisenstadt, Van Gennerp, and Erikson [11]—is that confirmation could very well serve as a "rite of passage." It could serve the purpose of separating the youth from the world of childhood, in particular the dependencies upon his mother, the relaxation of controls enabling him to become self-motivated and inner-directed, and the transmitting of the tradition of the elders both as to beliefs and ethics into a framework for living. Confirmation could *confirm* the youth in his new identity as a young adult within the social group, with all its privileges and responsibilities. Ideally, as Erikson so aptly describes, the ceremonies may "strive, within an atmosphere of mystical timelessness, to combine some form of sacrifice or submission with an energetic guidance toward sanctioned and circumscribed ways of action—a combination which assures the development in the novice of an optimum of compliance with a maximum sense of fellowship and free choice." [12]

The pastor or priest may be the substitute parent who permits the youth to break away from home, who sanctions his religious questions and doubts, who allows him the freedom to test out his new ideology or idealism within a wider context than the narrow prescriptions of family. A young person may need to be a disciple or follower of a strong leader—the Christ-figure, Albert Schweitzer, the pastor—before he can become his own authority. [13] The questions are: Does confirmation serve this purpose for children in this group? Does the pastor or priest fulfill the role of "guide" or even

[10] Jacob Arlow, "A Psychoanalytic Study of a Religious Initiation Rite," *Psychoanalytic Study of the Child*, VI (1951), 355.

[11] See *Youth: Change and Challenge*, pp. 27 ff.

[12] Erikson, *Identity and the Life Cycle*, p. 144.

[13] George J. Mohr and Marian A. Despres, *The Stormy Decade: Adolescence* (New York: Random House, 1958), p. 151. "An exalted powerful father-God may be substituted for the repudiated personal father."

"master" for the young adolescent represented here? What, in other words, is confirmed for the youth in confirmation?

2. CONFIRMATION AND THE CHURCH'S PRACTICE

Let us look now at the evidence from this group of thirty young adolescents who were interviewed and tested concerning their religious beliefs and practices to test out the formulation about crises. What about their capacity for abstract or philosophical thinking? During the interview, the examiner questioned each youth about the creation story and asked him how he squared this with science, particularly the theory of evolution.

Here are some examples of accounts of creation from both boys and girls:

[Dan, age thirteen and a half, Protestant] Well, he [God] was lonely, so he made something where man could be, and he got lonelier, he began making man and animals. Well, first he made animals and then man. . . . he took dirt and he made it in the form of man and something happened and he came to life [In response to the question, If science said one thing and the Bible said another, which would be right?] I think the Bible would be right.

[Greg, age fifteen and a half, Protestant] I'm kind of liberal about this. I don't take its word for everything the Bible says. I don't think it happened completely this way. Of course, God had a lot to do with it, but I don't think the Bible . . . is to be always taken literally. It's just an example, and I don't believe God hurled the world into existence. I mean, it was probably quite dramatic and everything, but I'm sure it was different than this, and I believe partially what the scientists say, and I'm kind of a compromiser. [He relates the planetary hypothesis and adds] I think God created it before it started growing. Of course, he is *nature.*

[Darlene, age fourteen, Fundamentalist Protestant] Well, it's in the Bible, it's in the beginning God created the Heavens and the earth and did something each day and I feel exactly what's in the Bible is right and before it was just dark nothingness and at least having to do with earth, the atmosphere and the universe close around us but nothing was here—and then in the beginning of time, he was here before this forever and ever

174

and he's always been. It's hard to even try to imagine but he was—and then in the beginning of time he created this earth and put people on it and then when fire comes in the end and demolishes it and ruins it and it's gone, well then it will just be ruined forever. But I feel that he did just as it says in the Bible, that he created the earth and he put man here and beast and everything.

[Janice, age fifteen, Protestant] That's one thing that bothers me. . . . I know there has to be a God because that's the way I was brought up. . . . I feel all these people in the world wouldn't believe in one if there wasn't one . . . so I believe everything that's in the Bible. . . . [In response to question about evolution] Well, we . . . talked about this at school and I've always taken it for granted that it was done in six days. But in order to go along with science, these six days had to be longer than 24-hour periods. . . . There is sort of a certain amount of years between each thing happening which could be maybe several thousand years that each thing did happen, you know, that he did this instead of just in six days.

One immediately becomes aware of the fact that there are instances of both concrete, even literalistic, thinking about the story of creation; Greg and Janice are attempting to form a synthesis between science and religion. One should say, however, that even with Darlene, there is evidence of abstract thinking around the themes of endless space and eternity.

We may test Piaget's conceptualizations about the growth of logical thinking by looking at the total group.

The Creation Story—Adolescent Thought

Child	Age	Concrete	Abstract
1. Ray	12.5	X	
2. Vivian	13	X	
3. Adele	13	X	
4. Diane	13		X
5. Lenny	13	X	
6. Dennis	13.5	X	
7. Don	13.5	X	
8. Maurice	13.5		X
9. Barbie	14	X	

175

Child	Age	Concrete	Abstract
10. Helen	14		✕
11. Ron	14	✕	
12. Stewart	14		✕
13. Darlene	14	✕	
14. Teddy	14		✕
15. Roddy	14		✕
16. Claudia	14	✕	
17. Delbert	14		✕
18. Sally	14	✕	
19. Terry	14.5		✕
20. Chester	14.5		✕
21. Rachel	14.5	✕	
22. Daryl	14.5	✕	
23. Vernon	14.5		✕
24. Janice	15		✕
25. Greg	15.5		✕
26. Martin	15.5		✕
27. Susan	15.5	✕	
28. Corliss	15.5	✕	
29. Melvin	16		✕
30. Milly	16		✕

Table 8-1

(C=Concrete   A=Abstract)

Age Totals Ages	12/13	14	15/16
	6 C — 2 A	7 C — 8 A	2 C — 5 A

Table 8-2

(C=Concrete   A=Abstract)

Boy—Girl Age Totals Ages		12/13	14	15/16
	Boys	4 C —1 A	1 C — 7 A	3 A
	Girls	2 C — 1 A	6 C — 1 A	2 C — 2 A

The data show that only half this group is capable of abstract thinking. It shows quite conclusively that the capacity to think in abstract categories increases with age. At age twelve/thirteen only one boy and one girl are capable of thinking abstractly about creation and evolution—one of three of this group. More than half are so capable at age fourteen and only two of seven are still thinking concretely at age fifteen/sixteen. Other factors than age (intelligence, training, family environment) are involved here so that we cannot draw any firm conclusions. Our sample is not large enough to generalize, but it is interesting to note that the girls were predominantly concrete in their thinking about God at all ages. It might be worth investigating the common-sense opinion that girls generally are intuitive rather than intellectual in their approach to religion.

We shall examine the identity crisis in more detail in the chapter on "Coping." However, it might be significant to look at four of the youth with respect to the identity crisis to test out Erikson's theoretical formulation. Two of the girls, Helen and Diane (studied in chapters 6 and 12), have fantasies which demonstrate their identity struggle and its relation to their faith. Helen identifies strongly with a nineteenth-century Sunday school heroine, Elsie Dinsmore. As noted in the study, she does this not to break away from her family but to become the "religious leader" of the family and to win the approval of a secondary identification figure, her pastor. Diane, on the other hand, strongly identified with religion through her parents in latency, chooses the heroine of *Breakfast at Tiffany's* to distance herself from both her parents and the church. She wants to live in the secular world, and not be fanatical as her mother is about her faith. Her sister now serves as an identification figure, as a way out of the "nest" into the excitement and intellectual feast of the world. And her struggles make her doubt much she has previously taken for granted. It is an instance of a "religious identification" with her mother at six which she now finds undone and a struggle for identity with a different "faith" than she has been taught.

The two boys, Terry and Teddy (chapters 2 and 4), have similar identity struggles but centered more on *vocation*. Terry's drive to be a priest was a way of pleasing his mother by "outdoing" her. He found the vocation to be too demanding. His religious counselors, although they provided good identity-figures in prepuberty (Knights of the Altar and God and Country studies) are now not close to him. The high school with its heterosexual grouping, its science, and its activities beckon him to find an identity here—and his early longing to solve the family triangle loses its appeal. Teddy, on the other hand, at age six, had a strong identification with his father, whom he lost when his mother divorced. His identity struggles now involve him with faith. God is a present reality—his stepfather is not satisfactory as an identification figure. Prayer and meditation are ways of seeking surcease from his conflicts and the strong erotic feelings about his mother. His faith is a release from anxiety but his identity struggle around leaving home still has to be faced.

The data from the interviews of the other twenty-four youths are not as complete as for the six biographical studies. It is the investigator's conclusion, however, that following puberty there is a moratorium on "identity" until the fifteenth or sixteenth year and that the crisis is not strongly felt by the young adolescent. The thirteen- or fourteen-year-old has become "inward" and extremely sensitive to his feeling about himself and *who he is*. But until he can turn outward and become sensitive to what others think of him and "feed back" to him, the crisis of identity will not be felt in its fullest intensity. Erikson has spoken of the "moratorium" on heterosexual relations following puberty. It would appear following the break-up of earlier identification patterns there is a similar moratorium on *identity*—at least, the adolescent does not deal with the crisis until about midpoint in the teen years.[14]

Finally, we want to look at current confirmation and membership practices of this group to test out the "rite of passage" concepts elaborated earlier. The total group's practices can be discerned from this chart and table 8-3.

Age at Confirmation

Child	Denomination	Age at Confirmation	Member
1. Terry	Catholic	7	Yes
2. Dennis	Protestant		No

[14] "The period can be viewed as a psycho-social moratorium during which the individual . . . may find a niche in some section of his society." *Op. cit.*, p. 111.

Child	Denomination	Age at Confirmation	Member
3. Chester	Protestant	13	Yes
4. Ray	Protestant	11	Yes
5. Don	Protestant	11	Yes
6. Greg	Protestant	13	Yes
7. Barbie	Protestant		No
8. Helen	Protestant	13	Yes
9. Rachel	Catholic	8	Yes
10. Ron	Catholic	7	Yes
11. Daryl	Catholic	8	Yes
12. Vivian	Catholic	7	Yes
13. Maurice	Protestant	13	Pending
14. Stewart	Catholic	8	Yes
15. Darlene	Protestant	9	Yes
16. Teddy	Protestant	13	Pending
17. Roddy	Protestant		No
18. Claudia	Protestant	13	Yes
19. Adele	Protestant		No
20. Delbert	Catholic	7	Yes
21. Melvin	Catholic	7	Yes
22. Vernon	Catholic	8	Yes
23. Martin	Catholic	9	Yes
24. Susan	Protestant	14	Yes
25. Janice	Protestant	9	Yes
26. Sally	Protestant		No
27. Diane	Protestant	7	Yes
28. Corliss	Catholic		No
29. Milly	Catholic	8	Yes
30. Lenny	Protestant		No

Three patterns generally emerge as practiced by Protestant and Catholic churches:

1. Early childhood confirmation and first communion (age seven to nine) by the Roman Catholics. The child is trained to "recite" his catechism and to attend mass and confession. The significance of what he has "learned" or "practices" is less important; the setting of right habits is more.

Table 8-3
Age at Confirmation

Age	Number
7	6
8	5
9	3
10	0
11	2
12	0
13 and above	7
Members	23
Non-members	7
Total	30

2. Middle childhood (age seven to eleven) "conversion from sin" with believer's baptism and membership as a sign of conversion. The child is made to feel guilty for his *sins* (generally disobedience of authorities) by adults. Repentance and reliance on God or Christ is held out as the buttress against further acts of "sinning."

3. Adolescent confirmation which prepares the youth for the adult social role of church member, introducing him to the belief system of the adults and allowing him to find his identity within the faith and the group.

The data on pages 178-79 suggest that the Roman Catholic group has a larger percentage of members by the time the boys and girls reach adolescence. Only one of a group of twelve remains outside the church, whereas six of a group of eighteen Protestant youth have not been confirmed. The conservative Protestant churches have also attempted to "secure" their children to the faith by baptism and membership before puberty, and have only "missed" one. The main-line Protestant groups have generally waited until the child reached puberty to train him for membership, and as a result have the largest number (five) not yet members.

When one examines what membership *means*, it is another matter.

I could not get from any of the Roman Catholic children significant memories of their confirmation; they were meeting expectations of parents and religious leaders purely and simply. As Terry says, "I did it because, well, it's one thing as a Catholic you're supposed to be confirmed." An amusing incident occured around Cindy H. (a Catholic). She missed the point of confirmation and thought being a "soldier of Christ" meant hitting others and being mean. Quite a few explanations from her parents were necessary to change her thinking. Diane is an example of those conservative youth who were *converted* as children. She said, "It seemed meaningful, but when I look back on it, it doesn't seem so. I don't feel I should have done it because now I don't think that it is fair for me to have done it . . . because I wasn't old enough to know what I was really wanting."

The group of youth thirteen and older appear to be using *confirmation* as a rite of passage with some exceptions. Susan (age fourteen, Protestant) says, for example, that for her "The church is a place to worship God" and that for her the sermon is now more interesting than a Sunday school lesson. And we remember Helen's identity with the church. "The younger people will soon be taking over for the older so they should pay attention to what the church is and does." One should say, in defense of the Roman Catholics that by the time they are adolescents, the *real* meaning of the church is becoming evident. As Melvin Rogers sums up, "It's kind of an organization instituted by Christ. And it's to help Catholic people get to heaven—help all persons get to heaven really. And we do this through various means—the mass and the sacraments, and well, just to help us get to heaven, I guess." The lessons have been well learned, but they have prepared him for the social role of membership.

3. THE AGE OF CONFIRMATION

Can we ask now, what is the proper age for confirmation? Theory and empirical data appear to point us to certain conclusions. What are they?

1. The onset of puberty occasions the break-up of latency struc-

181

tures in the personality including dependency upon parents and other adults for belief and value identifications.

2. The young adolescent, particularly at ages fourteen and fifteen, develops the capacity to think abstractly, whereas in latency he has been restricted to concrete thinking.

3. In middle adolescence the youth passes through an identity crisis in which he attempts to discover who he is in relationship to what others think of him.

4. The young adolescent is ready to go through certain rites of passage by which he is prepared for the adult social roles and learns the lore of the community.

5. These crises have certain implications for the teaching of faith and the meaning and purpose of confirmation.

The study shows that Roman Catholic children with few exceptions have learned their credal statements well and following confirmation at ages seven to nine have developed habitual patterns with regard to confession and church attendance. However, because of its early timing, confirmation precedes the crises of adolescence and tends to freeze the child in a latency-dependency relationship to mother church and father priest. Moreover, the child has learned his lessons in an intellectual sense and they do not become a part of his personality development until he reaches adolescence. Current Catholic thinking is questioning this. In fact, Father P. A. Liege says that this is in contradiction to early church practice which related the youth more directly to the gospel. [15]

"It is a fact that in the Catholic Church, little by little, primacy has been given to 'doctrinal teaching' and that the stage of kerygma has practically disappeared from the catechesis. Doubtless it was believed safeguarded when the children were baptized in Christian countries and received their Christian education in the faith as from a mother." Father Nebreda says that to transmit the kerygma requires a renewal of faith among the catechumens.

The more conservative Protestant children who have been forced to accept literal beliefs and harsh moral precepts at an early age by parents have either lost their identity within that of their parents

[15] *Encyclopedia*, G. Jacquemet, ed., Vol. IV, col. 757 (Paris, 1954). Quoted in *Apostolic Renewal in Seminary*, 125, a Christopher Book edited by James Keller and Richard Armstrong, New York, 1965.

or in the adolescent period. They rebel against this teaching by doubting who they are and what they believe. Particularly is this so when conversion is made an expectation of early childhood. The conversion crisis is precipitated before the child is prepared emotionally or intellectually for it, and he may recede from it during adolescence as an experience which once had meaning and now has become meaningless. A Baptist religious educator, G. Temp Sparkman, has noted this and suggested that the nonsacramental churches "recognize the value of religious experience prior to conversion rather than forcing upon that experience, though real it is, all the concepts associated with conversion." [16] This would give the child a chance to grow and enter adolescence with some more realistic expectations of his religious life.

The more liberal Protestant children have two basic patterns. There is a group of conformist youth who attend church half-heartedly as do their parents or who go because the crowd goes and take membership vows with little connection to their identity questions or their logical meanings and find their values and what ideology they have with the crowd. They have often dropped out of meaningful relationship to the church by mid-adolescence and certainly by the time they leave home for work or college. This group is quite similar to a group which a Swiss pastor writes about who take confirmation at age sixteen but with little expectation of participating in church and express this as "the lie of confirmation." [17] For this American group, as for the Swiss, there is, therefore, some sense in which the training is out of phase with the crises and conflicts through which they are going. One must add that there are, on the other hand, certain Protestant youth in this sample who have been allowed to engage meaningfully in relating their theological and ethical beliefs to their abstract thinking, to their questions of identity, and their search for a social role and, therefore, are working through to some real meanings of faith and practice.

[16] "Implications of Conversation Among Young Children," *Religious Education,* LX (July-August, 1965) , 313.

[17] L. Schmid, *Religiöses Erleben unserer Jugend* (Zollikan, 1960) . Quoted by Walter Neidhart in "A Declaration of Faith in Swiss Presbyterian Churches," *Religious Education,* LX (July-August, 1965) , 297.

4. IMPLICATIONS

The Bar Mitzvah of the Jewish faith, which uses confirmation as a means for the Jewish boy at age thirteen to be initiated into the rites and duties of synagogue worship, shows real wisdom. One Jewish educator, Stuart Rosenberg, however, questions the age of thirteen as being too soon for this and feels that it should be put off until age eighteen or twenty.[18] Similarly, Russell Becker feels that age thirteen is too soon, and he believes that confirmation should be held during the first two years of the four-year high school period. [19]

It is our conclusion that the crises of adolescence, and particularly the ones from puberty to age fifteen or sixteen, make this the ideal period for confronting the youth as a member of the adult religious community. One must recognize that, with a period of rapid social change when, as Friedenberg and Goodman say, adolescence appears to be vanishing in the sense of a period of transition, any specific age would be artificially selected and socially conditioned. However, it can be established as a response to the intellectual readiness of the child and the identity crises that he is going through, and in a real sense become a rite of passage for the youth. This will not be a transition period in the sense that it was in a traditional culture, but it will represent a movement of the young person from the world of childhood to the world of adulthood, with the established ideology and religious practices as a framework for this movement. The confirmation service, rather than being built on the isolation of the adolescent, should then help him discover who he is in the light of ultimate questioning. The pastor or priest or rabbi may serve as an identification figure in the classes which he conducts with the youth of this age and help bridge the gap from the primary family to the larger world through the church.

[18] "Judaism requires today a new ladder of religious education. Modern rabbis and intelligent laymen should revise the Talmudic scale. . . . All of which makes me feel that thirteen is not the right age for Bar Mitzvah. And if I could, I would settle for nothing less than eighteen!" Stuart E. Rosenberg, "The Right Age for Bar Mitzvah," *Religious Education,* LX (July-August, 1965), 300.

[19] "Placing the confirmation study program in the first two years of the four-year high school period is the best way to put the question of affirming one's faith to the maturing young person as a decision he makes in preparation for his life ahead." Russell J. Becker, "The Proper Age for the Declaration of Faith," *Religious Education,* LX (July-August, 1965), 294.

Our suggestion would be, therefore, that the classes be held the last two years of junior high school. These classes would not be for the entire year but in two quarters, a fall quarter and a spring quarter, with the classes substituting for the church school hour. Following the completion of four quarters of study of the scripture, church history, the policy of the church, the relation of the Christian to the world—particularly the world of his peers—the youth would be ready for confirmation. This confirmation would parallel the graduation from junior high and would give him the three years of senior high as a period in which he would actively work as a church member and gain some feeling of identity in this role.

The crises of adolescence, therefore, suit him for confirmation, and being confirmed is in a very real sense reinforcing the youth in the idea that he has of himself. To the question, "Who am I?" he brings the correlated answers from the gospel, "You are a child of God"—"You are, as a part of your baptism, sealed as a part of the family of the church"—"You belong not just to us but through your Savior, the Christ, to the world as his servant." His crisis as an adolescent, therefore, finds real significance within the confirming act of the church as it affirms his new identity, as he experiences it and his new citizenship in the larger community.

9

Diane
the Study of a Conservative
Protestant Girl

The reader is now asked to enter the life experience of a conservative, even fundamentalist, girl. He should lay aside any prejudices about the girl, for in one way she is a conservative, in another way she is a person in process. One might expect religion to play a central role in her life and it does. The unique way Diane has used religion to cope with her situation is most important. She is, in addition, the first low vulnerable child we shall study (see chapter 10); however, her vulnerability rating sharply increases at the time of puberty. The crisis character of adolescence which we have just studied is also important to study in her life.

The questions the reader is asked to consider in studying Diane's life history are as follows: (1) What does her early conversion (at age six) mean to her? (2) How has her religion helped her cope with her drives? (3) What can be said about the current stage of doubt she is going through? (4) How can we understand her shift in vulnerability? Does her doubt and loss of self-esteem have anything to do with it?

Diane is representative of about five children in this group who come from conservative homes. She should be studied carefully to understand the kinds of struggles such youth go through in today's world and the attempts at resolving these struggles.

Diane Taylor is a young girl, just entering adolescence. She is of medium stature, with long arms and long legs. Her face is square and with fine features; her eyes are blue, her hair ash blonde and cut in a youthful bob. She is slow of gait and of movement, deliberate in everything she does, but, when she gets excited, her speech gets more rapid and there is a flood of words. She carries herself well, with more assurance than one expects of girls this age. She looks at you directly and answers you directly. On the days I saw her—immediately following Christmas—she wore a new plaid kiltie skirt, a white blouse, and white sneakers. She wore no makeup.

She was with her sister, Phyllis, a college freshman, who resembles her but is fully six feet tall. This sister is one of her five siblings, there being a brother Ted, twenty-one, who was recently married and is working in a neighboring town; Phyllis, nineteen, mentioned above; the two children who bracket her—Janice, fifteen, and Paula, seven; and Molly, almost four. With Phyllis off to college, only the four girls are at home now. Home is in a small midwestern village, where her father migrated from Capital City to take up a combination management-labor position with an electrical company. He has worked for the company all his married life and has achieved, for a man with a high-school education, a significant position. They live in a new house on the edge of town with five acres, which they cultivate for vegetables which are canned by mother and children in summer for winter meals. Father is an active person in the local church, serving as head of the board of deacons, and mother is president of the woman's society. Father also is active in Lions Club, Community Chest, and he sings in a male quartet.

Diane is a seventh grader and this year was elected cheerleader for football and basketball games. She takes piano lessons and recently was asked to be pianist for the youth group at church. She excels in her grades at school, has learned to swim in the summer, and plays at other sports, though she is not good at them. Her present vocational ambition it to be a business secretary in a big city.

187

1. RELIGIOUS PRACTICES

This is a family which actively participates in church life, is fundamentalist in belief, pietistic in practice. Mr. Taylor's parents were active churchgoing farmers, the mother being an outgoing, loving, and fervent Christian. Mrs. Taylor's family were lower-class, laboring people, fundamentalist, with the mother being more fearful and magical in her beliefs. When the Taylors lived in Capital City, they liked the minister at their church very much, but Mr. Taylor felt the church was modernist and did not stress evangelism enough. When they moved to the small town where they now live, he found the local church more to his religious taste, and he and the entire family joined this church. On reaching mid-childhood, each child has been baptized by immersion following accepting Christ and has joined the church. Diane accepted Christ at age six, as we shall discuss later, and joined the church following a short class in basic beliefs. [1]

Each member of the family participates in the life of the church and is expected to attend church school, both morning and evening church services, and prayer meeting on Wednesday night. When he is old enough, he becomes a part of the young people's society. Prayer is taught in the home, the Bible is read, grace is said at meals, and devotional readings are read by the father. Besides that, the youngsters are taught hymns around the piano and enjoy singing them with the father. The mother listens to religious programs on the radio and subscribes to the *Back to the Bible* magazine put out each week by a certain program.

Religion suffuses the home. On visiting it one notices a Sallman painting of Christ at the Door on the wall and a woodcut with the words "God is Love," near the door. One feels that religion is as much a part of the family as the air they breathe and the food they eat. Being a Christian means that they do not engage in some practices such as smoking and drinking and do engage in others such as prayer and churchgoing. Diane has grown up this way, as have the other children. Theodore went through a period while he was in the service when he rebelled actively from the family's

[1] The text used was *The New Life*, by A. R. Knight and G. H. Schroeder (Philadelphia: American Baptist Publication Society, 1947).

religion, but interestingly enough he came back to the church upon marriage. Phyllis has not actively rebelled, although in her first year of college, she has told her mother she is having to rethink her religious position. Janice is at present in a stage of rebellion, and, as we shall discover, already Diane has seen this behavior in the others and is wondering about these practices.

She revealed upon questioning that she does not pray every night as she was taught but does engage in private meditation. She gave up her Bible reading when, as she told her mother, it did not seem to make any difference. She does attend church services regularly with the family and goes to the youth organization each Sunday night. She cannot stay away from church except when ill, although she says she wishes she did not have to go all the time. She is actively critical of the minister which they formerly had, and evidently with reason. She likes the minister they now have, and going to church is not the chore it used to be.

2. RELIGIOUS BELIEFS

Diane can be said to accept the orthodox Protestant beliefs, with fundamentalist undertones about biblical inspiration. These can be seen most clearly in the God-concept scale when she describes God as holy, eternal, redeeming, and divine. She does not think God to be mythical, but rather a Reality in which she implicitly believes. She believes things strongly, in the scale either agreeing very much or disagreeing very much. There are a few areas, which we shall discuss in the next section, in which she disagrees a little, showing the presence of doubt. But her church-school teaching, the preaching she has heard, and her parents' strong reinforcement of the beliefs have made an indelible impression on her.

When asked about what she believes about God, she said she finds him to be beauty and a sense of order. She sees him in the beauty of nature and also in the slums. When asked further about the slums, she said that seeing the children there aroused pity and that this was of God. She holds an orthodox view of God as Creator, redeemer, and as Holy Spirit but questions why there is no mention of the Holy Spirit in the Old Testament. She also questions the idea of God as vengeful and as damning, feeling this is no part of

God. In fact, on the Q-sort, she finds the stern, critical, and punishing adjectives to be least descriptive of God. She criticized the pastor who said that he would enjoy seeing God punish sinners in hell from his vantage point in heaven. This is most unchristian, she felt. When she was eleven, she wanted to be an archeologist so she could go to the Holy Lands and in her digs make discoveries to disprove the scientific ideas about evolution. But a year later, she was trying in her own mind to make some kind of synthesis between the biblical story of creation and evolution. "Whether man came from the ape or from dust, I still believe God made him. God is the creative mind behind it all." (CWS, 1962)

She also holds the orthodox ideas about Jesus. At eleven she said, "I believe he is the only one on the whole earth that's perfect and that ever will be perfect until he comes again." (PT, 1961) At twelve, however, she is having difficulty with the idea of the preexistence of Christ. How can a man exist before he is born? She believes in Christ's divinity more from his life, death, and resurrection, and the fact that he saved her at age six in her conversion. This for her has its own self-authentification.

She says she would not be afraid of death if there were no heaven and hell. Heaven is a place she cannot even dream about, hence she does not know about the streets paved with gold and the gates of pearl. But hell is for her a place of eternal destruction. "There one is tormented forever, forever, forever . . . it rings like down a long hall." (CWS, 1962) She thinks she is going to heaven, for she has been saved when she accepted Christ. There is not an otherworldly quality about talk of heaven. She sees it as a reassurance against death.

She has strong ideas about good and bad which are not exactly those of her parents but which have recently been influenced by her peer group. She holds to the Ten Commandments and the Golden Rule but has paraphrased the latter for herself as follows, "Do unto others as you would have others do unto you, if you feel like it." She feels it might be all right to smoke or use cosmetics—this differs from mother—but she thinks dope and drinking are out. On questions of sexual morality she says, "To go out and make out is not for us" (her peer group) , feeling that she is too young to get serious with boys. In fact, she is quite serious when she talks about "those who think they are big enough and understand life enough to have sexual intercourse." One gets the impression that she and her sister Phyllis (rather than the mother at this stage) have had long talks about this.

She believes in meditation rather than prayer, which is long reflection and bringing the powers of her mind to play upon a problem. She thinks that prayer can be used selfishly, as praying for a new car, but that if one asks for strength for a test or prays for an orphan, God can answer prayer. At this point in interview she did some active problem solving about the way in which she thinks God runs the world. She does not believe in magical solutions to prayer but believes that God uses natural law as a means of restructuring a situation. She said, "God can answer prayer many different ways. If you pray for someone sick of cancer and dying, he'll send somebody, a chemist or druggist to find something to heal this man . . . the spirit of God can use men or different ways differently." (CWS, 1962) She said once she meditated before a basketball game—the team had previously dropped two games to second-rate schools. As a result—the team also prayed before the game—the team won. She believes that prayer and meditation made a difference in their doing their best this time.

3. RELIGIOUS ATTITUDES

Diane summarized her prevailing religious mood with the following words "I believe in it because I think it is true, yet it's very hard to believe in it." She has always been precocious, as will become evident in the developmental material. One finds her making a transition from latency early with the conflicts and irresolutions of adolescence already upon her. Her speech is colored with the phrase "I guess," as though nothing is absolutely certain. That is, unless she is pushed, and then she falls back on a moralistic, churchy tone more characteristic of mother than her. To certain things she hears in church—such as strong statements about hell and death—she thinks she has closed her "spiritual ears." (CWS, 1962) It has been said over and over again, and she feels often the sermon or lesson is not relevant to where she is intellectually. But to other statements, such as words about growth in religious

191

attitudes, as she heard from one of her older sister's church school teachers, she listens and sees its relevance. She has deeply emotional doubts about what her parents have taught her and therefore doubts their ability to be her guide in realms of religion and morals. But she is trying to use doubt creatively to work her way through what she hears now, whether in school or in church.

She also is experiencing a conflict between duty and desire. She has previously been intense in religious practice, using mother's and father's behavior as a guide. But she has seen what her older siblings do in rebellion and also measured her family's active practice of religion against that of her girl friends. She sees a girl whose parents do not practice religion coming to church of her own volition. And she feels this would be better than going out of a sense of duty. The reason she goes to church now, she says, is because her parents make her. If she had her dream come true she would go Sunday morning and that would be all. She would stay home sometimes and sleep. She would be a member but not president of anything as her mother and father are. If she were asked to do something, she would do it, but that's all. Her desire would be to get pleasure out of life and not be bound in by the rules of conscience.

Religion as she has experienced it has been stifling to a certain extent, but she has also been dimly aware of it as a creative encounter with reality. She experiences this in religious music or in art or in private meditation. So she has a basic conflict in regard to the value of her own creativity versus conformity to the group. On the one hand she sees the church as an extension of the controls of her parents, particularly mother, and on the other she feels the stirrings of her own creative urges which would have her make something of life. Formerly she had ideas of a church vocation, a biblical archeologist or a nurse to Korean orphans, which attempted to blend the creative urges into a conforming life. Now her ideal is to live alone in a large house, have a new car, and five hundred dollars a month for doing nothing. She would have no tax and could go to school free. (CWS, 1962) It is a life such as Audrey Hepburn lived in *Breakfast at Tiffany's,* but perhaps "not quite that wild," she says. But it involves freedom without responsibility. The freedom is from parental control, church control, community control, but in the hiatus which is adolescence it would give her a chance to find out who she is and allow her to seek out the creative resources in herself which she can develop. She does not want to accept responsibility for others until she can be fully responsible to her own genius. Whatever shackles her now into believing what others want her to believe, doing what others want her to do, is to be shut out. She may act a part, as a "TV actress" (LBM, 1962), until she can be sure of herself, but, when she is sure, she wants to live authentically until about age forty when she wants to die. That will be enough, she thinks, before she gets old and has to act like an old woman and feel old. One gets the impression that she would like to be "translated" into an angelic state without the pains of death as well. It is the struggle of growth which she is feeling so painfully now, and which provides the ache which she must hide from the world.

4. QUESTIONS

There are certain questions which one must ask again of the developmental material to help us understand the present stage of her religious development. With Diane, one gets the impression of a girl in transition, characteristic of the adolescent upheaval. Yet there run through her personality certain trends which have been a long time developing and which need tracing to their origins.

1. What did conversion mean to her at age six? This is early for this kind of experience, even within her fundamentalist church. Is the experience, as usually described, a resolution of a conflict or series of conflicts which bothered the little girl at this stage of her life? Or is it to be understood as a family phenomenon or a community phenomenon, aside from its theological derivatives? And since she has been converted this early, does this have any effect on her experience in latency and early adolescence?

2. How has religion as practiced by Diane affected her coping with internal drives, namely sex and aggression? Has she used religion as an "escape" from tension states? Has she prayed or engaged in Bible study as a means of coping with her inner problems? And as a part of this, we should ask where she has learned these patterns of control? From mother or father or siblings?

193

Can religion be looked on as a "flight from herself" or as an active coping device?

3. What can be said about the current stage of doubt which she is going through? Is she doubting her way to faith? Or is she doubting her way to unbelief? How much is doubt a correlate of her state of conflict between duty and desire, between conformity and creativity? How much is it a deeply emotional schism in her between her identity with mother and father and her identity with siblings? Or peers? And how much is doubting and criticism as she is practicing it a product of her own perfectionistic standards which she feels herself failing to reach and now wonders whether anyone can reach?

4. Finally, with respect to vulnerability, one should state that she was at infancy and preschool rated one of the least vulnerable in the group! At puberty there is an increase in vulnerability, shown perhaps most dramatically in a drop of thirty-six points in "performance" IQ, a shallowness of affect and tendency to role-play rather than get through with her own ideas and feelings.

The question arises as to what is causing this, particularly in the area of self-esteem and narcissism? What part has her religion played in making her able genuinely to love herself and to love others? Is there any loss in this ability in the breakup of the latency integration around accepting Christ? What has moved her from positive self-esteem to the adolescent narcissism with resulting egocentricity? Is there anything in her world which can help her integrate a religion of love into a positive self-picture? Will this move her toward the family and toward their religious schema or away from them in a rebellious fashion? In other words, is her newly emerging religious integration moving her toward a religion of love or away from it?

5. DEVELOPMENT OF DIANE'S RELIGIOUS ORIENTATION

Vulnerability. Perhaps it is best to begin with the vulnerability question, for this gets us back to Diane's infancy. She was her mother's fourth child and third girl. She was a sturdy, vigorous baby and, according to Dr. Escalona, could move energetically but also spent much time in gentle activity. She took a long time to nurse, yet turned from the breast decisively when sated. She had good tolerance for stimuli such as light and sound but was distressed by loud noises. She showed little reaction to the subtle nuances of human behavior, smiling little. She seemed more interested in objects than people. She was not extremely sensitive, her thresholds appearing in the medium to moderately high ranges (SE, 1950)

Following her birth, her mother was unwell and depressed. Soon the father and the older sisters took over her care, necessitating weaning at eight weeks. At first she put up a fuss but after a short period of colic and "throwing up" she adapted to this. (PS, 1950) Mother's fears seemed to center about the death of one of her children but after about six weeks she was able to return to her duties with the baby. The Taylors had prepared the older children for the birth of Diane and engaged in the typical family behavior of "queening" her, that is, having the children put her in the center of things and treat her like a little queen. No doubt this tended to compensate for the lack of contact with her mother.

Mother treated her somewhat insensitively when she came back. On the first observation at eight weeks it was felt the mother handled her abruptly to which Diane reacted with vocal protest. Mother reported, "She's got spunk. If things don't please her she'll throw herself back and stiffen." (GH, 1950) In the first home visit the mother seemed concerned about Diane and asked the visitor how to tell whether a child will be ill-natured. The mother, because of the press of duties, seemed to neglect the baby at times. She said, "When the milk is boiling over and the baby needs fed or they want their bottle and there are two kids to get off to school right now or they will be late. Or you're washing, the door bell rings and then the phone when you're trying to work in the baby's bath." She propped Diane up and let her drink by herself, when she drained the bottle too slowly. Or Diane would cry for father's attention when he came home, and the father would give it. The father, incidentally, is slow like Diane in contrast to the mother's quickness.

Dr. Grace Heider rated her as low in vulnerability and summarized her behavior as follows: "On the whole this sturdy baby more often showed resentment at not getting what she wanted or

195

of handling which she did not like than at ordinary overstimulation or fatigue, and she was able to handle herself in an effective fashion. In some ways her life seemed more a matter of defense and attainment than of enjoyment of activity and relationships" (p. 203).[2] Again she said of her, "an energetic, not very sensitive baby defending herself against an unhappy somewhat negative mother" (p. 205). She had a constitution more like her father than her mother, quiet and unobtrusive and not of wiry temperament like Ted and Janice. Endomesomorphic, according to Sheldon's study, she was by constitution slow, easygoing, and able to adapt herself to stress. She had three illnesses in the first year—measles, chickenpox, and mumps—and became run down physically, but other than some disturbance in eating she did not suffer badly. She did begin to use "eating" as a means of keeping attention focused on her. The picture is of a healthy child, with some stress in the environment because of the mother's depression, but this was partially made up for her by the father and siblings in their queening behavior. She was considered low in vulnerability at this time and again at preschool, and this position does not seem to suffer until prepuberty. We shall return to the vulnerability problem and the place which religion seems to play in it later on, when we have more material. But now let us turn our attention to the learning of controls.

Controls. Diane was trained easily, being trained for daytime bladder control at fifteen months and nightime at two years. In fact, she became quite fussy then if her pants were slightly wet. In learning to dress herself, however, she was slow, preferring to wait for someone else to do it for her. She also learned to talk later than the other children, not forming sentences until two years. "All she had to do was beam and wait for someone to give her what she wants," said the mother. (GH, 1953) So far as discipline was concerned, the mother thought she nagged and scolded too much, but Diane learned to "mind mother," and only when pushed too far would she get stubborn. She reacted to Janice's aggressiveness by withdrawal, generally to her corner of the room with her things. She also reacted to crowds—as when her cousins would come to visit—by withdrawal.

[2] *Vulnerability in Infants and Young Children: A Pilot Study,* Genetic Psychology Monographs (1966), 73, 1-216.

Her father said to her in criticizing a drawing in which she colored outside the lines, "Well, you won't be ready to go to school if you can't learn to keep in the lines."

Her mother spanked her when she got whiney or put her to bed. She reacted to discipline generally by withdrawing, but then coming back wanting to be reinstated with father, in particular as the "good child." Mother thought her spoiled by the ritual of queening, but it seemed to hold her within a certain role and she performed up to the behavior expected of her in the role. I observed the mother and father's discipline of Melba, the present baby, at age four. The father was extremely accepting and loving toward the child. The mother spanked her gently when she clamored for attention, but controlled her and got her to go take a nap with little pushing. The child cried a great deal when the father left and did not wave goodbye, as though devoted to him heart and soul. One can imagine Diane receiving similar treatment when she was this age.

She recalls her one big sin at about age five. It occurred when her father, mother, and grandparents were going to the stock show. They let her out of the car at the house and told her to go in and stay there with her older sisters. She went in, only to discover that they were next door playing with a girl friend, so she went out planning to go there, too. She got to the corner and her parents stopped in the car and discovered her. They asked where she was going and she lied, saying she had not been home yet. When she was found out, they were quite put out with her not only for disobeying but for lying about it. Later at prayer meetings, when asked to tell of her sinful life before accepting Christ, this is the guilty act she would recount.

When she came in for testing at age five, she impressed the examiners by her self-assurance and easy confidence in her abilities. She tested at superior level, with a Stanford-Binet IQ of 121. When commended on her ability to string beads, she replied to Dr. Moriarty, "Oh, yes, I do very, very well." She welcomed structure, however, and rose to the approval of adults. She seemed to be the little princess to whom everyone defers. (AM, 1955) At a large gathering, such as the preschool party, she was not noticed by many, preferring to play dolls alone or with her cousin, Ray. (LW, 1955) As Dr. Murphy commented, she resembled Charlotte Bühler's de-

scription of the "beloved child." "She seemed poised between intro-
version and extraversion but starving much for the outside world, yet
selecting and using it in her own way." (LBM, 1955)

At the age of five she was dealt her first major blow—a sister
was born. The parents prepared her as they had prepared her
siblings for her birth, and she seemed to rejoice in the prospect
of the baby. However, when the baby was born, Diane developed
digestive difficulties and Janice became enuretic (GH, 1955) She
was asked to defer to the baby as others had deferred to her.
On the surface she seemed to enjoy doing this, but about this
time other things became noticeable which seem to indicate aggression toward the mother. Probably the most dramatic was the
invention of an imaginary playmate, Tuffy Tyler. She would talk
to this female Perry Mason in her bedroom, and when she was
naughty she would blame Tuffy for it. Mother became depressed
again, for the new baby also was unplanned. Mother had always
felt her mother and sister had had too-large families. She blamed
her mother for not preparing her sufficiently about sex, and she
did not know suitable birth-control measures, evidently until
after Diane's birth. One can imagine Diane's trouble in identifying
with mother at this stage, when identification with the mother is
so important. She must have developed hidden hatred in being
dethroned by the sister. There is evidence that she would like to
have been a boy so she could have identified directly with father,
and yet she was afraid to make these wishes known. She became
withdrawn as she entered latency, with directly observable conflicts
about her role identity. At the second party, at age six, she showed
some ambivalence: "Sometimes, I'm playing with dolls, the rest,
I'm the boldest . . . you know like a boy." At the birthday table
she said, "I'm a boy, I'm always a boy." She seemed dreamy and
unrelated to the rest of the group.

One should add here that about this period, Diane's mother used
the fear of hell as a means of controlling her behavior. The mother
says that "God was used as a whip" in her own home to control
her, and that it took several years into marriage before she could
get over her own fear of God and learn to love him. From Diane's
recounting of her own fear of hell and death, it must have been
taught to her not only in church but through the mother. Diane

used prayer and Bible reading through latency to help her overcome her fears of God's punishment. Sin for her was disobedience of parents and expression of hostility toward siblings. This she tried to keep in control as she matured, but often with hard results. She recalls that at age eight she would lash back at Janice, when she hit her at the table. She would also get angry at her father's kidding and speak back. At age ten she recalls hitting a playmate so hard that she bloodied her nose. This lost her a friendship, and besides it didn't work, she said. (CWS, 1962)

She became competitive in the one area in which she excelled, scholastics. She took the highest grades in her class and, according to her mother's account, is the brightest child in the family. But teachers sometimes did not understand her either, and in fifth grade she had an "awful" teacher whom she could not stand. She began to have migraine headaches about this time. On examining the child, her physician told Mrs. Taylor that something was bothering Diane and wondered if it was school. They traced the trouble down to her dislike of the teacher. In addition, during the period from ten to twelve, they had a minister who was anything but exemplary to her, and his teenage son, according to Diane, was a juvenile delinquent. She grew critical of this authority as well, and could not stomach the hypocrisy she saw in church.

She was not able to criticize either her parents or her authorities openly, but developed the practice of going to her room and talking to herself or crying it out. She found that her headaches became less recurrent when she did this. But her mother reports that she knows little of what Diane is thinking anymore, and that in a crowd, because she does not talk up, many times she is not noticed by others. At puberty Diane, therefore, is quite critical of herself for failing to live up to the high standards she has for herself and is equally critical of her mother and the authorities for keeping these controls upon her of which she would like to be free. (CWS, 1962)

She does feel that existentially she has some freedom, like that of any human being. That is, she can choose to live a certain way and go to heaven or another way and go to hell. But she realizes that hell as a means of controlling her behavior is only a fear mechanism, and that as such it will not always work. (CWS, 1962) She has given up some specific religious devices such as prayer and

199

Bible reading as means of coping with her drives. She told her mother she wanted her to remind her to read the Bible. When her mother forgot to do this, she said it didn't make any difference. One could interpret this to mean that she no longer finds the Bible to be a magical helper; or it could be a feeling of apathy in relation to mother.

The sexual drive has not really emerged with full intensity in Diane, she menstruated the first time only last summer. However, her difficulty in establishing the feminine sex role, which we shall investigate later, has made her look at sex as something which causes trouble. She did not learn about sex from mother but had to learn from her sister and a friend. She saw the menstruation film at school and then went to Phyllis for further information. But as she recounted to me in discussing right and wrong, the sexual drive is something not to be fooled with, because it may precipitate marriage before Diane has had time enough to be free of family and its enforced social living. Her faith has not helped her handle the sex drive, it would appear, except perhaps to help her place it within the confines of marriage. Mother, she feels, is trying too hard now to be sure she turns out all right. If she could just relax and let her have more freedom, Diane thinks that she would not have any difficulty. The attempts now to control Diane are felt as "overcontrols."

Conversion Experience. Diane has grown up in a church in which the commitment of one's life to Jesus Christ is a major step for each individual. Diane knew this quite young; in fact, when she was interviewed by Dr. Murphy at age four, she mimicked a talk she had heard in church. "He was unconscious . . . in a stable! Saved from four cows . . . saved from everything . . . Oh, mother! She was scared. She was perfectly saved." At points her tone of voice was churchlike. (LBM, 1954)

At the age of six Diane took this major step, which she later recalls as the happiest moment of her life. She told the psychiatrist how it happened,

Every Sunday after church, I mean before it closes, the Sunday school, the preacher asks an invitation and there had already been some of us asking about it for the past two Sundays and then I decided I would go

200

down and accept Jesus Christ, and I went down there and I was crying. I don't know why, but I think it was that I had saw that I was here and Christ died for me and it was then that I realized that I was really happy and I was shedding tears of joy. I think that is one of the happiest times of my life. [When asked how she felt, she replied] Ah, you know how you feel after you've had a bath and you're nice and warm and all cuddled up. And you feel just about that way. You feel like now I'm really on the road upward. . . . Now I can really do something for Christ. . . . And I think it was just that people were happy for me and they showed their affection by coming down and shaking hands and talking to me. And it was then that I realized that it was really very nice. . . . And that I could do something now because I had given my heart to Christ. (PT, 1961)

She recalled at twelve that she had asked her mother to go down to the altar with her the first Sunday, but her mother told her if she was old enough to be a Christian she was old enough to go down herself. Next Sunday, however, mother did go down with her and supported her in the decision. Her father recalled that Diane did not seem to be suffering from any sense of guilt at the time but wanted to do something which set her off as a Christian. (CWS, 1962) She joined the pastor's class, even though she was quite young, and the pastor recalled that she was very alert as to the beliefs discussed. The booklet studied has a place for the new disciple to write his acceptance of Jesus Christ as his personal savior, which Diane did. At the end of the study there is a new members check-up chart, in which daily prayer and Bible reading, tithing one's income, and church attendance is recorded. Diane shows that she faithfully kept her new vows, even to the extent of recording that one week she "witnessed for Christ" thirty times in her new-found zeal.

The question for us to unravel is, What did this experience mean psychologically at age six for Diane? We can be assured theologically that God does call the child as well as the adolescent, as seen in the story of Samuel or the youthful Jeremiah. But psychologically, we need to know why the precocity of alertness and readiness in this particular child? We will recall the "queening" which Diane received from her father and siblings, the regal self-assurance she had during the preschool period. At the preschool party a quaint bit of animism in Diane was recorded. When the wind blew her napkin and lifted it into her ice cream, she shouted, "Quit blowing, stop, listen wind, did I tell you!" (LW, 1954) She felt secure in her position in the family and in the world, and things were right with her.

Then her sister, Paula, was born, and she was asked to give up her position at the center of the family to this newcomer. The father and the other siblings began to show her how they were to give way to the baby and to begin to "queen" someone new. The record states that she developed digestive difficulties, the only way she showed the blow to her narcissism and the wound she suffered from the dethronement. She needed some recourse, some way to bolster her security in the family, and in highly precocious fashion at age six she turned to religion, the parent's mainstay and guide. The question is, Did Diane feel severe conflict at this time which she was striving to resolve, or was the conversion experience a reinforcing of a position which she wanted to maintain? It could be argued that she suffered the conflicts usual for this age, and wanted the father and sought to remove the mother, and therefore found accepting Christ, the father's Lord, a means of doing this. There seems to be some basis for this explanation, but the conflicts are not of a guilty sort, as one finds in adolescence. The major sin Diane remembers is disobedience at this period, which removes her from family acceptance. The religious act seems to be a means of finding healing for the displacement by the new baby and a crowning of her earlier experience as queen of the family. She learns that decision is expected of her, and she wants to do it now. The mother counsels being grown up enough to do it, but Diane finally gets the mother to support her. She still remembers at puberty all the affection and support from family and church members which she received as a result. The experience is of the immanence of God, much like what she felt when supported and loved by mother, father, and the others in the family. And for her it is truly the happiest moment of her life.

The conversion experience was for Diane a reinforcement of her self-image as a *princess,* one whom God visited and told she was accepted by him and belonged to Jesus Christ, his Son. She may have been displaced by the baby, but she was important in God's eyes, and indirectly in her father's eyes, for the step she had taken. She was the one in the family most interested in religion. While the family still lived in Capital City, she went to a church group that met for a prayer meeting. She was always with her mother on these occasions and would sit quietly at mother's feet coloring while the meeting was going on and the other mothers in the group became absolutely devoted to her and thought she was a perfectly wonderful child. And when she was nine she took all the religious training involved so seriously that the minister's wife told Mrs. Taylor afterward that the minister would like to have her for his own—that she was the loveliest child he had ever known. (GH, 1959)

This self-image is a hard one to maintain, however. For instance, she wanted to read the Bible every day, and asked her mother to be sure and not let her forget. The mother, obviously harried with many family duties, promptly forgot. Diane felt the lack of support from the mother, though she must have also found the father full of praise for her precocity in religion. She used her religion sometimes self-righteously to criticize a member of the family when they fell from grace. For an example: when Theodore was eighteen, he went into service, bought a car for himself, began going with a fifteen-year-old girl in a neighboring town and had occasional escapades. Diane saw this rebellion from her parents' religious standpoint rather than from her brother's. She also saw members of her school class in the same judgmental fashion and divided them into hoodlums with nothing to live for and citizens such as lawyers, teachers, and housewives who have a sense of accomplishment (AM, 1961) The falling into moralism is one not easy to avoid for the fundamentalist Christian and following her conversion, she fell victim to it.

The decision for Christ so early in her life may have been an attempt to storm Olympus on Diane's part. At least, at age twelve, she now feels she may have acted impulsively. She reports that she did it too soon, and that now she wished she had waited. It is the one point in her life when she felt a personal experience with God, and everything from that point on has been in the shadow. If it were precocious, she now feels that she could benefit from it as a means of resolving doubt and conflict. As we shall discuss in the next pages, the whole area of religion is caught up in her adolescent identity crisis, and the previous solutions are no longer working. The crown of her queenly position in the family has disappeared. Last year it was a happy memory; this year it gives her further nostalgia and loneliness. But the occasion of her doubt and its emotional derivatives we shall now have to trace.

One finds Diane at age twelve involved in massive doubt, not only of her parents' religion, but also of social institutions and of her own identity. She feels the in-betweenness of adolescence sharply. "I do feel sort of left out, since I'm not old enough to graduate and I'm not young enough to be one of those cute little kids that go around saying cute stuff" (PT, 1961) She is highly critical of her mother for her messy housekeeping and her disciplinary methods; she feels her father kids her too hard and does not take her seriously; the former minister and his family were hypocrites; the town council doesn't do its job correctly. She begins every conversation with this kind of doubt and ends up doubting herself. In fact, as said earlier, "I guess" is her favorite expression. The problem is to discover why she lost her early assurance and narcissism and seems bogged down right now in doubt and self-criticism. In fact, the psychological manifestations of the problem show themselves in a thirty-two-point drop in "performance" IQ at the prepuberty testing, which Dr. Moriarty links to "the need to be orderly which takes precedence over speed," and a "criticism of even minor deviations." (AM, 1961) In place of the earlier realism and feeling of self-assurance in confronting tasks, she now resorts to fantasy as a means of magical gratification of her need to be free of rules and parental expectations. The world would be palatable, she told me, if she could live alone, be given a new car, plenty of money, and nothing would be expected of her but to attend school and do what she pleases. "This would be pretty sharp," she thinks.

Role of Doubt. Our problem is to discover what function doubting serves for Diane? Is it a moving from faith to doubt? Is it a feeling of loss of identity? And are there any coping aspects to the doubting; i.e., does it help her solve her current problems?

One can say at the outset that in the last year Diane has felt that her earlier latency religious orientation has not been adequate for the pressures both inner and outer which she is undergoing. As reported above, she feels she prematurely solved the religious problem—and, though the conversion experience continued to give her a special place in her father's eyes as "princess," with the birth of the second child she lost this place for good and was forced to grow up. The aggressive and sexual drives are being felt with new intensity, and her place in the family is seen to be no longer one of prominence. She fantasied herself for a while a nurse to twenty orphan Korean children, a means of making reparation for the displacement she felt—perhaps during her mother's depression following her birth, certainly at her disenthronement at the sisters' births. She thought, too, of disproving some of the things she learned in school, by being an archeologist and digging in the Holy Lands to disprove evolution. The doubting came to the fore, however, following puberty, when she began to see the dissonance between what she had been taught and what she could see in the world outside. The family lives of her school classmates, which differed from her family life, the life of movie stars such as Audrey Hepburn, and the life of her older siblings—Ted now married and Phyllis away at college—gave her some inkling of freedom from controls of parental religion. "How come?" was her recurrent question of the examiner.

Diane now becomes involved in a genuine crisis, a crisis in her feelings of identity. A psychologist reports, "This decline [in intelligence test scores] . . . seemed to represent difficulties in generalizing, reaching conclusions and organizing when no model was available for imitation." (AM, 1961) We spoke earlier of her sex-role conflicts at the beginning of elementary school. They appear to return with great intensity at this stage, when mother loses her value for Diane as an identification figure. At age seven she told stories on the CAT in which mother is seen as a rather harried figure who is taken advantage of by her children (I). Father is the one who always wins arguments (V), in fact, the children side with him against the mother. However, at prepuberty, she is able to verbalize the conflict with the mother directly. On card 19, the blank card, she tells of a family rescued by a huge bird and flown south where they live independently. She then uses the occasion to criticize her mother as a housewife and disciplinarian.

The sex-role conflict comes out most vividly on the Godin test. She sees the Madonna-like character as having two kinds of eyes;

in the one she looks down on a brightly lighted city at night, in the other she looks down like a mother at her children. The one eye has lots of excitement in it; the other is calm, the one which looks at her children. "Neither predominates, they're just different," says Diane. (Card 7) Diane has often wondered about mother's happiness as a housewife and her sacrifice of herself for the house, the father, and the children. The depressions which she suffered after the birth of her two younger sisters now cast some doubt on the role of mother and add to Diane's ambivalence. She has felt the father to be the independent one and the happier one of the two. She identified with him, we will remember, at the age of six. But when father deserted her for the younger babies, she was lost. She searched around for a point of identity, and, as her self-doubt grew, she doubted her ability to fulfill the role of woman, except as independent of biological mother. At first she thought of mothering orphan Korean babies, if a husband would agree to this. Then at twelve she admits she is afraid of marriage and of the responsibilities of looking after children at all. She intimates this most vividly when talking about right and wrong in the area of sexual relations. She says if they—those who make out at parties—"think they are grown up enough to do that, they should have a vision of what life is all about." Here she seems to speak with conviction, but it has the sound of bravado, as though she is wise for the time being in her unrelatedness to boys. It gives her time to find independence of the primary family, which for her mother as she has viewed her has been a ball and chain. Mother may not have wanted a career, as Diane thinks she does, but she has not had time to think of anything but religion and family during her married career.

Which brings us to Diane's conflict about the religious area. Several factors have together brought her to her present doubting frame of mind. We have mentioned the dissonance between her parents' attempts to require religious practices and other girls' parents' lack of concern here. Diane feels she would like the freedom to go to church or stay home on her own volition. Besides she has met youth who do not go to church at all who are "sharp kids." She has seen the hollowness of the former minister's religion and its underlying negative feelings. She has felt the failure of her own perfectionistic standards to keep her angry feelings in control and has projected this unconsciously upon mother, father, and environment. She is guilty over these rejected parts of herself and is striving for some kind of wholeness in an identity, now fashioned after sister Phyllis. Phyllis is going to college, is moderately free from parental controls, and yet is not a "beatnik" but someone bent on a career and not immediate marriage. The conflict in the religious area focuses Diane's present conflicts between desire and duty, between conformity to adult norms and her own adolescent creativity. She does not see her parents as teachers of religion now, nor the church as it appears to be an extension of her family. But she does grapple with religious issues as seen in the study of her beliefs.

This brings us to study the creative use of doubt in which she may be engaged. She is using doubt to clear away the rubble of old beliefs and action systems and, at least in her solitude, and perhaps with Phyllis to try on new ways of looking at things. To cite one example, one can find this certainly in her thoughts about death at forty after a full life. She is also using doubt to sever connections with mother, with the depression surrounding being a woman, which seems to underlie her thought and action. And she is trying to find a model by which to integrate her feelings about being a woman and a creative one at that. Phyllis is helping her here, much more now that she is away from home most of the time.

Is Diane highly vulnerable as she moves into adolescence? It would seem that her prevailing doubt may temporarily cloud her creativity. Unless it becomes obsessive, and unless she seeks defense in compulsive study or activity for its own sake, one would not think that she is in for any breakdown. She has weathered the displacement in the family, and she does not appear to generalize this in terms of a displacement as a daughter of God. God still is love for her, though she may not feel this love nor be entirely free to express her love for him. Hell still is something to fear for her, as banishment from the circle of love, but she is striving in her own fashion to find a way out of her egocentric predicament. Christ no longer seems to lead the way for her, but he may as she goes further into adolescence. Some of the psychologists are quite taken with her ability to work her way in typical easy-going, methodical fashion out of a quandary, using her intellectual gifts in brilliant fashion.

Said one, "Her performance in the schematizing test is very much like an adult if not a little bit superior. We read in this child consistently the highest, most thematically organized expressive child in the entire group." (RG, 1962) Another summarized her Rorschach, "The number of responses, range, content, and spontaneity indicate a superior intelligence but also a high energy level, imagination and creativity, a readiness to please and to identify with the task at hand." (MM, 1962) Truly, she has gifts, which she is aware of, and wants to find an avenue in which to express them. Her parents' religion, though it may have fundamentalist strictness, also has, especially through the father, a foundation of love. One might imagine that when Diane becomes able to perceive this her original Christian commitment may take on new dimensions and depth.

Diane, although a middle child, does have the advantage of older siblings going before her and breaking new ground—in marriage, college, and testing the tenents of the family's faith. Her nineteen-year-old sister now has become a realistic identity figure for her, just as Audrey Hepburn replaced her imaginary playmate, Tuffy Tyler. One would speculate, therefore, that she will follow this sister to college into a freer, more liberal atmosphere.

The reader may wish to compare Helen and Diane. Why, for example, is Diane struck with doubt in early adolescence, while Helen appears to believe with even more vigor? Does their difference in vulnerability provide a clue? Or is their family situation enough different that Diane does not have to become the family's savior? Is Diane's queen identity still prevalent, and, if so, does it provide a more integrated identity as a child of God? What about the masochistic drives (guilt, punishment, and atonement) in the two girls? I have explored this theme in more detail in an article entitled "The Religious Experience of Two Adolescent Girls." [3] The reader may want to study these questions further.

We now turn to a study of the relationship of vulnerability to religious experience. The vulnerability of the six youth in the biographies has been studied intensively. The reader will want

[3] *Pastoral Psychology* (Sept., 1966) , pp. 49-55.

to turn to the biographies after reading this next chapter to see them afresh from this perspective. Religious psychologists have tended to see a crisis-prone youth as subject to a crisis-type of religious experience. Is this the whole story, or are these other factors operating in today's youth? Let us turn to chapter 10 to find out.

10

Vulnerability and Religious Experience

The young adolescent is vulnerable. He is open to hurt from his parents, from his teachers and minister, and particularly from his peers. He is uncertain of himself as to just who he is; he does not have an esteem for himself as yet, or even a steady self-picture which will help him withstand the slings and arrows of daily existence. As we have noted, after puberty he may withdraw from immediate social contact and appear reserved, even shy, with those whom he has known quite well before. He suffers poor estimates of his appearance and of the way in which he affects others. Unless he has a history of achievement in various areas he does not have too great an opinion of himself as a student, as an athlete, or as a socializer. This vulnerability to hurt or stress makes adolescence within our culture a difficult period to go through. Particularly is this so immediately following puberty, the period which we have been studying.

The vulnerability of adolescence has been studied in relation to religious experience. However, because of the emphasis upon the storm-and-stress aspects of his vulnerability in relationship to crisis conversion within Protestantism, the full meaning of vulnerability has not been understood. As Margaret Mead points out,

The Reformation with its emphasis on individual choice was unwilling to accept the tacit habitual church membership which was the Catholic pattern, a membership marked by additional sacramental gifts but demanding no sudden conversion, no renewal of religious feeling. But the Protestant solution is to defer the choice only so far as necessary, and the moment the child reaches years of discretion, it makes a strong dramatic appeal. This appeal is reinforced by parental and social pressure, the child is bidden to choose now and wisely. [1]

What is not apparent, as has been pointed out, is that vulnerability within an individual youth has multiple determinants. It has been present from infancy in many instances; it has a developmental history and it can change from high vulnerability to low vulnerability. What we propose is to study the relationship of vulnerability to the religious experience of adolescence.

What we shall attempt to do is to look more closely at the biographical studies as they are written up within the text. We shall be concerned with how these boys and girls have developed to the point where they are, what the factors are within their developing personhood, and whether we may understand more about their religious experience by getting the complete complex of factors which will provide us with an understanding of the dynamics and determinants of their religious development. The fact that we have access to longitudinal materials in tracing the development of these six persons will, I believe, enable us to understand religious experience from within the youth's frame of reference. It will also help us see the relation between religious experience and the idiosyncratic needs and adaptive problems of youth today.

VULNERABILITY DEFINED

The early studies of this group of children centered around the relationship of their vulnerability to problems of adaptation. [2]

---

[1] *Growing Up in New Guinea* (New York: New American Library, 1930).

[2] Escalona and Heider, *Prediction and Outcome.* Also Grace Heider, "Vulnerability, Sources of Strength and Capacity to Cope in the Normal Child," proceedings of the 14th International Conference of Applied Psychology, 1961.

By vulnerability Dr. Heider means *the openness of the individual to stress from both inner and outer conditions.* She explains that vulnerability is the Achilles' heel in every person. However, it is not simply one area where one is open to being hurt; it is rather a complex of physical factors, environmental factors, and management processes which make up this *global concept.* A sugar cube is an example she uses. The cube has a certain physical arrangement of molecules which make it strong in the atmosphere. However, if one puts the cube into his cup of tea, it dissolves. It is *vulnerable* to *heat* and soluble in water and changes its shape. A living organism as small as the amoeba, however, brings another set of forces into operation, namely, "management." If one pricks the amoeba or puts a noxious chemical in its path, it "reacts"—changes its shape and moves in another direction. Vulnerability to stress, therefore, calls for successful or unsuccessful adaptive behavior. A human being capable of reflection and decision, is even more complex, he can change both his organism and environment within limits.

Dr. Heider and her associates, working with the Child Study group, analyzed certain factors which make the individual vulnerable to stress. They included certain *organic factors* such as:

1. instability in body functioning (for example, blood pressure)
2. low energy reserves (i.e., easily tiring)
3. a tendency to deterioration under stress in special functional areas such as speech or sensory threshold
4. developmental imbalance (for example, quicker development in the intellectual than the motor areas)
5. lack of congruence between the child's aspirations and capabilities
6. lack of balance in physique (as by Sheldon's categories)

In the environmental area factors which made the child vulnerable to stress are:

1. an emotionally disturbed or physically ill mother
2. the lack of fit or congruence between mother and child (for example, a rough, quick mother with a slow sensitive child)
3. place in order of siblings with the rivalries and openness to hurt which this engenders
4. socioeconomic factors which determine size of house, play space, toys and equipment, sleeping arrangements, etc.

5. acts of nature (for example, the Capital City flood which directly or indirectly affected many of these children)

Management factors in early infancy include defensive, demanding, and aggressive reactions to stress, obstacles, and difficulties. These variables represent weaknesses in the developing child which show possibilities for intrapsychic conflict and pressures which will produce interpersonal difficulties. One must recognize that these reactions are not "pure" very long but involve the building of defenses and the learning of behavior from the first day of the infant's life.

Grace Heider rated thirty-one of the original group on a five-point scale at infancy so far as their vulnerability was concerned. She rated them again at the preschool stage.[3] I read through their prepuberty testing and interview materials and rated the original thirty-one children without any personal acquaintance with the child. From my preliminary investigation and with the guidance of Dr. Murphy, six children were selected for intensive study, three high vulnerables and three low vulnerables. The purpose was to discover if there were any correlation between vulnerability and the type of religious orientation at adolescence. The children selected are the ones whose biographies appear through the text. They are ranked as shown in table 10-1. (Highest is rated 1, lowest is rated 5)

Table 10-1

	Infancy	Preschool	Prepuberty
High Vulnerables			
Helen	1	2	4
Terry	1	1	2
Roddy	1	1	4
Low Vulnerables			
Diane	5	5	4
Barbie	4	4	4
Teddy	4	4	3

[3] *Vulnerability in Infants and Young Children: A Pilot Study.*

A capsule summary of their physical, environmental, and management factors and resulting "vulnerability" will give the reader some idea as to how this concept applies.

Helen

Helen is a girl who is considered highly vulnerable at infancy with a rank of 1, a rank of 2 at preschool. I would rank her at 4 now as one who is among the least vulnerable of the group. She is not extremely bright, with an IQ of 110. Her school grades are in the B's. She is realistic so far as her vocation is concerned, wanting to be a nurse or a schoolteacher or an artist. She comes from a large family and until two years ago has had to share a room with her sister and a younger brother. In the country, however, there is more living space. She has adapted to this little community and the little church quite well and is entering puberty with much more strength than she showed in the earlier years. The psychologist says she has an open enthusiastic approach to the world with limited experiences but full use of those in which she is involved. She is realistically aware of frustration and friction, which she on the whole can handle lightly with humor and affective warmth, as well as considerable differentiation and range. Her mother has thought of her as different from the other children. She was hungry for affection as a child but has become much freer from defensiveness, much more flexible and interested in response. She still handles anxiety by withdrawal. She has a highly active fantasy life and at times is emotionally distant from people. She has had a warm religious experience but also desires to be the good girl in contrast to a close friend who had to get married.

Terry

He was ranked as highly vulnerable at both infancy and preschool, and now I would rank him between 2 and 3. He is one who was a blend of mesomorphic and endomorphic. He wears glasses. His health has been up and down. He has broken some bones. He feels fragile. He has had some stuttering. His vocabulary has not been big enough for his thought life; although of high intelligence, he has never been able to use fully his creative potential. He has been action oriented but quits before he loses his temper. He comes from a mother-dominated home and has been quite active in the Roman Catholic Church. His father has been somewhat distant. He has been a striver in Scouts and passed all of his badges for Eagle Scout at age thirteen. He has low frustration tolerance in his driving toward a goal. He wants to be a priest after having served as an acolyte for several years. It is this use of repression, denial, and avoidance which has kept him from coping more adequately with his environment. It is thought that he will have difficulty during adolescence.

Roddy

This is a boy who was highly vulnerable in infancy and preschool, ranking 1 at both times. However, I would now rank him 4 with moderate vulnerability. He is a boy who has made tremendous strides. He has a good body build, being classified ectomesomorph. His general health has been good. He has a muscular body type with both sensitive skin and nervous system. He had a severe eczema as a child but this has been controlled. He has also been subject to allergies. His speech problem in childhood has been corrected. He comes from a family with one sister four years younger, a strong mother, and also a father who is interested in sports and has served as an identification figure. His family is middle class. He has achieved well, using his good intelligence (127 IQ) to get A's and B's. He relates well with his peers and has a strong drive to master various tasks. His goal is to be a physician, and, after reading Schweitzer, he wants to become a medical missionary. He is president of his class and high scorer on the basketball team. He is popular with both boys and girls. The only poor report is from the psychiatrist who feels there is a mixed identity here and has some reservation about his vulnerability in adolescence. He feels he has achieved his current adjustment at the sacrifice of his creative potential. However, he has adjusted as a normal adolescent might in the American culture, and from that standpoint I would rank him of moderate vulnerability at present.

215

Diane

Diane Taylor ranked with a vulnerability of five at infancy and five at preschool. I would now rank her at three or four. She comes from a family with six children. The oldest boy, however, is married. Her father is a skilled worker, and the family now live in a small town. They are active in the church; the mother had a postpartum depression and has been depressed at other times since the birth of this child. She was an extremely normal baby, was slow in learning skills. However, she developed well in childhood and currently with an IQ of 114 gets A's and B's in school. The father is head of the household—the mother, being more impulsive than the father, lets him make the decisions and work with the children more directly. There has been a history of some anemia, and currently Diane has migraine headaches. Entering puberty she has some acne and her body image is rather poor at present. Psychologically she is a relaxed, slow, calm person, very voluble in conversation. On the psychological tests she appeared to be a person with a good deal of tolerance for delay and of need satisfaction, realistic most of the time with occasional lapses into magic, no strong attachments except as mutually profitable. She shows strong aggression, yet an underlying anxiety which may force her into dissociation. She is extremely critical of others. The psychiatrist feels there is strong control here but at the expense of her own feelings of self-acceptance. If she does not win the fight for control, she may be a candidate for adolescent breakdown, he suggests.

Barbie

This girl is the least vulnerable of any of the group which I have examined. She has the best proportioned body build, she is an intelligent girl with an IQ of about 110-115, but she does not exert herself in school, getting B's and C's. Her vocation is to be a housewife, to marry, and raise children. She is an active girl, interested in sports, in nature study, physically and socially mature at twelve. She has no strong desire to achieve; she is concrete rather than abstract in her thinking. She is better at motor skills, has good capacity for planning and organization. She appears to avoid being too vivid or too outstanding, says the psychologist, seeking the role of comfortable anonymity. The only conflict appears to be over sex role. She feels that her parents wanted a boy rather than a girl, yet her relationship with her mother has been so positive that the feminine role was never totally rejected. She was somewhat of a tomboy, aggressive and controlling with both boys and girls. She may enter adolescence with some vagueness as to sexual role. Her orientation to church has been social rather than intrinsically religious. She is beautifully accommodated for the culture in which she will live, upper middle class, her father being president of a company. She has one sister four years older than she.

Teddy

He is a boy who was not very vlunerable in infancy and had a preschool ranking of 4 at each level. Now, since the prepuberty study, I would rank him at 3. He is endomorphic with some ectomorphic qualities. He has one of the highest IQ's of the group at 135 and uses it to get high grades. For example, he is in a special math class in school. His parents' divorce struck him very hard. He overate at age six and became somewhat obese. He is still somewhat overweight. Although his father was in the service, he identified with him highly during childhood and feels the loss of his father keenly, referring to the stepfather simply as "George." He is a highly serious boy, has worn glasses since he was ten, has been slow and awkward with poor coordination. However, he does participate in sports with other boys; he is highly sensitive to social situations; he is dependable, achieves identity but at considerable expense. He controls his emotions, isolates himself as a defense. The psychiatrist feels there may be an undercurrent of depression here, some self-disparagement, some grief at his father's loss, certain stoicism in delaying gratification and controlling anger. He copes with his environment by holding himself apart from affection and closeness, by using intellectualization and rationalization. He gets along poorly with his peers. His level of aspiration is lower than he could achieve—religion for him has been a matter of support and moral obedience for the most part.

It will be noted that vulnerability is not a fixed aspect of the child; it changes perceptibly from one period to another as the individual and his environment undergo changes. In addition, management process, or "coping," is a balancing factor between the individual and his milieu. The child can and does change in his vulnerability rating in the process of growing up, as he learns to handle internal and external stress, particularly at puberty, and to face the stresses from physiological changes and the influences of his environment (school, peer group, clubs, church). We shall deal with "coping" in more detail in chapter 12.

Gordon Allport's recent investigation of intrinsic and extrinsic religious behavior provides us with workable and relatable religious categories. [4] Earlier, we defined religion as "what the individual symbolizes as ultimate and his relationship to that ultimate in ceremony and social behavior." Insofar as the religious experience which youth undergo, if we redefine Allport's categories, we can say there are at least three types: (1) growing, maturing, reflective religious experience; (2) utilitarian, drive-oriented, and need-gratifying religious experience; (3) conforming or group-oriented religious experience. William James, in placing institutional religion aside and investigating only personal religion, missed this entire group. Allport's, and other, studies of the institutional religionist in the past decades have corrected the balance. Moreover, as our study shows thus far, if youth are predominantly conformists today, we must take into account "conformist religious experience" in order to understand the kinds of data which we have at hand.

What is the relationship of early vulnerability to the type of religious experience youth undergo? William James quite rightly saw the relationship between certain organic or temperament variables and religious experience. The "healthy-minded," he pointed out, will have a gradual growth into the religious life. Temperamentally, they look at the world more optimistically. "The great point in the conduct of life is to get the heavenly forces on one's side by opening one's mind to their influx." [5] In our study he might be the low-vulnerable child; that is, he has a balanced

---

[4] Allport defines *intrinsic* experience as being an end in itself; *extrinsic* experience serves another end, as prestige or safety. See *Religion in the Developing Personality* (New York: New York University Press, 1960), p. 36.

[5] William James, *Varieties of Religious Experience*, p. 108.

constitution and a supporting environment and would be expected to be free from overwhelming inner needs or conflicts and thus free to grow into a maturing religious experience within the general orientation of the family in faith and practice.

On the other hand, the "sick soul" or "divided self," James says, lives in a double-storied world. "Peace cannot be reached by the simple addition of pluses and diminution of minuses from life. . . . Renunciation and despair of it (our real good) are our first step in the direction of truth." [6] Incidentally, the divided self is not temperamentally different from the sick soul except that he experiences a division within the self between his intellect and conscience, or his "higher and lower feeling," at a critical period in his life. The sense of guilt and desire for reconciliation arises from this inner division, James says. The sick soul may have developed in the highly vulnerable child; that is, he is one who has experienced crises in his encounters with his environment, and he would be expected to have the crisis type of experience in adolescence. In this crisis his religious emotions would be expected to be closely related to anxieties, unmet needs, and unresolved conflicts. [7]

On the basis of Allport's studies we might expect the "institutionally religious" to be one for whom religion was a matter of form and going through the motions without any inner meaning. For this individual conformity to the group's ideology and values becomes of primary importance not for its own sake but for "extrinsic ends of prestige, success, or talismanic favors." The discrepancy between the beliefs and values of the institution and the behavior of the peer group does not necessarily produce conflict. Rather it may, without any crisis, push the adolescent into the peer group in isolation from the adult world and its responsibilities and demands.

The James-Allport concepts would lead us to make the following hypotheses:

1. The adolescent who has, during his early years, tended to be highly vulnerable will be likely to have a religious crisis related to his intense inner drives and problems which he will attempt to

[6] *Ibid.*, pp. 163, 164.
[7] We shall not deal with the individual who undergoes "mystical experience" but on the basis of preliminary study, one whould expect him also to be a "high vulnerable."

219

solve by "surrender" and decision to what he holds ultimate.

2. The low vulnerable adolescent, if autonomous, will tend to have an intrinsic, or personal, reflective religious experience, developing as he grows and learns, and related to the beliefs and practices of the church in which he is reared.

3. Or the low vulnerable adolescent, if not autonomous, will tend to conform to the codes and practices of his parents or peer group seeking his security and identity in this manner.

In order to test these hypotheses and further refine our thinking about adolescent religious experience, I submitted to a panel of three [8] a sketch of the three boys and three girls whose biographies are in the text. They judged the six according to whether they found them intrinsic or extrinsic in their religious experience, according to a three-point scale.

The scale did not use intrinsic-extrinsic in its materials but attempted to measure these variables along a continuum of conformity-nonconformity, utility-objectivity, egocentricity-unselfishness, distance from God-intrinsic relationship with God, and parochialism-worldly-mindedness.

Helen's sketch will give the reader an example of the kinds of material with which the panel worked, and some idea as to the ranking of the material.

Thumbnail Sketch: Helen

[Mother's Sketch] Well, she is fair minded, she is affectionate, easy to get along with, I guess you would say compatible. She is very good with children, especially small ones, the babies. [She then paused and continued.] She is happy, easygoing most of the time. There are moments when she loses her temper but it is not often or very strenuous. Ordinarily, she makes friends easily and keeps them. [Her sister then offered, "She is a real sweet kid," which the mother affirmed. When I thought I had a complete picture the mother then added,] She is not a saint though, she is a very human girl. She is messy, doesn't keep her room picked up but this is getting better. She is taking more pride in her personal appearance. She still thinks boys are for the birds though but that is all right with me.

[8] Seward Hiltner, Paul Pruyser, and Phillip Woolcott of the Menninger Foundation staff.

[Pastor's Sketch] She is a brilliant person. She has a great potential so far as IQ is concerned. She is very sincere and has a very inquiring mind, her grades show that. With other people she is on the shy side. She is not as easygoing or outgoing as the other kids. She would like to rattle on like the other girls. I can't say whether she is insecure or secure. At times she seems firm in her thinking, at other times she is insecure like she is searching for something that she has not quite got.

[Psychologist's Sketch] Helen is a very fascinating girl as you know. I think she is most fascinating to us because she seemed so very vulnerable as an infant. There were all kinds of respiratory ailments, she had a serious kidney infection, later was hospitalized for awhile. She is one of a large family in which the mother is certainly a very competent individual but one who strikes you as almost too calm and collected at times.

Over and again we had the feeling that Helen didn't get enough loving, perhaps. Her next younger brother I believe was born less than a year after Helen, almost as soon as possible which meant that she didn't have an opportunity to have all that babyhood love and care that we think children need. This may account for the fact that she reaches out so much for everybody and she has extended herself in all areas to take in everything. I think this is fabulous in that she emerges as a beautifully vivid child with lots of interests and of all the kids in the family I would say that she is the sublimator par excellence. She has all these needs and feelings for people but I don't have a feeling at this point that they have overwhelmed her since she is using these. She wants to know about absolutely everything. She was a girl at seven who knew what we were doing, and we felt that she did. She seemed to know the role of these persons who were talking to her and what they wanted from her, and this struck us as very mature, and it seemingly had continued as she talked to you. She talked to you about things she thinks *you* are interested in. When she talks to the psychiatrist, she talks about her problems. When she talks to me it's intellectual academics. This was a very amazing fact.

One time she told me she would like to visit the Foundation and meet some of the patients, know what was going on here. I think all this could be indications of instability, perhaps in that she is trying so hard to find out about everybody else that you wonder is she secretly or subconsciously trying to learn more about herself. But if she is doing this then she is working very positively about herself. Another thing we might say about Helen that has impressed us is her ability to know how other people feel—this relates to what I just said, of course, but she seems to be unusually aware of two sides of the issue. You get this when she talks about highly personal feelings. She seems to have some awareness of how her mother feels in this big family. The results of the ranking are shown in table 10-2.

Table 10-2

	Judge 1	Judge 2	Judge 3	Mean
Diane	11	11	13	11.7
Helen	11	11	12	11.3
Terry	11	10	11	10.7
Teddy	10	9	7	(8.7)
Roddy	10	12	9	10.3
Barbie	8	8	7	7.7

On the basis of the scale, with correction for Teddy, it would appear that Helen, Diane, and Teddy were largely intrinsic in their religious life, and that Terry, Roddy, and Barbie are extrinsic religiously. The judges thought Diane and Terry felt close to God, but missed Helen's and Teddy's devotion in interview since they reported the most personal religious experience. They did, however, pick up Roddy's and Barbie's feelings of distance from God and their pattern of conformity to the group. They further caught Helen's and Roddy's worldly-mindedness but failed to distinguish the unselfish factor in Helen which comes out forcefully in the interview. The need-centeredness of Diane was quite apparent, but the judges missed it in Roddy and Terry where it operates with as much force. Finally, the judges failed to do justice to Teddy's intrinsic religious experience, probably because the pastor's material was sparse and because Teddy had hidden his religious feelings from the other investigators and even from his mother. In his instance, we have corrected his score, even to the point of placing him in the intrinsic category, rather than the extrinsic, where the scale would have him fall.

One must say that as stated the hypotheses are too simple; there is no one-to-one relation between vulnerability and religious experience—or temperament and religious experience as James attempted to show. There are too many variables, particularly the intervening variables of management or coping with stress as shown in the diagram.

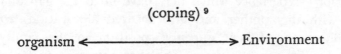

$$\text{(coping)}\ ^9$$

$$\text{organism} \longleftrightarrow \text{Environment}$$

The child is unbelievably persistent in the same respects in which he is vulnerable, as Erikson says.[10] That is, his weakness in part processes subjects him to danger, but it also provides a loosening up within and a challenge without enabling further growth. Helen is an example of a girl, highly vulnerable at infancy and orally disturbed and deprived in relation to her mother, who has become less vulnerable in early adolescence and for whom religion has not only met personal needs but has also been of intrinsic value.

On the other hand, Terry is an example of a boy who, although "toned down" in early adolescence, is rated just as vulnerable as in infancy and who has developed a "religion of tradition" to meet his intense personal needs. The resurgence of sexual and aggressive drives at puberty tends to undo this conformity to parental expectations, and the vocation of the priesthood at first appeals as a means of distancing himself from his mother while "outdoing" her as to religion. The use of religion to meet personal needs would make one still classify him as extrinsic, although linked to *crisis* and *decision*.

Roddy, from a nonreligious family, was highly vulnerable at the periods of infancy and preschool and is "toned down" also, but by selecting the school and peer group as his area for conformity

---

[9] *Vulnerability* is in indirect ratio to coping and, therefore, as Lois B. Murphy shows, is the opposite of ego-strength. We shall investigate the strengths of the adolescent in chapter 12.

[10] *Identity and the Life Cycle*, p. 55.

rather than the church. His religious experience is lacking, but as we shall consider later on, his imagination and fantasy life have religious possibilities. On the behavioral level, however, he is one who has become a conformist as a means of pleasing his mother, but in the absence of a religious faith. He demonstrates the prevailing importance of the peer group to contemporary youth.

The process of development may move the child from low vulnerability in infancy and preschool to increased vulnerability at puberty. Diane is an example of a girl who at age six had a "conversion" experience which may have filled the gap of limited contact with the mother and also insured admiration from the father. She retained her "queenly" position in the family until replaced by two younger sisters. She then retreated to fantasy and at puberty is questioning her acceptance of Christ and is doubting many elements of her parents' faith.

The crisis which a low vulnerable child must face may precede adolescence and subject him to stress which may increase his vulnerability until he can develop adequate management devices. Teddy is an example of a boy from a moderately religious family who lost his father at age six by divorce. Following his mother's remarriage to a man not entirely acceptable to Teddy, he turned to Jesus as an identification figure and used prayer as a frequent means of support and strength in a stressful world. The stress from the environment and the availability of religious resources in the home, we conclude, are important, therefore, for both vulnerable and nonvulnerable youth.

The nonvulnerable child who is neither greatly stressed nor is exposed to religious teaching falls into the easy conforming type of religious observance. He may not raise the questions of suffering, sin, sorrow, and evil which the vulnerable and stressed child does out of his suffering, anger, and reactive guilt feelings. Barbie is an example of a very healthy girl from an upper-middle-class family who remains "childish" in her religious beliefs and conforming in her religious behavior. She faces outward to her peer group for her values and tastes. Her struggle with her older sister results in lower academic effort and not using religion as a major area of interest as her sister has done.

IMPLICATIONS OF VULNERABILITY

What are the issues for adolescent religion which our study of vulnerability has raised?

In the first place we have seen that vulnerability is not a simple fixed variable but is a conceptualization for a complex of variables. If we deal with the factors which make up vulnerability—namely organic predispositions, environmental conditioning, and management factors—we can understand the relationship between "openness to stress" and predispositions to certain kinds of religious experiences.

We have observed that constitutionally infants are born with relative "vulnerabilities." Physical illness, difficulties in the speech area, slowness to walk, for example, are behaviors which have constitutional determinants. The reaction to stress causes physiological disorganization, spread of tension throughout the various body systems, and the eventual breakdown of defenses. These are present from the beginning with children—in their genes—and do not appear suddenly at adolescence.

Physical maturation proceeds "on the tracks" of the child's ground plan. It is the unfolding of his potentialities and adaptational patterning of which puberty is simply a part. The "upheavals" of puberty are a primary and secondary maturation, but of an organism with at least twelve or more years of growth behind it. Although of dramatic character, adolescence is another instance of breakup of previous consolidations and integrations which have occurred at age two/three, age five or six, even at prepuberty (age ten/twelve) prior to this period. The "breakup" of puberty, although it makes adolescents highly vulnerable to stress, has its precedents in the youth's life prior to this time.

Interpersonally, we should point out that children are highly "vulnerable" to their parents' influence. They are smaller, weaker, and dependent upon adults for physical and emotional nurture. They need food and shelter, but they also need love and trust and dependability. The "family romance," which Freud so astutely pointed out, is an impossible solution to the child's vulnerability. He cannot compete with father for mother's complete love and attention. He must lose this battle. Depending on what he does with this conflict (repression, incomplete identification with the father, or satellization with parents) it will occur again at adolescence. The adolescent's "vulnerability" has its precedents in his dozen or more years of life with his parents—a divorce, a death, a physical or mental illness, the emotional absence of a parent— all have played their part in his increased vulnerability in the "teen years." Physical maturation pushes him to desire independence from parents yet he is ambivalent because he does not want "to grow up," but wants to remain dependent upon them.

Vulnerability to the "peer group," its tastes, standards, and mores, is contemporary youth's bugbear. As Parsons and Riesman are saying, today's youth are "other-directed" and responsive to their own "teen culture." In today's rapidly changing society they have difficulty in finding structure and standards from their parents. The sheltering within the "teen society" provides them relative distance from parents while also allowing them the relative "vulnerability" of a dependency relationship. Whether this represents integral "coping" behavior we shall have to examine later.

The intensive study of these six youths makes other variables apparent—namely sexual differences, socioeconomic differences, and religious differences. The young girl is more "vulnerable" to certain stresses in her environment because of her sex. Marie Bonaparte points out,

Woman has a far greater hunger than man to be loved, cherished, and petted, like some grown up child. The male, bearer of the phallus, is far more self-sufficient; he has his social task which he loves and which occupies his mind and thus has more chance of satisfying and sublimating his sexual instinct. Woman, for her part, subsists and depends far more, and much more exclusively, on love: love of the male, love of husband and child. [And love of God?] [11]

David Riesman feels girls are more vulnerable and have extra burdens "partly because women are the accepted consumption leaders in our society, partly because women, much more than men, feel pressure to play any role they are accepted in by the men." [12]

---

[11] In Helene Deutsch, *The Psychology of Woman,* I (New York: Grune & Stratton, 1944), 54.
[12] *The Lonely Crowd,* p. 81.

Men are physically more aggressive, but socially they are allowed to be rebellious or resistive to authority and to the manipulation of the "taste-makers."

The young girl looks more directly to her mother for love in the early years, and if it is not forthcoming she is open to difficulty. The young boy, on the other hand, must turn from his romance with mother to an identity with father, and if he is "absent" the youth is open to trouble. All of these vulnerabilities come into the open during the youth's search for God when parental gods fail him.

Social and economic factors predispose the youth to vulnerability. Advantages of housing or possessions are not important in themselves, but their absence or scarcity may predispose the child to feel vulnerable. Again, Riesman says social class and spatial arrangements may influence children. "As compared with the one-room house of the peasant or the longhouses of many primitive tribes, he (the child) grows up within walls that are physical symbols of the privacy of parental dominance. Walls separate parents from children. . . . The conversation between parent and child, interrupted by the social distance that separates them, is continued by the child with himself in private." [13]

For many children, being displaced too soon by a sibling, being "lost in the shuffle" of children, particularly in a lower-income-class home, is stressful through adolescence. It will be noted that the one upper-middle-class child still felt vulnerable at not having a horse. Yet she did not suffer the stress of the other children and therefore did not respond to theses of suffering and pain as did the others. In some homes of the larger group, divorce, illness of a parent, or being placed in a foster home are particularly stressful to lower-class youth and make them highly vulnerable at adolescence.

The religious conditioning of children makes them open to certain kinds of stress. As we have observed thus far, the Roman Catholic children have been provided strict controls and rigid structure for their worship and the practice of the "faith." We might speculate as to whether this would support the "latency" child, but make it difficult for the adolescent to gain enough freedom for his own

[13] *Ibid.*, pp. 43-44.

thought and independence from his parents' traditional views of things. The conservative Protestant children have been expected to "decide for Christ" at an early age and subject themselves to rigid moral controls which should help them with their impulses. We again might speculate whether this would not leave them "vulnerable" to the stress of the outside world as they faced adolescence. The main-line Protestant children have been given greater freedom—perhaps too much too soon. Moreover, they have not been given structure and firm guidelines but allowed to decide for themselves. We might wonder whether they are not overly vulnerable to the peer group and "set up" for conformity by this kind of conditioning.

Our study of vulnerability has led us quite directly to an understanding of the relationship of faith to "coping styles." Coping or management is the way adolescents handle the stresses from their environment and from their inner conflicts. This process becomes increasingly important as puberty engages the child—as the earlier styles or integrations break up under the duress of his sexual and aggressive drives, and as the support and structure of his parental home ceases to satisfy or support him. Coping efforts and defense mechanisms both need to be looked at—particularly in relation to the religious variables of belief, attitude, identity, and practice at adolescence. What sense does the young adolescent try to make of his life? How does he find his identity within a larger context than the home? How does he intellectually and emotionally use the symbols, myths, rites, and experiences offered him by the religious community? How does he find integrity and commitment enabling him to grow up within both the religious and secular society? These are the problems that will engage us in chapter 12.

11

Barbie
the Study of a Conformist Girl

Barbie is typical in many ways of the girl one expects to find in many junior high schools, although a little atypical when compared with Helen and Diane. She is very much tuned to her peer group, a "conformist" kind of teen-ager. Yet she is more than just a conformist, as Roddy proved to be more than a conformist. It is to understand how she got to be so "average" and so sensitive to the radar of the crowd that the reader is invited to study her.

The questions we want to ask of the biographical materials are: (1) How has Barbie developed her particular stance toward authority? (2) How has she become so conventional in her religious ideas and practice? (3) What are the stress elements in Barbie's life, and are they related at all to religion? (4) What about the identity crisis in Barbie's life?

229

Lest the reader think that such a home as Barbie's could not produce a religious youth, we should add that Barbie's older sister has always been interested in religion and has developed through church and school into quite a religious authority. We may want to ask: Has the sister's interest in religion reflected positively upon Barbie? Or has the upper-middle-class home not provided her, the second child, with enough challenge to turn to religion?

Barbie is a pretty, blonde teenager, about five feet two with the expected eyes of blue which dance when she laughs and at other times look out at an exciting social world. She dresses and wears her hair like the style-conscious crowd with which she runs at the junior high school. That is, she has a bouffant hairdo, loud red shirt, capri pants, canvas shoes, and the ring the gang wears, a Cleopatra snake type. She is slow moving, and during the interview yawned catlike as though she had stayed up too late the previous evening and had to get up too early (nine) that morning. Her developing figure and her easy social grace give evidence that she is not having any trouble attracting the boys. She tends to speak in a babyish fashion, particularly when she tries to be cute. And when called upon to perform in a testing situation, she can get a frog in her throat or giggle nervously while shrugging her shoulders in bewilderment.

Barbie was the second daughter of an executive father and a mother who had been trained in social work. Her sister, Ellen, preceded her by four and a half years, a beautiful and highly intelligent girl. Barbie's father proceeded up the ladder during her early years and at present is vice-president of his company. The family moved from a comfortable home to a luxurious one which they built in the suburbs two and a half years ago. Since this daughter had not done nearly so well scholastically as their older daughter, the parents became concerned and, with professional advice, sought out a private school in a neighboring state which Barbie might attend. She entered this school at thirteen, though it is of a different denomination. The family attends a suburban church, near their former home, and the father has been treasurer of the church. At present, however, the father is occupied with business, and the family is only nominal in attendance at services. The older girl planned to attend an eastern college in the fall.

1. RELIGIOUS PRACTICES

The Howard family is not seriously religious but practices it conventionally. Barbie's father was orphaned from his father at age twelve, his mother helping him by means of a substantial estate to finish college. They were Protestants. Mrs. Howard came from a neighboring state to Capital City, from a stronger religious family. She met her husband in the church youth group to which his cousin had brought him. They knew each other from high school days, therefore, and courted through the church youth group. They became members of a church right around the corner from where they lived. After they were married both parents accepted responsibilities in the church organization, but since they moved to the suburbs they haven't been nearly as faithful in church attendance. In fact, the time of their decline began with the building of their present house.

Barbie was taken to Sunday school at age three, after being christened as a baby. She sang in the children's choirs in the first three years of school. She followed Ellen in the various church activities, with the exception of church membership. Ellen was very interested in religion at thirteen and joined the church only to regret it at age eighteen, so she has counseled Barbie to wait until she knows what she is doing. Barbie stopped regular church school attendance in sixth grade when the boys got to cutting up in class. She started youth fellowship the next year, but the youth minister's records show that she only attends about once a month when there is a party or something exciting is going on.

The family does not practice religion in the home. Barbie recalls the mother attempted to institute grace, but it ended in a week when they all registered embarrassment. Barbie received a Bible when she was twelve but she has not read it except when required to as a part of YF worship. She recalls that Ellen tried it but gave it up in preference for Gibran's *The Prophet*. Even this book seems too deep for Barbie, she said, and she put it down after a brief sampling.

Prayers were given up, too, when mother did not tuck her in, and are only said when she attends church with her parents.

2. RELIGIOUS BELIEFS

Barbie shows the results of a haphazard religious education, with little support from her parents. There are large gaps in her knowledge of religious things, and the beliefs she does hold she holds with not very much thought going into their framing. It is remarkable that she comes out as well as she does in knowing some parts of Christian tradition. Her lacunae in theology will be more understandable when we survey her developmental history.

She holds to a belief in a personal God; in fact, when she is questioned about it, her God is pretty anthropomorphic. He has a body and is not even a giant but a manlike creature, much as walked through the Garden of Eden in the "cool of the evening." He is immortal and understanding, his power is controlled by his goodwill. The most descriptive word for him is "real," the least descriptive is "mythical." He is much like a father that is kind, guiding, and just, not above punishing the disobedient child, but not from wrath or jealousy. In fact, Barbie dislikes the idea of a lenient and permissive Lord as much as she dislikes anything. She further disagrees with any thought of God as remote, unavailable, or mysterious. She is quite concrete in her thoughts about God, and the concreteness extends to having trouble picturing him without a body. (CWS, 1963)

Some of her thought of a human God may come from confusion of God with Jesus. God looks like Jesus, she thinks. In recounting the story of Jesus she tells of his birth, his beginning his ministry and being tempted, his miracles of healing and forgiveness, particularly of the woman taken in adultery, and his being killed by his enemies. She shows gaps in her story, and does not recall the story of the Resurrection until prompted, and then the Resurrection is explained as returning to encourage his friends and then he really dies. What appeals to her about Jesus is his strength and understanding; she does not like the gentle side of him or of any boy, evidently.

She got her ideas of right and wrong from her parents, her sister, and her friends, but mostly from mom, she says. She thinks the worst sin is disobedience of her parents, though there are some "in between areas" which have her confused. She has tried smoking but has been caught and lectured about it by her father. She has not tried drinking, though her parents do, and she feels it might be all right after she is nineteen or twenty. These are practices reserved for later on, evidently. Regarding boy-girl relations, she feels that kissing a boy whom one likes is right, but heavy petting or sexual intercourse for her age is going "too far." She has come to these ideas after talking with her older sister.

She believes in an after life, and thinks of heaven as beautiful, wonderful and fun, and hell as the opposite. She believes God is the judge who sends you one place or the other. She does not know whether she is going to heaven, but feels it depends upon one's whole life and not on one incident.

She believes in prayer, but has stopped praying since she did not get what she wanted, namely a horse. She knows that there is a difference between what one needs and what he wants. She believes praying for others helps and used as an illustration praying for her grandmother who was sick. She can see how praying is not magical but depends upon human and natural factors for its fulfillment. In this area as in others, her belief follows her practice. Since her parents do not pray in her presence, she has stopped praying and seeing its relevance to her life.

3. RELIGIOUS ATTITUDES

Barbie reflects two ambivalent attitudes on acquaintance. She needs structure and limits within which to function, and yet she dislikes prohibitions and demands made upon her. When given an unstructured situation such as an interview or a Miniature Life Toy Situation (LBM, 1954) she sits back and waits for the adult to prompt her what to do. Then, given an example in a test as to what to do, she follows the adult's choice before she can make a choice of her own. She has found it easy to bow to authority, represented by her parents, the school, or the church. There is some resentment of her mother's authority, but she does not rebel against it overtly, rather, as we shall see, by passive nonresistance. All of this comes out in her attitude toward religion—she has accepted what she has heard in church, when she has gone, with little questioning. She now finds some difficulty between the Genesis story of the creation of man and the stories of the cave men. She has asked her teacher once about it, and she said, when she got no answer she just let the question settle in the "back of her mind." She has not questioned the belief in an anthropomorphic God. In fact, her beliefs appear to be those of a child with respect to God, Jesus, prayer, and immortality. There appears to be no thirst for knowledge in the realm of religion, which is vastly different from her sister, who has already read widely in world religions.

She is conventional in morality and religious practice. She does not stand out from her crowd in her ideas or attitudes, says her pastor. In fact, he had a hard time placing her in the youth group, she had so blended in with the other boys and girls. One should add, however, that her minimum attendance has something to do with this, and the fact that in this large church she had never been in to consult with the minister. Her morality is, however, quite conventional: there are some things which a *lady* doesn't do and some things which she does. Her mother reflects this attitude par excellence in her derision of the community teen dance club. The fact that some boys have been "rough necks" at the dances is enough to keep Barbie from such a *public* place. What the neighbors think is of great importance, and standing out from the crowd—the right crowd—is not tolerable. So Barbie, when she attends an Episcopal church, is not impressed by the litany and symbolism but rather by her own unease about doing the wrong thing and standing out from the crowd. She took the elements of communion with her friend, she said, for she would have felt foolish refusing them. She does not want to go back, because she "bruised her knees" on the kneeling benches. Yet she realizes she will be required to attend chapel at the private school which she will attend in the fall. One wonders if conventionality and conformity will make her assume the attitudes of her classmates, or whether she might be able to tolerate dissonance with the total group.

Another attitude which she has developed is a feeling of security at home in which she has all the privileges and comforts of the upper middle class. She has been an active girl, as we shall note in the developmental history, and enjoyed the motoric much more than intellectual or artistic modes of achievement. Yet her life has been one of relatively little stress, and she has become accustomed to having her needs met, when she has experienced them, with little frustration. This is the external picture, at least. The only thing she really wants that she hasn't got is a horse, and when God did not give it to her, or Daddy accede to her wishes, she gave up praying. She has learned there are differences between wants and needs, but her needs in the material sense have been so satisfied, that she has not really felt deprived as have the girls in the lower middle-class families with many children. The stress has been interpersonal in the tremendous sibling rivalry with an exceptional older sister, but religion has played no part in helping her cope with this. In fact, the sister has tried religion and in moving from Christianity to interest in wider religions has kept Barbie from moving naturally into a membership class and an exposure to basic Christian concepts. The fact that Barbie has no acquaintance with the problem of evil in terms of suffering or hunger of young people in other countries or other parts of her city shows an insulation from one of the areas which might have stirred religious and moral questions.

Finally, there is no feeling in Barbie of religious vocation; in fact, she has relatively little ambition to become anything but a housewife. She reports that she has had no experience of God, except to recognize that there is one because she has been taught there is. Therefore, she has felt no intense sense of worship, nor come to experience God in church or in the beauty of nature or in other realms where adolescents report a sense of divine encounter. As a result she does not report a religious call or a sense of having to do something for God or for mankind. Barbie is perhaps of all the adolescents interviewed the least troubled about the condition of the world and the most complacent about doing anything particular about it. She simply wants to marry when she finds the right man, hoping that he will be a businessman who can support her well, and provide her with outdoor living such as riding and active sports. She does not want to go to college but wants to work as a salesgirl in a store until she marries. This should be after about a two-year courtship, but there is no lower limit on marriage for her, so long as it is the "right guy." (The lack of ambition contrasts sharply with both Helen and Diane who have "so much to do" before settling down to marriage, and also with Terry and Roddy who have religious calls to service.)

4. QUESTIONS

It is now possible to frame some questions which stand out in our minds and to put them to the developmental material in order to understand how Barbie developed her current religious attitudes and orientation. It is to be admitted that she is one of the least religious in the group; however, we are concerned to know why this is so, as much as to understand why the more religious have developed in their way.

1. How has Barbie developed her particular stance toward authority? Is this from her own constitutional givens? Or has her family been responsible for her acceptance of structure and limits? Has she given in to this easily or has there been a struggle? Furthermore, in adolescence, as the voice of the crowd has become louder—has she found the "hidden authority" of the gang to influence her more than that of her parents or her sister, and particularly the church?

2. How has she become so conventional in religious ideas and practice? Why is there so little doubt? And why has she done so little religious thinking? What caused her to fall off in her church attendance? Is it simply parental example, or the raucousness of the boys in her Sunday school class? Or are there psychological reasons within the makeup of the girl herself?

3. What are the stress elements in her life? If they are not at the level of basic wants and needs, as they are in the lives of Helen and Diane, are the interpersonal areas of the family magnified? What is the result of the strong sibling rivalry with her gifted elder sister? Has the older sister's attitudes toward religion impressed Barbie? And has religion been seen as a means of coping with internal stress? If not, what other means have been used by Barbie, in the atmosphere of this upper-middle-class family?

4. What about the identity crisis in Barbie's life? If she has felt no religious call or, in fact, vocation other than that of housewife, how has she arrived at this stage? And is this a conflict area for her, or a compromise in her struggle to get independence from her parents? How much has her mother served as an identification figure—has her mother's use of religion as an "unprohibiting" thing any centering function in Barbie's life? Is there any prediction one can make about the influence of the church upon her as she starts to boarding school this fall?

5. DEVELOPMENT OF BARBIE'S RELIGIOUS ORIENTATION

Relation to Authority. First, how did Barbie develop her stance toward authority? To get at this question it is important to go back to the infancy and childhood records and to look in particular at the mother-child relationship. Barbie was born four and a half years after Ellen, and the birth was complicated so that her mother had to remain in the hospital for three weeks, without nursing the baby. The mother felt this a godsend in one way, that she gained strength before undertaking Barbie's care. However, Barbie so differed from the first child from the beginning, that the mother has often felt she has never had the strength or wits to care for her. Barbie is ectomorphic by constitution, slow in movements, and from the beginning used delay in responding to outside stimuli. She liked sleep, was "just wild about it," sometimes sleeping through the night until 10:30 in the morning. The mother did not hold closely this "feminine" child, who vocalized so much, but worked her right into a schedule. There is some discrepancy in the reports about whether the parents wanted a boy; they say they did not, but, since this represented their last opportunity to have a child because of the mother's physical difficulties, it is thought that unconsciously they did. At any rate, Barbie was quite different from all the others in the family from the beginning. Says Dr. Escalona of her at twenty-four weeks,

She was a wide-eyed, slow, delicately moving baby capable of real relaxation and somehow "self-contained" in that she seemed content to look about, suck her thumb, finger, her dress, or near-by objects without need-ing attention or without engaging in vigorous activity of any sort. Per-ceptually she was alert without showing distress at intense stimuli, the one exception being social sensitivity which was thought to be very high. (SE, 1949)

The mother having studied child development was not awed by textbooks or psychologists but had a working philosophy of child care which she had worked out herself, namely "listening with one ear and saving the text books." She impressed the visitor, however, as self-conscious and covertly anxious, and very reserved about personal topics. Though gentle and quiet in her approach to Barbie, Dr. Heider felt the mother quite ambitious for her and in her own way stimulating. For instance, she never allowed her to remain without toys and tried to get her to hold a cup at six weeks. (GH, home visit, 1949)

It was Barbie's difference from Ellen that gave the mother difficulty from the start, particularly in controlling her. However, Barbie trained easily, weaning from breast to cup at five and a half months, walking at fourteen months, and being toilet trained at fourteen to fifteen months. (PS, 1954) However, as a child, she reacted to discipline more sensitively than her sister. When spanked for naughtiness, she would rub her little bottom, at two, and found it hard to believe her mother's statement, "We love you, but we don't love the way you act." (GH, 1955) Ellen was a perfect child, according to the mother, and quite beautiful, and her friends thought Barbie to be quite an ugly duckling as a baby. The mother had trouble with this estimate, and in particular accepting Barbie's difference in interests. When Barbie was four and a half, the mother told Grace Heider,

"Barbie has more pep than Ellen and a mind of her own. She is difficult to cope with and more set in her ways than her sister. She just doesn't think it necessary to mind all the time and she is kind of stubborn when she once makes up her mind. You can't reason with her. She is spon-taneous and probably more affectionate when she is affectionate at all than her sister, but when she rejects them she does so wholeheartedly. She has so much spirit. She is impatient at being watched and wants to go off on her own." (GH, 1955)

The mother felt that her girls should behave in a lady-like fashion, as befits the upper-middle-class families which they represent, but Barbie, as she developed, was the strange one—less reserved, more motoric, interested in dolls and feminine things, but also interested in playing with boys and in the outdoor life of the boys. The clash between the mother and the daughter and the mother's disappointment with her behavior—at least from the age of four on—represents the first strand contributing to Barbie's attitude toward authority.

Reaction to Stress. Perhaps it would be possible not to deal with the stress elements in Barbie's life and return to the authority question later. At the age of four Barbie seemed particularly sensitive to the male role and the female role in the family. In the Miniature Life Toy Session (LBM, 1954), Dr. Murphy elicited the feelings that "mommy takes care of everybody, but daddy just sits down." She was aware of the fact that babies come from mommy's bottom, but the erotic was very subtly suggested by much kissing between the dolls, and by her kissing the "little fur mousie" on the mouth. The power of the males was very interesting to her, and in her play she acted out male intrusiveness and aggression by poking her finger into the hole of an alligator toy, yanking the tail of the mouse, and shooting a gun. Her father now handled the discipline, and she recalled her fear of a huge gorilla in her closet when she went to bed. Then when she went over to sleep with Ellen and talked loudly, her father came up to spank her and return her to her bed. (CWS, 1963) She wanted her father's attention and may have continued this activity to get it. But her father by this time had developed an ulcer and was spending huge blocks of time at his work. She attempted to reach him at his work, as only a sensitive and aware little girl can do. He took her to the office a couple of times but then the employees were not there so she did not feel any real part of his work world beyond seeing an empty office. (LBM, 1954)

In her play she developed masculine interests, turning away from dolls somewhat and finding her fun in rugged games, tree climbing, and outdoor interests. She told Dr. Moriarty at one time she had caught forty-eight frogs, besides having a hamster and a shepherd dog. At the preschool party she displayed real pleasure and comfort in the presence of other children. She was well coordinated both in

239

her gross movements and in riding a trike. (BW, 1954) Being a lady produced some strain in her; at the time she was attending the country day school and even there succeeded in playing cowboy with boys at the school.

A particular stress element in the life of this five-year-old was rivalry with her only sibling, Ellen. Up to this time, Ellen treated her like a doll, but when Barbie developed keen desires for toys and parents' time, difficulties arose. When she was angry, Barbie would shout "Don't look at me. I don't want you to." When in an argument, Barbie would want mother to enter her side, and she would get furious when Ellen would want to stay with a little girl friend and leave her at home. (GH, 1954) She said on the MLT that she did not know if the big girl loves the baby, "I guess the baby loves the big girl." The temper tantrums which Barbie threw at this time were most difficult for her mother to handle, and on one occasion she consulted one of the project's psychologists about this.

When Barbie started to school the sibling rivalry became most acute. Ellen was an A-student from the very beginning and her teachers, like the mother's friends, thought of her as a model child. Barbie could but suffer in comparison. It was inevitable that some teacher would say, "Ellen would not make a dumb mistake like that," and one did. It was not that Barbie did not have good intelligence, but that her interests were social from the beginning and not academic. The psychologists noted even at preschool that she took little personal satisfaction in the testing situation. Said Dr. Moriarty, "Barbie . . . accepted and handled test demands in an efficient perceptive way, demonstrating always maturity and clarity of cognitive processes, yet with an apathy and remoteness which permitted no real pleasure or satisfaction in the situation." (AM, 1955)

Her preschool intelligence test on the Binet showed 132, whereas in the latency period, and since, she has shown an IQ of 110-113, with performance scores exceeding the verbal scores. The frustration her mother experienced from the start was that she did not study or work in school as Ellen did, and from the fourth grade on has had to have tutoring to keep up with her class, particularly in mathematics. The mother says that she and her husband have tried not to push Barbie, but to allow her to develop intellectual interests on her own, but Barbie has in her own slow, motoric way dragged her feet here, knowing that it got her mother's goat. She would not be compared with Ellen, and to show how different she is, she would slow down in her intellectual drive, even though it might hurt her in other ways. We shall come back to this point when we discuss her reaction to authority as a teenager, but let it be noted that the means of handling authority at the time of starting school was by dragging one's feet.

Conventionality. Let us look now at the conventional outlook which Barbie has developed and see its precursors at the preschool and latency period. There are indications on the Rorschach that Barbie was conventional at age five. On the repressive-impulsive axis, the examiner found her basically normal, sound, and undisturbed. "My first impression," he said, "was that of an extremely well-trained and equally well-trainable girl who has a very easy time to take over the conventional ways of thinking and experience, who fully identifies with what people do and what is proper and decent." (PP, 1957) On the one hand, in manners and social training it would be expected that this mother would teach Barbie that there are certain things which a little lady just doesn't do. She showed at age five a tendency to talk like the mother, although at times her laughter and loud voice would break through the exterior. The role of "little lady" seemed something of a strain, according to one examiner. (AM, 1954) And according to another, "her spontaneous interests appeared restricted as was her originality very restricted despite her high level of integrative capacity . . . and intelligence." (PP, 1957) The absence of color responses on the Rorschach was noticeable at preschool and has continued to prepuberty, an indication of dampening of her feelings, perhaps even a repression of them, particularly around the family.

The family has held to upper-middle-class manners and behavior, and during Barbie's development has moved from one house in a good neighborhood to another in an exclusive suburban area. The building of the house has absorbed the mother's time and interest. She reported to me that the house has been like another child to her, so deeply invested has she become in its development. (CWS, 1963) This upward mobility, with the importance given to easygoingness in clothing and recreation, included "radar-sets"

241

turned on full and directed actively toward the neighbors that count and what they think of one. The mother, therefore, took Ellen out of the state for asthma treatments, so as not to draw attention to herself, and has been actively concerned about Barbie's potential school failures for fear of what it might do to the family name. We have already indicated that religion is also conventional, not held with any zeal or intensity, nor practiced with any more regularity than the neighbors. When Ellen showed signs of taking it as seriously as her fundamentalist boyfriend, the pastor was asked to talk with the girl about the seriousness of "mixed" religious interest. And now when Barbie begins to attend a different church, her mother "flips," she says, when she discovers she takes communion with her friend. Religion should be "unrestricting," meaning undemanding and rational, thinks the mother. The values which she holds are the values of her upper-middle-class culture, and the demands of the Christian faith are not to be taken seriously when they are at cross purposes with the culture. It should be said she sees the small service needs of an auxiliary as needing to take her time, but the values are limited and the insulation from the social needs of the community is nearly perfect.

In training Barbie to conventional manners there has been a masking of her creativity and a resulting inhibition of her awareness of the deeper values of life in the community. The dissonances between the values of their group and those of another—such as intense religious groups—have been dealt with directly by sheltering the child from such groups. When rowdies spoil a party, the mother forbids such parties in the future; or when Barbie wants to go to a dance in which she will be thrown in with children of a different class with unconventional values, again she is forbidden to attend.

The lack of conflict in thought or values has tended to keep Barbie on the childhood level in her beliefs and has meant that she has doubted little of what she has been taught. She still holds to anthropomorphic ideas of God, and to magical ideas about Jesus, his miracles, and his resurrection. That these should be questioned has never come to her mind. Her thought life in religion has stopped at the childhood level, at the time that her attendance in church school and youth fellowship has dwindled into the conventional once-a-month pattern of her parents. She has not been taught other than "culture morality" at home, so it is no wonder that she is no further along than she is religiously. It is at the interpersonal level that Barbie is going through the most maturing at the present. And this can best be understood by looking at the last question, regarding the identity crisis, and by pulling the various strands of Barbie's development together under its discussion.

Identity Crisis. The roots of the identity crisis in Barbie go back to the preschool years when she turned from her nurturing mother to look for the identifying mother to help her learn the sexual role.[1] As we have noted Barbie was not wholly acceptable to the mother as she was, largely because she seemed so different from Ellen and so difficult to handle. Barbie in her confusion turned to her father in search for a model and tried during the latency years to play boys' games. She found she was not acceptable, but she was confused in her understanding of sexual role. At the preschool psychiatric exam, she would not play the game of "cats and witches" where boys and girls switch roles for fear of her mother's finding out and disapproving. However, the tomboy behavior appeared to be her way of coping with her oedipal feelings and her way of showing that she felt the man's world superior to the woman's which her mother and her sister occupied. All of this was veiled behind a sweet and feminine voice and manner especially around her mother.

She might have turned from the mother to the older sister for an identification model during latency. But, as we have observed, her rivalry with her sister brought her into the arena of books, music, and scholastic excellence. On the surface Barbie conformed to her parents' expectations that she would follow in Ellen's footsteps, but, underneath, her hostility toward her mother and her sister was expressed by sabotaging her efforts in school. Dr. Toussieng points out that "the area of vigorous games with boys, the climbing of trees as well as eager rides on horses" (PT, 1962) provided a place where she found gratification. Her mother and her sister were models which she could not hope to emulate, but she did find that her good physique and motoric control enabled her to

---

[1] Helene Deutsch, *The Psychology of Women*, Vol. I.

win swim contests and to excel in outdoor group games. Her mother describes her as "harem-scarem, unable to settle down to things, and active and having to be doing something all the time" during this period. (PS, 1961) The result, she felt, was that her study habits were not good, though her social relationships became something to behold. Again her mother told an observer, "we are all in awe of her and she is so skilled in social relationships we think, 'Where did you come from?' because she is not like most of the other members of the family." (MF, 1960)

Barbie turned quite naturally to her peer group for the acceptance and approval which she felt she did not get at home. Her tomboy relationships with boys in latency became by age eleven heterosexual, and she very precociously became aware that boys were attracted to her. She observed about swimming at that age, "I think when the boys tease you and are ducking you and playing in the water that means they like you." Her mother helped her in her heterosexual relationships to a certain extent, providing Greenberg's book, *How You Grow,* to read. She also saw the Brownie film on menstruation and was not surprised when she began her periods the summer she was 12. She blossomed in her development and with a pretty face and growing figure became a popular girl with the boys. Beginning with boy-girl groups at age eleven, she had by the time she was thirteen started dating by seeing a boyfriend on the sly downtown. She would tell her mother she was going to a movie and then meet the boy and shop through the stores. She was also planning parties—the one we described earlier is an example—and seemed to be the center of social attention in her class at school.

Because of her popularity with boys, and also her social ease, the girls found her to be a good friend. Slumber parties, record sessions, and times in which they would spend hours talking on the phone became central for her. Her dress became that of the rest of her crowd; the bouffant hairdress, the long nails, and the capri pants the other popular kids in her "set" wear. All of this went against the taste and conservatism of her mother and sister who wished she would be more of an individualist and show more of the artistry of Ellen. But between eleven and thirteen Barbie had turned from the mother to the peer group for her tastes and her opinions. Her mode of relating is to conform—not to the parents now but to her contemporaries. Her parents have taught her this mode and to listen to convention and the sound of the crowd; now Barbie shows how well she has learned her lesson.

There is dissonance which plays up the dependence-independence conflict in her as an adolescent, and this shows up most clearly in the area of sexual ethics. Barbie's mother does not think she should kiss the boys and has told her as much. Barbie thinks it is all right to go this far and admits that she does. (CWS, 1963) It was not, however, until an incident when Barbie had a girl from her class over to her house with two boys, and one couple went into the basement and engaged in some heavy petting (making out) and the mother discovered this, that Barbie discovered the mother's strong feelings about sexual behavior. Barbie's father has told her on matters such as smoking that she should work this out for herself, after she was caught doing this with another girl in the basement. (CWS, 1963) Her projective tests reveal at this time a good deal of testing of limits and desire to go outside the home without the parents' chaperonage. The punishment shown those who do go outside limits is jail, or in her own language "getting grounded," meaning the loss of the privilege of going out. (Godin)

Barbie's feelings for her parents are changing: at times she feels that she would like to be adopted like a six-year-old who never experienced genuine acceptance. At other times she would like to feel old enough to have a love relationship with a boy and get away from her parents. She sees marriage as a final escape from the home, but the boy she marries must be kind and understanding. That is, he will be like father or, as she perceptively caught herself saying, "That sounds like I am talking about God again." It is interesting that the male, whether father or lover or God (since she thinks of him in anthropomorphic terms), is a savior who rescues her from the necessity to have to compete with the other women in her orbit.

Religion is definitely on a childhood level for Barbie and has not developed beyond the utilitarian form of helping her get what she wants. Her mother has helped her feel this way toward the church—as an institution which is useful for social projects or parties or an occasional visit but as making no more demands than this. The lack of any genuine feeling about God or the religious life and the tendency to conform, rather, with what the culture demands of one she has learned from her parents and learned well. The fact that she now turns from her parents as teachers and toward the peer group which provides her with more solid identification and acceptance is to be expected. In fact, it is small wonder that she feels isolated from her mother, when her previous performance has been so little appreciated or herself no more understood.

Her mother and father have discussed the fact that they do not want her joining a different church. However, despite Barbie's first impression of communion in the cathedral, one might suspect that this group will have a strong influence on her young life. She needs structure and authority in the realm of behavior, and this group can provide her this. She also needs something which will give her moral strength against the demands of her crowd particularly in the realm of sex relations. She further might benefit from the liturgy and aesthetic emphasis of a formal worship to broaden her childish conceptions of God and help her understand him and approach him. She showed some interest in a more liturgical church.

However, she has now gone through the confirmation class at her church, as children her age "should do." We should ask, "Does the reader still feel Barbie to be as normal as blueberry pie? Does her low vulnerability rating make her less susceptible to Protestant religion so long attuned to crisis and decision? Is she at all like Diane, in that she is more adjusted to the peer group than to the adult society? What of her future? Will she have questions of identity in mid-life, if she follows the fairly easy road of marriage and the life of a matron?" The reader may want to puzzle out these and other questions pertaining to Barbie.

The study of vulnerability leads quite naturally to an examination of faith and coping style among these young people. It has become apparent that each youth copes with his world in his own unique way and that the beliefs and religious practices he adopts either help him or hinder him in coping. For some of the six faith is freeing, and for some it is restrictive. For some religion has become a creative opening to the outside world; for others it has been an easy way to conform with parents or the teen group. Let us focus on the reasons for these differences in the next chapter on faith and coping styles.

12

Faith and Coping Styles

"When the going gets tough, the tough get going." This motto of the politically tough and creative Kennedy family might be transliterated, "When the going gets tough, the weak get tougher, or the vulnerable learn to cope with the situation." This would make the motto a coping statement. What we plan to study in this chapter are the strengths of adolescents, their possibilities, their resiliencies, their creative adaptation to the emergent drives which they confront and the new social roles to which they are called. What are the coping efforts and the defense mechanisms which they put forth? And, in particular, what is the relation of coping to the religious variables of belief, attitude, identity, and practice in adolescence? The defensive use of faith will be explored, as well as its coping use. Moreover, we shall want to examine how conformity may be blanching out the creative efforts of young people in coming to grips with the social realities which they face, making some sense of them, and planning ahead so that the faith which they declare may be in healthy correspondence to the world which they face. Admittedly some of the statements and conclusions which

248

we shall make will be interpretive. They will make explicit a theology which has been the framework of the study thus far. However, it is necessary to fill in some detail to the charcoal picture that has been sketched so far in order for the portrait to come alive.

COPING DEFINED AND ILLUSTRATED

The problems of adolescence, its crises, the lack of fit of the adolescent with his environment have been the predominant emphases of clinical psychology and the studies of the delinquent and mentally ill. The studies of normal adolescence have waited upon the work of Anna Freud, Erik Erikson, Jean McFarlane, and Lois Murphy, who in their careful systematic way have discovered how the developmental process involves the active coming to terms with challenge and opportunity provided by the environment. The child is stressed, but he develops ways of dealing with stress. He is hurt and vulnerable to hurt. But, as our study has indicated thus far, at the point of his vulnerability he has grown and developed both defensive and coping devices.

Lois Murphy defines coping as "the process, the steps and sequences through which the child comes to terms with challenge or makes use of an opportunity. Coping devices involve *choices* in ways of using these resources and also new structures and integrations developed by the individual organism to master its individual problems with the environment." [1] In the studies of the children presented here the coping devices which they have developed have been enumerated and factor analyzed. "Each child has his own table of problems emerging from the exchange between his specific nature and his particular environment," says Lois Murphy.[2] Coping resources include ego strength and the ways in which the child and his environment perceive each other, what they expect from each other along with the objective resources on both sides. And all are part of the pattern which will determine the ability of a given child in a given setting.

[1] *The Widening World of Childhood*, p. 316.
[2] *Cultural Sequences, Expectancies and Patterns in Relation to Childhood Stress* (Chicago: University of Chicago Press, 1957), p. 22.

Factor analysis of coping variables contributed six major trends or sources of strengths and resiliencies which the ego develops in response to its being subject to stress. Alice Moriarty listed these as:

1. Openness to new experience: eagerness in meeting the world with concomitant capacity to act upon this world.

2. Identity unity versus diffuseness: firmness and constancy of identity promoting optimal cognitive functioning.

3. Adequacy of reality testing: sensory-digestive system and ego's utilization as directed to realistic understanding and weighing of situation.

4. Affective modulation: empathy and adaptability in adjusting to and using a situation.

5. Compulsive exactness: aspects of neatness and care in approach with suggestion of an optimal point between overexactness and sloppiness or vagueness.

6. Sporadic versus sustained control: disruptive nature of erratic and uncontrolled behavior, especially where it is associated with fearfulness and tension.[3]

With the emergence of the sexual drive and the pressure of the world of one's contemporaries and the adult world to assume more responsibility within the community, the adolescent faces specific challenges which will either prove the inadequacy of former coping procedures or throw him back on old defenses which may or may not work. The mental health of the adolescent, as Karl Menninger and his collaborators point out, may be dependent upon the adequacy of his coping devices. Dr. Moriarty has shown in her study of how children cope with intelligence tests that these devices are (1) problem-solving methods in which the adolescent attempts to work his way through a problem by bringing various parts of the environment together with the resources within himself, or (2) coping with internal stress within the organism by using various devices such as delay, distancing, reverse role playing, etc. When these normal coping devices break down, the adolescent may revert to more primitive levels including nervous patterns, the various compensating devices of neurosis, acting out against society, the retreat from reality in psychosis, or even the abandon-

[3] Variability in Cognitive Function, Genetic Psychology Monograph (Menninger Foundation, 1964).

ment of the will to live. These devices are more and more primitive; they cost more effort; there is more discomfort and loss of control in their use. [4]

Ready examples of how two children cope with newness of environment are shown by Helen and Roddy. When Helen and her family moved to the country, she was lonely and sought the help of her mother in coping with the matter of making new friends. Her mother, busy with the other children, advised her to seek the help of God in prayer. Helen took her loneliness to her room and in meditation and prayer was able to get some relief and surcease until she could handle this more adequately herself. Roddy, on the other hand, at the time of his move, went out into the peer world and met other children who were in the same boat. There he began to make friends and seek the approval and esteem of his peers. Thus when elections came up he was recognized as a leader and one who had developed superficial but successful means of coping with newness and with group behaviors and, therefore, was selected as the president of his class. Each child coped with the same problem but brought to it his previous vulnerabilities and coping styles, one of which might be called religious, the other might be called peer-oriented. The coping style had been developed in relationship to earlier critical phases of development, but at this particular phase in early adolescence the youth attempts to use the style with more or less success or may radically modify the style or develop a new style more appropriate for the kind of challenge which he faces.

FAITH—SOURCE OF BELIEF AND PRACTICE

Now let us look in some detail at the source of the adolescent belief and practice in his development from infancy. Belief, by the nature of the case, is an intellectual formulation of primary attitudes and motives; religious practice has its source in prior commitments and conditioning. Preceding the child's saying, "I believe" or "I pray" is the stance of faith, that constellation of attitudes and motives peculiar to religion. Is this faith a religious instinct, or is

[4] See Karl Menninger, Paul Pruyser, and Martin Mayman, *The Vital Balance* (New York: Viking Press, 1963).

it the product of conditioning? Does it blossom at adolescence as a result of the crisis precipitated by a call to conversion? What in theology maintains the objective referent to the kinds of experience the adolescent reports? The setting of these questions in some kind of framework must precede our bringing the coping material of these six youths together with their adolescent stance of faith.

Is there a religious instinct? The preponderance of the evidence appears to show that there is no such instinct. William James wrote in *The Varieties of Religious Experience* that his empirical reports demonstrated that the religious emotions were the same as any other emotion; the only difference was the object of the emotions. Gordon Allport further concludes, after his study of the religion of youth, that "the religious outlook is highly derivative in its origins. Born of organic unrest, of self-interested desire, of juvenile interpretation . . . it nonetheless undergoes extensive transformation." [5] So also does András Angyal hold that, "The trend toward homonomy is manifest in common everyday behavior but can best be studied in social, artistic, and religious attitudes." By this he means, "the sharing in a meaningful cosmic order—perceiving an individual fact not as it is but as it appears in a cosmic perspective." [6]

Whence come these voices saying that the search for God is implanted in the soul (from Augustine to the present day)? Rudolf Otto, for example, in *The Idea of the Holy*, builds his whole thesis on the fact that the feeling of the numinous is nonevolvable, that it proceeds from the divine order to the human order. Theologies of revelation are formally posited on this premise that the human psyche is too distorted and disoriented to search out God; God must, therefore, search out man and in meeting him reorient his "sinful self" so that he may more nearly understand and obey his creator.

It is possible that both the continuity and the radical discontinuity theories have part of the truth. We have seen that there are precursors of faith as attitude and motive in the child's developmental history. However, these undergo a transformation—an enlargement, even a radical transmutation—as they are related to Ultimate Reality (God), particularly in early adolescence as the

[5] *The Individual and His Religion,* p. 64.
[6] *Foundations for a Science of Personality,* p. 178.

objects of faith are depersonalized, and de-family-ized, and as the reality of the Wholly Other becomes apparent to the youth. Let us examine this development now in more detail.

The roots of faith are found first in the preverbal sense of security or "trust" which the infant feels with his mother. He experiences this through responding to his mother's empathy and physiologically by being nursed, having his hunger satisfied, and by contact with his mother's body. He needs this trust as basically as he needs food. Spitz and others, in their experiments with hospitalized infants have proved that without "mothering" and the development of trust an individual will die. [7]

The development of "distrust" and preparanoid attitudes lies at this critical juncture in the child's life. If he is able to trust, to "let go," to surrender himself to the life process at all, the baby must have a healthy give-and-take with his nurturing mother. Incidentally, Jules Masserman holds that a basic ur-defense is developed at this period. "When I cry, mother comes," which adults later hold in terms of prayer and providence. "When I pray, help will come." This defense is a necessary illusion, he holds, for a person's sanity. The trust or faith element in the defense is quite evident.

The second root of faith is in the autonomy drive demonstrated by the child, particularly from age two to four. He develops his sense of self over against his parents—particularly when they oppose his desires and drives. He does this despite the anxiety of separation from them. He leaves the previous undisturbed paradise of "dreaming innocence" and learns to say "I want this and I want that." This involves the child with risk or courage in its positive side; in its negative side it thrusts him into defiance and rebellion. However, he does not develop a sense of *self* unless he risks separation from the authoritative parents. His superego is formed in this nexus and struggle, says Freud.

The third root of faith is the identifying move he makes especially from four to six, where he strives to become like the parent of the same sex. In psychoanalytic theory identification with the same sex parent is the process by which the child manages to give up erotic

[7] Renée Spitz, "Motherless Infants," reprinted from *Child Development*, XX (1949) 145-55.

claims on the opposite sex. He first imitates, then introjects the parental ideal and is able to pattern his life from the internalized image of the trusted parent. He develops the capacity to commit himself to a projected ideal, model, or person by this means.

The fourth root of faith, developed in the latency years from six to twelve, is the capacity to surrender one's selfish good for the good of the group. It underlies the capacity to conform to the group's ideas, goals, and activities and provides an avenue from the home to the community. Conformity, or in religious terms, obedience to law, is a very important factor in faith; it makes the difference between the hermit's delusions and isolated practices and the churchgoer's devotions and actions within the common body. However, in perpetuation, conformity may keep the growing youth from the firsthand experience with the object of faith.

The task of adolescence is, as Erikson so ably points out, for the individual to discover a sense of identity. In the realm of faith it is to discover an ultimate loyalty—some person, cause, or cosmic Whole to which to commit himself. Erikson calls this fidelity, "the virtue which enables one to devote oneself to something or someone as true." In the moratorium of youth he tests the rock bottom of truth, "before committing himself to it." [8] We have already discussed in the chapter on confirmation how the intellectual development of the youth enables him by age fifteen/sixteen to conceptualize God in something other than anthropomorphic or familial terms. He is challenged by the "crisis of identity" to discover not just who he

---

[8]"Youth, Fidelity and Diversity," p. 7. Also *Identity and the Life Cycle*, p. 120. Erikson has developed a crisis model of ego development, in which the psychosocial stages are a meeting of the ready organism with its phase-specific needs and urges and the environments which can meet these needs in established ways. This parallels the coping model but makes of each period a crisis, with particular tasks to be negotiated.

Infancy Birth—1	Trust vs. Mistrust
Early Childhood 2—3	Autonomy vs. Shame/Doubt
Play Age 4—5	Initiative vs. Guilt
School Age 6—12	Industry vs. Inferiority
Adolescence 12—24	Identity vs. Role Diffusion

is, but to what he will commit himself. The previous religious training he has received provides him with the data—symbols, rituals, and theology—with which to ponder the problem. His prior emotional history has further given him the experience of trust or distrust, risk or rebellion, conformity or nonconformity, that he will bring to this critical period.

The adolescent experiences a critical turning, one in which he must either cope with the challenges of his new environment or drift in conformity to his parents or peers. At this juncture the symbols will take on unique meanings as they relate to his life. The drama of creation, redemption, death, and resurrection will touch the well-springs of his emotions as he lives through the roles of repentant sinner, forgiven believer, journeying pilgrim. He experiences "feelings of awe," which Phyllis Greenacre calls "a basic religious emotion and which is grounded in strangeness in the face of a powerful being." [9] This awe (for Otto a tremendum in the face of mystery [see p. 281]) is an openness to the Ultimate. In sensitive inwardness youth responds to the created order, to the scriptural narrative of Christ, to love demonstrated in heterosexual relations as revelatory of that Ultimate. It is not a replaying of an old tune, but a new symphony which floods his soul with its rapture and beauty.

This means that for the youth there has been a transformation of old motives and attitudes although he has built his present faith stance on them. Gordon Allport calls this the "functional autonomy" of the religious motive. It is no longer the servant of other desires— as for security or autonomy—but becomes a master motive, interpreting what comes to view and becoming the power to live in accord with a framework of meaning and value. [10] So, too, Erikson holds that the main religious objects retrace our earliest experiences of trust and autonomy, guilt and retribution, doubt and certainty. However, transformed, "the pure self is the self no longer sick with the conflict between right and wrong, not dependent on providers, and not dependent on guides to reason." Without parental benefactors or priestly intermediaries, the adolescent self is confronted

[9] "The Experience of Awe in Childhood," *Psychoanalytic Study of the Child*, XI (1956), 19.
[10] Gordon Allport, *The Individual and His Religion*, p. 64.

by the Ultimate. And his loyalties and commitments are transformed by the confrontation.[11] Dietrich Bonhoeffer sees the Christ as symbolic of the pure self or ideal self, calling him the Man for others.[12] For these adolescents, reared in a Christian culture, this is the reality they report. (See particularly Teddy's and Helen's biographies.)

Fantasy, Adaptation, and Coping Styles

One of the tests presented to the thirty adolescents in the study was the Religious Projective Pictures devised by the Belgian psychologist-priest, Father André Godin.[13] The purpose in using the test was to discover the youth's use of fantasy and its relation to his adaptation to his environment, particularly his use of religious symbols and myths in coping with his world. This test is an adaptive test like the Thematic Apperception Test rather than a true projective test, using Bellak's categories. In other words, it is interested in the kind of response the stimulus (secular or religious picture) produces in the subject. And from this response, a made-up story, something of the direction of the personality, in particular his patterns of adaptation, can be inferred. This particular test was standardized with a Catholic female population in Europe. Godin suggests that this "psychologically negligible factor" (difference in denomination) should make no real difference. However, our results wait on standardization in America and with both sexes and, therefore, our results should be looked on with a certain tentativeness.

The Godin studies have been interested in the different uses of the "religious cards and the secular cards," and the relationship between reaction to religious authority and parental authority. [14] We are interested in the adaptive patterns which the tests show about the six youth in the biographies and what this may tell us about the relationship between faith and coping styles. This is a different approach to the test from the European studies, and its results must

[11] Erik Erikson, *Young Man Luther* (New York: W. W. Norton and Company, 1958), p. 264.

[12] *Letters from Prison* (New York: The Macmillan Company, 1962).

[13] Godin and his associates are located at the International Centre for Studies in Religious Education, 184, Rue Washington, Brussels, Belgium.

[14] Margaret Robinson, "The Lumen Vitae Religious Projective Pictures Presented As a Group Test," *Studies in Religious Psychology*, Vol. I, Brussels, 1959.

be checked against other populations. However, for our purposes, projective tests and interview materials) so that the results have an we shall use other tests (i.e., checking the results against other internal validity for each subject. Following this, it will be possible to use fantasy materials from the Bible, from myths and fairy tales, and from the contemporary store of fantasy, namely movies and short stories, to devise some contemporary coping styles.

The ten pictures divide themselves quite naturally into three groups:

First Group—shows a picture of an individual in solitude:

Card 1—a girl alone in a woods.

Card 5—a girl with her head in her arms alone on a bench.

Card 7—a close-up of a woman's face, her hands being clasped before her.

Second Group—shows a young woman involved with a family situation:

Card 2—a girl talking with an older man.

Card 3—a girl speaking seriously with a man and woman.

Card 4—an older man with a young man and woman, surprised at their work.

Card 6—a young girl reading to an old woman.

Third Group—(two of which I did not use) are religious cards, according to Godin:

Card 8—two girls saying their rosary in a pew in church.

Card 9—a girl lies in a hospital bed with a nun standing looking at her.

Card 10—a young man and woman on a hilltop with a stone cross in the background.

Card 11—a young girl at the bedside of a sick adult, with a priest coming through the door.

Card 12—(used with Terry but not the others) a woman speaking with a Catholic priest.

The responses of the six were coded by three judges [15] using the following categories:

What does the subject do with solitude?

1. He reaches out dependently toward his parents.

[15] Mrs. Katherine Stafford, Mrs. Alma Stewart, and myself.

2. He withdraws to fantasy and narcissism.

3. He engages in problem solving.

What does the subject do with the parental relation?

1. He remains dependent upon them.

2. He rebels or escapes to the peer group.

3. He distances himself from them although he cooperates.

What does the subject do with religion?

1. He seeks magic help or miraculous solution.

2. He uses it to control drives of sex and aggression.

3. He is open and cooperative with the divine powers.

Results

(Only when there were two agreements
out of three are the results reported.)

Subject	Solitude	Parents	Religion
1. Helen	"problem solves"	dependent	magic/cooperates
2. Terry		rebels	magic/control
3. Roddy		dependent	magic/control
4. Diane	"problem solves"	rebels/dependent	control
5. Barbie		rebels	control
6. Teddy	"problem solves"	dependent/rebels	cooperates

When we look at individual responses of each youth to one picture we can put these data into a characteristic coping style. We have selected a different picture for each, but this one picture does represent something unique about the youth.

Helen—Card No. 10

The father of these two has died of the disease that's spreading through the land; the son has just buried him; the daughter, his sister, comes to him and they are talking to each other. The son is telling his plans to continue his father's business because his father had a very good reputation; the daughter is feeling rather sad and she says she will help in every way she can. . . . This girl is sort of sad about their father's death, of course, and the son finds he's interested in certain science, medical science, and they're working experiments while—no, during the day he'd continue his father's work and at night he would stay up and experiment and he's found a medicine to help the disease and he's saved some people around; he saved a baby and some others.

Interpretation. There is tragedy in the picture with respect to the family; however the children do not abandon the family but attempt to do something constructive to make the best of a bad situation. The girl is not as well equipped as the boy, but she does her part. The boy, on the other hand is able to do something, using his powers and the elements of the environment to work out a cure for the disease. The cure saves a baby, something close to Helen, which she can care for.

Terry—Card No. 12

Oh, Humphrey Bogart is not a priest at all, he's a racketeer . . . and the rackets got too hot and it kills him, so they thought, and they dumped him in front of this monastery. So the monastery takes him in, and he finds it different in the monastery, and he starts to become a brother, not a priest, a brother—and that's what he is now—and at the present moment he's probably been out of circulation for a number of years, and she was actually a girl friend, and she's the one that in the beginning set the whole ride up for him. She'd asked him to come to this place and as he was coming, these guys picked him up and thought they had killed him, shot at him with a machine gun. And so she is in the monastery now after she has located him through a friend and she's trying to tell him that she didn't really, you know, lead him into the trap, and he doesn't believe her. And so eventually the cops come around, since he's been wanted for murder, gambling, and everything else. The priest doesn't lie for him, the father, but doesn't tell the absolute truth. . . . He makes a last stand, after saving the monastery, and they had actually tried to kill him. So they have a good fight and he gets killed, of course, and he kills the bad guys and the cops come and get everyone else and she finds him while he's dying and they have a rather— as those death scenes go.

Interpretation. Terry repeats the story of a movie plot, but the bandit-priest theme so catches up his own attempts to control his sexual and aggressive drives that he spins the story out with great flourish. The tempting quality of the woman. The priest makes a last stand, saves the monastery and dies with a smile on his lips in his lover's (mother's) arms. This sacrifice (being a priest, saving the monastery, and finally dying in a burst of aggression) shows the mother his love, and her loss in his death.

Diane—Card No. 3

This girl ran away from home and now she's back and she explains to her mother when she asks, "Why did you run away?" She says because she thought they were too poor and they couldn't support her and all that stuff. Everybody feels sad, but in the long run everything turns out all right, because their dad finds gold and then they are rich and everything I guess. [In answer about the feeling tone of the picture] Well, they are sad because their little girl isn't happy in their home, and the little girl is sad because her parents are sad . . . I guess.

Interpretation. Displacement in the home, disappointment of a daughter so that she rebelliously runs away from home, and the return of the prodigal daughter are all a part of the story in Diane's case. A magical solution to the problem of poverty and of the disappointment by the father is hoped for by the daughter. The father will eventually make things right by putting her back in the center of the family.

Roddy—Card No. 4

They look like they were surprised, but I don't know what's happening . . . [twenty second pause]. Poor father came home telling them, I finally got a good job or a poor job, or didn't get a job at all, and they all look surprised. Whichever way it went [in response to a query about which way it went] father comes home and tells them that he didn't get a . . . that he did get a good job, and that they won't have to stick around in this old shack again, and that they will get a good home without weaving baskets. The man is surprised, the boy is about to smile, the girl frowning. He'll drop his cigar, if that is what it is.

Interpretation. This is another theme of disappointment with the father, but this time although Roddy gives it a magic solution, he is not sure about it. He is afraid that the father cannot make it and that he will have to make it himself, which he also fears. He is sensitive to the reactions of the people in the picture, using his highly sensitive radar system well, making one wonder if the peer world is not of more interest to him now than finding a good home.

Barbie—Card No. 10

Like in Italy. And this guy looks like he's done something wrong and except everybody else thinks it's wrong but it really wasn't. Like he killed somebody, but it was in self-defense. And so he thinks everybody is going to think that he did it, and you know because he didn't like the guy. And that was at his girl friend's and he was asking her to come with him and she does. And she persuaded him to come back to town. And he has a trial. Oh, he gets about probably a year in jail because of the running, but I mean he didn't care when he got caught because it was in self-defense. The girl stayed with him and did not date when he was in jail.

Interpretation. The rebellion of youth is symbolized in the boy who kills and runs away, but with the support and help of his girl friend. She comes with the rebel, stays with him while he serves out his sentence. Barbie is firmly entrenched in the world of her peers as the place to work out her salvation; although the rebellion is directed against the over-controlling parents.

Teddy—Card No. 10

Well, anyhow, it's her time of trouble and she's a sort of atheist and lone believer and this trouble seems insurmountable to her. She's exhausted every possible solution so in the moment of desperation, friendless, on her last legs, she turns to God for help. And suddenly a friend comes along, forgives her and she topples this insurmountable obstacle. He accepts her, some friend she hadn't counted on for help or some friend that she had alienated in some way—And he comes back, and (they) make up and they join forces against this troublesome object, whatever it is. And naturally they break it down and then again everything comes out okay.

Interpretation. Teddy's life story is apparent in this make-believe. He comes to the help of his mother and relieves her of her troublesome "object," but not before he has forgiven her. The turning to God in time of desperation and the appearance of a "savior" in human form is a religious sub-theme.

It becomes quite obvious that the early adolescents represented here are highly involved with their families, either dependent upon them, rebelling against them, or making some restitutive, even sacrificial, attempts to atone them for the youth's unruly drives of sex and aggression. Solitude is used in a problem-solving way by Helen, Diane, and Teddy, as their biographies confirm. But Helen's dependency upon the family and Diane's and Teddy's ambivalence of dependency/rebellion reveal that they are not free of family as yet. Religion is a cooperative means of coping for both Helen and Roddy, but for Diane it is still used as a means of controlling her unruly drives.

Terry is perhaps most caught in a replay of the oedipus struggle, and his use of the bandit-priest theme shows how highly charged his use of the priesthood to distance himself from the mother has been. He rebels when with his family, uses fantasy while alone, and in the religious realm has attempted to control his unruly drives—even to the point of dying in order to show his "sacrificial love" to his mother. The struggle with parents in Roddy's and Barbie's cases is nearly as strong, but it has been suppressed in both instances. Roddy cannot criticize his father's failure; Barbie cannot openly say her mother over-controls her. But in fantasy they can be critical and rather than using a religious theme, they use the peer group as the place in which they may find acceptance, esteem, and eventual freedom. Religion still has magical qualities for the highly imaginative Roddy, it might be a means of control for the social Barbie. The biographies of each bear this out.

What are some themes which emerge from our reflection on the Godin responses? Elaborating the stories of the six and doing some imaginative reconstructing, we may focus on some young adolescent themes and infer the kinds of adaptive patterning they suggest: [16]

[16] Chase defines myth as "an esthetic devise for bringing the imaginary but powerful world of the preternatural forces into a manageable collaboration with the objective (i.e. experienced facts of life) in such a way as to excite a sense of reality amenable to both the unconscious passions and the conscious mind." Quoted in J. Bruner, "Myth and Identity," *Daedalus,* vol. 88 (Spring, 1958). p. 349.

1. *Cinderella:* The contemporary version may involve the youth not in "besting her sisters" but in a clandestine relationship with a boy, probably not approved by her parents, one who turns out to be a "good guy," tough and able to make his way in the "cool world."

2. *Prometheus:* The contemporary version may be a superman who masters a situation—poverty, crime, or the attack of enemies—but the motives are never pure. It is probably to gain esteem of a parent, or, if outside the family, to gain popularity with one's peers or the love of a maiden. Superman, like Prometheus, may have to suffer for his threatening the powers of the gods (authorities).

3. *Pollyanna:* The youth may not recognize the tragedy and trouble of his existence but suppresses or denies it. He sees some magical solution to his difficulties, brought about by his parents or by the divine powers whereby everything turns out well. There may be a pleasurable journey in Elysian Fields by some "conformist" "affluent" youth.

4. *Prodigal Son:* Running away from home still appeals to the youth beleaguered by parental controls or disappointed in not having their approval. For some, however, the conversion is as much in the parents as the youth when he returns. They now recognize that they have wronged the youth and make things up to him since he is back.

5. *Catcher in the Rye:* The identification is with Holden Caulfield who catches the children playing in the rye from falling over the cliff to their destruction. [17] The youth is a contemporary "savior" who has sublimated his drives in an identity whereby he uses his energies to save his peers from a dangerous situation. He is still highly vulnerable himself even when helping others.

6. *The Prophet:* Although not symbolizing the prophet as an identity figure, this youth recognizes that he must both equip himself and be used by the community in order to make his life and the life of others better. There is an open, active cooperation with creative powers, rather than a shrinking from them.

[17] J. D. Salinger, *The Catcher in the Rye* (Boston: Little, Brown and Co., 1951), p. 173.

FAITH AND COPING STYLES

What correlation is now possible between the coping procedures we see in youth and their faith, attitudes, and motives? Is it possible to begin to see some emerging coping styles in young adolescents as we have experienced them in our study? These are the questions with which we shall conclude.

William James is correct in attributing the "moods of contraction and moods of expansion" to the religious man's motivation. [18] One may perceive both moods within the Godin projective stories. However, it would seem to us that one may better understand the religious motives of youth if we discern them as either *defensive* or *coping*. Speaking functionally, at puberty the youth, through the emergence of his sexual drives as well as his drives for status, power, and recognition in his peer group, experiences a break-up of the defenses and modes of relating that were satisfying and useful in childhood. If there is a *crisis in adolescence* this is its origin. He may either try to shore up his latency defenses or fall back to a more primitive level of ego organization.

Anna Freud, in her definitive study of adolescent defenses, says there may be two distortions of character during this period: asceticism and intellectualism. The *ascetic* believes he masters his unruly drives by cutting himself off from them. She says, "This may be interpreted not as a series of repressive activities qualitatively conditioned, but simply as a manifestation of the innate hostility between the ego and the instincts which is indiscriminate, primary and primitive." [19] The adolescent, like Terry, fluctuates in this solution—at times primitive in his denial, at other times just as excessive in expressing his drives.

Intellectualism represents an attempt to use the newly emerging analytical and deductive powers to solve basically emotional problems—the oedipus conflict in particular. However, as Anna Freud points out, "adolescent intellectuality seems merely to minister to day dreams. . . . The abstract intellectual discussion and speculations in which young people delight are not genuine attempts at

[18] *Varieties of Religious Experience*, p. 74.
[19] *The Ego and the Mechanisms of Defense*, p. 172.

solving the tasks set by reality." [20] The defensive use of reason is a shield by which the adolescent tries to keep from dealing with himself or his environment. To a certain extent Roddy uses his good intellect in this way to perform "loop the loops"—behind which lurk the ambivalences of his struggle for independence through the peer group and his dependence upon his mother.

Conformity is another means which is predominantly used by youth to defend themselves from the adolescent struggle. We have discovered two kinds: conformity to the beliefs, standards, and practices of parents—a kind of "traditional conformity" which keeps the youth tied to the parents in a dependent relationship. This is a carry-over from childhood and was noted in several members of the larger group. The other kind of conformity is the adjustment to the tastes, beliefs, values, and activities of the peer group. However, as we discovered with Barbie, this is merely trading one conformity for another without any real grappling with the issues which confront the adolescent. There is no "crisis"—or it is delayed —no meeting the new environmental challenge. There is merely a change of the coat of tradition for the "threads" of the gang. It represents the largest number of this group, and I would surmise it to be today's dominant youth stance toward religion.

The youth may, on the other hand, recognize the break up of latency structures and the unworkability of latency styles (dependency on parents, peer-group morality and conformity) and face the changes within his new organism and the challenges of his new environment. He copes with the new reality and uses both environment problem solving (coping A) and self-orienting adaptive devices (coping B) appropriate to what confronts him. This, on a religious level, utilizes his intellectual struggles with new ideas of God, his integral perceptions of himself as a child of God, and his commitments to what he perceives as Ultimate. He begins to live in terms of an expanded and expanding world view. The challenge confronting youth is to become a whole man, to realize his total powers within the environment in which he is placed. His previous vulnerabilities, defensive styles, and mechanisms (sins of omission and commission) can be mastered as he assumes re-

[20] *Ibid.*, pp. 176-77.

sponsibility for his actions and commits himself to Ultimate loyalties—a boyfriend or girl friend, a community, a church, God.

The change from egocentricity to concern for other persons, from separation from persons to reconciliation with them, or from isolation to community may occur in the adolescent by a sudden overturn of his emotions and by the emergence of a new and different orientation. This is what has been called "conversion" in the literature and has been studied exhaustively by psychologists of religion. William Silverberg calls it the "schizoid maneuver" by which, he says, "the effort is made to remedy utter helplessness by abandoning the effort to manipulate external reality and by manipulating in its stead one's own psyche wherein one is all-powerful." [21]

The possibility of a retreat into schizophrenia or schizoid states as a magical solution to problems has been recognized by psychologists since Anton Boisen. Boisen's work has been subtantiated by the psychiatrists Leon Salzman and Carl Christiansen. Salzman links the inner struggle with authority and the attempt to gain independence therefrom. Regression ensues when the hostility and resentment become too great and the ego's defensive walls crack. He recognizes, as does Christiansen, that there is a positive function to this crisis; it is "regression in the service of the ego." "At the same time, there is in the adolescent period a flowering and maturing of the person's attempts to set up meaningful values in his life. And so in many cases adolescent conversions may actually represent a maturation of religious, social and ethical ideals." [22] Christiansen feels all conversions are attempts at a reintegration of the ego's defense systems, some of which succeed and some of which fail. [23]

Using a coping model, one may say that the adolescent tries to "problem solve" the difficulties he confronts—manipulating his environment, mastering the problems with his analytic and synthetic powers until he runs into a blind alley. It may be the problem of evil (Why do I have to suffer when I have wronged no one?). It may be the questions of God's power or his love (Why doesn't God

[21] "The Factor of Omnipotence in Neurosis," *Psychiatry*, XII (1949), pp. 387-98.
[22] Leon Salzman, "Religious and Ideological Conversion," *Psychiatry*, XVI (1953), p. 186.
[23] "Religious Conversion in Adolescence," *Pastoral Psychology*, XVI (September, 1965), p. 25.

answer my prayers and give me the desires of my heart?). It may be the problems of death and eventual annihilation of himself (Why must I die? And is there anything else?). These mysteries do not pretend to solution by one's intellect. As Rudolf Otto says so beautifully, "A problem eludes our understanding but is intelligible in principle. A mystery is beyond our apprehension, not only because we come upon a 'wholly other' whose kind and character are incommensurable with our own and before which we recoil in wonder." [24]

The youth may attempt a "schizoid maneuver" either by retreating to fantasy or mental illness where he is omnipotent and can really bend the environment to his whim, or by magic, trying to coerce the mysterious powers to come to his aid and respond to his will. However, the mature use of coping powers is to recognize one's limits—and the limits of the human situation. He learns that one gets sick, one gets tired, one grows older, one dies. He finds that one needs other humans for fellowship and for loving. He discovers that one needs wholeness and the refreshment and recreation of the powers underlying his existence.

To become mature—through and beyond the passageway of adolescence—the youth needs to cope with the changes and challenges of his existence with his total self: judgment, perception, and will. As Donald McKinnon points out, "Whenever a person uses his mind for any purpose, he performs either an act of perception (he becomes aware of something) or an act of judgment (he comes to a conclusion about something)." [25] I would add he also performs an act of willing (he commits himself to some idea, person, or Ultimate). The youth may develop a preference for a judging or a perceiving or a willing style—however, all acts are necessary at appropriate times, flexibly handled by the maturing self.

Openness to experience is a means in adolescence to become aware of new combinations and possibilities. In the matters of faith it provides an openness to mystery, to the spontaneity and creativity

---

[24] *The Idea of the Holy*, John W. Harvey, tr. (2nd ed.; New York: Oxford University Press, 1950), p. 28.

[25] "Nature and Nurture of Creative Talent," *American Psychologist*, XVII (July, 1962), p. 489.

of the Universe. Acts of judgment should be formed and place these possibilities in some kind of order and pattern. These are thoughts and also values and modes of behaving in the new situations confronting youth. But unless the youth makes some commitments, he will not act in a faithful way to meet the challenges he faces. This may be commitment to a "leader" or to an ideal or to a Savior. Surrender may be involved, but identification and the finding of an identity are even more a part of his process. The human teacher or leader may later be repudiated but only after his "ideals, goals, and values" have become an intrinsic part of the adolescent's character structure. The "impossible ideal" of the God-man may, however, always remain for the youth a means of perceiving new insights about experience, a judgment on his immature and "sinful acts," and call him to deeper, more universal commitments. [26]

AN EMERGENT TYPOLOGY

From our study we may now formulate a typology by which it is possible to understand contemporary youth's religious experience. One must recognize that each youth may at any period have a particular trend dominant and with a matter of time shift, through growth and response to challenge, to another type. Adolescence is a period of change and challenge and any typology is modal and only approximates reality. Nevertheless, this typology does take into account the intrinsic-extrinsic forms of experience and their individual and institutional expressions.

The adolescent self-in-process, while still in his primary family, must discover his identity, begin to function with integrity, and find his ultimate loyalties. In response to his challenge, he may accept the traditional ideology and values of his parents and church, or he may conform to the conventional tastes and values of his peer world. *Both are conformity.* In crisis he may isolate himself from parents, church, and peers—the isolation may take a psychotic turn, or he may, with his peers, rebel against the adult world in a predelinquent or delinquent manner. Autonomy calls him out of the security of his parents' home—and within the established church

---

[26] See Dag Hammarskjöld, *Markings* (New York: Alfred A. Knopf, 1964) for an illustration of a life-long struggle with commitment to Christ as an impossible ideal.

TYPES OF ADOLESCENT DEVELOPMENT

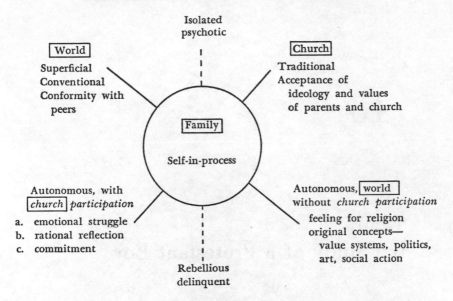

Isolated
psychotic

World
Superficial
Conventional
Conformity with
peers

Church
Traditional
Acceptance of
ideology and values
of parents and church

Family

Self-in-process

Autonomous, with
church participation
a. emotional struggle
b. rational reflection
c. commitment

Autonomous, world
without *church participation*
feeling for religion
original concepts—
value systems, politics,
art, social action

Rebellious
delinquent

he may find through reflection, emotional struggle, and commitment a faith of his own. He may, outside the formal church, in various political social-action groups, artistic colonies, or intellectual communities develop an ideology and value system with which he is identified. This often waits for late adolescence (the college years) and is reserved for the *few* in our "conformist day." This final group may be the prophets of a new religion or the reformers of the old. But in history youth have been the "homo religiosus," the iconoclasts, and the charismatic leaders of the new day.

13

Teddy
the Study of a Protestant Boy

With all the data in and the formulations made, let us now examine Teddy, a boy who has had a typical Protestant rearing, but whose life story is atypical of the other youth. He is not so atypical of many children in our population, however, in that his parents are divorced and his mother remarried. The effects of this trauma on his life should be examined closely by the reader Particular attention should be paid to what this did to Teddy's religious development.

The questions we want to focus on are: (1) From whom did Teddy learn about God, and is God in any way a projection of a parental figure? (2) What about the origins of Teddy's attitudes toward evil and suffering? (3) Whence came Teddy's attitudes toward authority, both parental and social? (4) How did Teddy develop such an acute sense of inwardness? In what sense is it a corollary of his religious development and in what sense is it an outgrowth of coping devices developed in other areas of life?

Teddy has joined the church but has dropped out of church school and youth fellowship—much as an adult. He practices prayer

270

and thinks about life religiously, really more so than do his parents. Is there any sense in which we see here a third-generation child, returning to religion and becoming intrinsic and inner-directed?

Teddy is a tall, sturdy fourteen-year-old boy, with dark hair and blue eyes, and a very serious face, who shows tension from time to time with a nervous tic around his mouth or squinting around his bespectacled eyes. He was the son of a young soldier father and nurse mother. The father tried civilian life for a short time while Teddy was an infant but reenlisted, and at the time Teddy's sister Laura was born he left for the European theater. The mother continued nursing to eke out the family living, and when family difficulties proved too great, sought separation and then divorce from the absent husband when Teddy was six. She married again a year later, this time to a stable car mechanic and salesman, and continued to work as a nurse at night, so as to be with the family in the afternoon and early evening.

Teddy lives with his mother and stepfather in a pleasant lower-middle-class neighborhood at the end of a street. He and his sister slept together in a downstairs room in their bungalow until two years ago, when an attic was converted into two bedrooms for them. His mother keeps an immaculate house, pleasantly furnished, and they wear comfortable though inexpensive clothing. They own several automobiles, four years old or older; however, the stepfather talks of getting a used Thunderbird. Teddy attends the local junior high, ninth grade, plays tenor sax in the band, and is on the student council. The parents belong to a Protestant church, which Teddy and his sister attend with them.

He does not date as yet, though he attends mixed parties. His interests appear to be mathematics and his studies, his music, and baseball. He plays at sports, though he does not excel in them. He speaks in precise, pedantic, objective tones, much like an adult, possibly a professor of economics. This may be anticipatory of his vocation, because at the present he says he would like to go into accounting. For him this represents his best subject, mathematics, as well as a place in which he thinks he could make a successful career.

271

1. RELIGIOUS PRACTICES

The mother and stepfather went through a membership class and joined their neighborhood church of their own volition some five years ago. Teddy goes with his parents about three times a month, and when the mother must catch up on her sleep, or the father stays home to do an odd job, he will go alone. He listens intently to the sermon and will talk about it when he comes home. Of the whole group, he is best able to tell when the minister's thought is good and his delivery is poor. The mother thinks him too critical; however, this represents his serious approach to the whole service.

Teddy no longer attends church school, stopping last fall when he felt that the lessons were repetitious and the teacher lax in her discipline of the class. He has attended youth fellowship sporadically, but he has not found the group compatible with his serious interest in life, either because the boys are younger than he is or the girls more interested in social activities. He has high goals for such a group, thinking they should be an extension of the "church," and, since they do not meet his standards, he has not become involved. He would rather study or practice his "sax" on Sunday evening, he says.

There is some discrepancy between Teddy's memory of joining the church and the pastor's records. He and the mother remember his attending the classes when he was in sixth grade; however, since the records do not show his name, the pastor thinks he probably did not come before the session and was not examined on his faith.

This is a family which tries to practice their religion at home. The little sister says "grace" at ordinary mealtimes, but at special holidays with grandparents Teddy is called on to officiate. Teddy got a "prayer book" from a teacher in primary grades, and he still uses it for his evening prayers. His mother still comes upstairs to "tuck him in" along with his sister, and at this time she will talk with him about the day, and he will read one of the prayers from the prayer book. The mother claims that Laura will go to bed alone, but Teddy is not satisfied until they have this nightly ritual. As indicated above, Teddy likes to discuss "religious subjects" at the table, and, according to the mother, at age nine he knew more about the Bible than she did. It became quite apparent in the religious interview that he enjoyed "theologizing" about life, and he reported at the end of the second hour that he had thought more about his faith in this period than he had for the past four years.

He participates in the communion service meaningfully, and knows it to be a reenactment of the "last day of Jesus' life." In fact he feels that the words are just dead words unless they come alive in the reenactment, and one feels as vividly as did Peter and John that he is a disciple. He also sees baptism as a dedicatory act, and the dedication is of the child to the Christian life and involves the parents' commitment as much as it does the child's! Worship seems to be meaningful to him also, imparting a sense of majesty and holiness of God through music and prayer and praise. His favorite hymns, "Holy, Holy, Holy" and "Come Thou Almighty King" help him feel this majesty; "I Would Be True" is as much an affirmation to him as is the Apostles' Creed.

Prayer is a daily practice with him also. He says he prays from two to three times a day, including the nightly prayer time with his mother. He is aware of the difference between selfish and unselfish prayer, saying he tries not to use prayer as an "implement," meaning simply to satisfy his desires, but rather to get some knowledge of God's plan for him. He feels intercessory prayer should also not be to bend God's will to his, but to think clearly about God's will for others. Reading, sometimes of a secular book, will raise the thought of God in his mind. God seems to him to be a presence from which he is never very far.

2. RELIGIOUS BELIEFS

How does Teddy conceptualize his beliefs? He has probably the clearest religious concepts of any of the Protestant children. God for him represents the Absolute with no physical image but the power behind creation and the preservation of the universe. He would be a Father figure, except that this father makes no mistakes. Teddy does not believe in a devil, therefore, because a fallen angel would reflect on the perfection of God. God is infinite, omnipotent, majestic, and divine. (CWS, 1963) All the negatives represent for

Teddy the human emotions, like wrath or criticalness or formality or impersonality. Even so there are paradoxes in Teddy's beliefs about God: He is above us, yet he is near us. He can make no mistakes, yet Teddy does not put evil off on the devil but thinks evil has some higher purpose which man does not understand. God is One, yet Three in the Trinity, with Christ and the Holy Spirit. The difficulties in explaining the creation story with the theory of evolution are handled by Teddy by assuming that God's days may have been millions of years rather than twenty-four hours. Yet Teddy knows that the Bible was written by men and that they were writing a religious story and not science. God for him is a judge, finally, who though he understands man's humanity, wants men for fellowship with him. Those who know the truth and do not do it will be punished in hell. Those who own God as their Lord will know the serenity, beauty, and peace of heaven, away from earth's troubles.

Christ for Teddy is the second person of the Trinity, truly God and truly man. He was part of God, and this rests not upon anything which Jesus did but on faith in him. Teddy is most impressed by the Resurrection, feeling that this is more than miracle but separates mortals from godly status. Jesus died on the cross as an example to us to show us how to go through hard times, to stand up and not give in. He feels all men must undergo little crucifixions, part of the tragedy and sufferings of life, but when it is almost impossible to bear up, Jesus on the cross provides men an example. Teddy said he used to turn to Jesus all the time in trouble but finds that now he turns to God. He gives him something to hold onto when he is "beat." God created you, as he created Jesus. He gives you a second chance, in fact a three hundredth chance. So he must think you are worth something.

Teddy acknowledges he gets his ideas of right and wrong from his parents, particularly his mother. But he also sometimes says in Sheldon-like fashion, "What would Jesus think of this?" He thinks there are big wrongs such as stealing for which society punishes, and little wrongs such as disobeying parents which they punish. He tends to acquiesce in his parent's standards, however, feeling they have lived longer and had a chance to prove things through experience. He feels obliged to obey them, since they were put

274

here by God to guide him. He knows their authority rests in their power, but also in their wisdom and that they can control him while he is still a child and unknowledgeable about the world. He differs with them on matters of opinion, but not on matters of fact. So far as individual matters go, he does not believe in smoking for health's sake, nor in drinking, though his parents drink in extreme moderation. This, too, is a matter of health and keeping up in school and athletics. He believes in dating when he is older for the sake of friendship, but not to "go the limit" until he is engaged and the wedding date is planned. He knows this is lax, he says, but he believes it. (His mother did not teach him this and does not know where he got it.) He believes marriage is a union between woman and man and should be forever.

He thinks of the church as the teaching outpost of Christianity, and as the place for the worship of God, where men learn right from wrong and get the support to live their lives according to God's plan. The sacraments to him are reenactments of significant moments in Jesus' life and appear to be means for making the great events of Jesus' life come alive for believers. The minister is one set apart to do God's work, he feels, though if everyone were a minister, whom would they serve, he asks. So in his instance he feels he can serve God and the church as a layman. If God wanted him for a minister he feels he would have a special call, that he would feel he must give up many things and study and feel a strong sense of duty to God.

3. RELIGIOUS ATTITUDES

For Teddy, as for Sören Kierkegaard, there is an infinite qualitative distinction between the divine and the human. He thinks of God as absolute, and by that he means as transcending his world. "He is above us, so much above us he can be of help," Teddy says. "His majesty and absoluteness bring forth the utmost emotions, a feeling of being in awe, feeling incapable, and unworthy to be in his presence." (CWS, 1963) The distance between God and his creatures, however, is one that makes them acknowledge their *dependence* upon him. Teddy thinks there is nothing else to believe in, that God is something to hold onto when one is in desperate need. God's perfection is found in his power, his capacity to create and to sustain, whereas man must depend upon powers outside himself, upon the powers and creations of God in order to survive. The weakness of man therefore is an acknowledgment of the need of God, and God as experienced by his immanence, his surrounding and sustaining presence. This is not personified as a father, however, for Teddy, but is seen as above emotions, except for love. This love is impartial, just, and truthful, transcending human expressions of love.

A second primary attitude which Teddy displays in his religious stance is fortitude in the face of evil. Perhaps, his best statement is that "storms make a strong oak." Evil is not a separate power, but a means by which God tries to turn something bad into something good. He feels this is the message of Job, and even the meaning of the Crucifixion. God allowed his own Son to die, yet nothing can replace his love for his children. In all of this one is aware of the events of Teddy's own life, which we shall explore below, in which he was the victim of conflicts between his father and mother, which he had no part in. As he said in an aside, in replying to one of the Godin cards, "Unfortunately there are too many things to be sorrowful about in the world." This tragic sense of life does not challenge his belief in God, but has challenged his fortitude, his courage to stand the testing. Jesus Christ is the supreme example to him of one who was put to the supreme test of suffering and who withstood the very worst that men could do to him. Teddy feels he has had his tests, and that in the face of what seemed insurmountable trouble, in which every solution seemed exhausted, and in moments of last desperation, he has turned to God and found support and help. He feels that "him whom the Lord loveth he chasteneth." There is the possibility then in Jesus' life (what he calls his fifth gospel) to find an example of how to live, to go through hard times, to stand up and not to give in. He says this is not necessarily a need to be perfect as Jesus was: "You can make a couple of mistakes and come back and win, that is, be in God's loving sight."

A third attitude which Teddy has developed, somewhat as a corollary of his dependence upon God's transcendence, is a submission to authority in matters of morals and beliefs. This young man has an excellent mind which he can use in analysis of problems and in constructive solution of them. He will, as we shall discover in the developmental material, set about a problem-solving task in his own reflective, step-by-step fashion. However, in the area of morals and beliefs he has not doubted the authorities who have presented him with a body of doctrine and ethics. He shows this attitude particularly toward his parents, feeling that they have had more experience and are able to look at more facets of the problem than he. He accedes to their demands, and is able sensitively to feel their disappointment if he does not live up to these demands. He will put down his own desires, if the parents do not agree with them, and he will listen to "reason" as they explain things to him. There is a curious lack of doubt of the authorities, and a strange blunting of his analytic powers in the face of the authorities whom he respects. One gets the impression that he accepts God as the highest authority, and to doubt God would be to leave himself vulnerable to the threat of meaninglessness and despair.

A final attitude which Teddy expresses most poignantly is an inwardness which gives him strength to face the conflicts which have been a part of his life to date, and which seem to be coming to the surface again in puberty. In the religious exam the interviewer commented that he thought of his self as a kind of citadel, inviolate against the storm and stress of the world. Teddy agreed with this but added that there was an opening upward to God and smaller openings to man. He is able to withdraw from the world (to his room for the most part) and there consider his problems, perhaps pray about them, and gain the insight and the strength to face them. He realizes that he cannot escape other people, that they follow him even in his thoughts, but he can be alone for awhile and this is strengthening. He adds, "Next to God, or almost equal to him, men influence me."

There is then this curious polarity in Teddy's feelings about people: he needs them, but he must get apart from them from time to time, in order to understand his own feelings and to analyze problems that he faces. He feels an autonomy then, and this autonomy is strengthening and enabling. Prayer and worship are a part of this same kind of inward contemplation and provide him with this same kind of power. It is as though "the world is too much with him, late and soon," and if he could not retreat to himself from time to time, he could not stand the stress of it all. Yet he knows how much people mean to him, in particular the "authorities in his life," mother, a favorite teacher, or band instructor. To these he returns and feels better able to cope with the demands which they put upon him, without any rebellion or questioning of their authority. It is much like Ernest Hocking's principle of alternation in work and worship which he practices in his life.

4. QUESTIONS

There are several questions which we want to ask of the longitudinal material in Teddy's case. He has had excellent religious training and, even despite a divorce between his mother and father and a second marriage, has made a considerable adjustment in his life by the age of fourteen. He says he feels really he has had two lives, split in two by the divorce. We are, therefore, intrigued primarily as to what this emotional trauma has meant to the boy, and how if at all his religious faith and life stance have helped him weather this crisis. Perhaps we can break this major question down into several subquestions so that we can manage them in some kind of developmental study of Teddy's life:

1. From whom did Teddy learn about God, and is God in any way a projection of a parental figure? Is there any sense in which the divorce, coming as it did at the height of the oedipal crisis, altered Teddy's primary feelings in relationship to God? If the parental relationship with the father has been disturbed, has he sought any other significant relationship to give him a model for the Divine? How are the distancing modes of immanence and transcendence affected by the divorce?

2. What about the origins of Teddy's attitudes toward evil and suffering? How have his own difficulties in the struggles between mother and father, mother and grandmother, and the remarriage influenced his ideas of evil? Are there any conflicts which he has had to face early in life which have left their mark upon him in handling the problem of undeserved evil? How has he found a religious rationale for suffering? What does he do with the problem of Job? With the crucifixion of Jesus? What about his own "little

crucifixions"? How are these fitted in to his faith stance? Does he see any way out of "this veil of tears" which will leave him some autonomy?

3. Whence came Teddy's attitude toward authority, both as regards parental relationships with children and as regards the "established social and political order"? And how has he used his excellent mind to solve some problems which he has faced, and how has he distinguished other problems which are to be submitted to higher courts of authority? What had the learning of controls to do with the constitutional givens in his nature, and what had they to do with the particular environment into which he was born? In what way has the divorce made itself felt on this phase of Teddy's development? And finally, has this stance toward the "powers that be" brought Teddy to a healthy or unhealthy attitude toward religion?

4. How did Teddy develop this inwardness, and in what sense is it a corollary of his religious development and in what sense is it an outgrowth of coping devices developed in other areas of his life? Is this inwardness a protective device against unbearable stress (divorce, separation from father, remarriage of mother), or is it a positive mastery process which he employs in problem solving and outreach? Is he entering adolescence with the resources of religion which will take him outside himself? Or will he use his religious faith in a crippling, exploitative fashion to keep him from the larger challenges of his world?

All these questions are important for this exceptionally bright and able boy as he faces the new thrust of adolescent growth, and in particular as he ponders how his faith can help him meet these challenges.

5. DEVELOPMENT OF TEDDY'S RELIGIOUS ORIENTATION

If one takes Teddy's own analysis of his life seriously, he might well consider it split in two by the divorce. Can some of the developmental questions be posed to the predivorce period and some to the postdivorce period? Significantly, the divorce occurred when Teddy was five, in the midst of the oedipal struggles, so that it adds fuel to an ordinary crisis of the little boy's life. It might be well to see Teddy predivorce first, so that the questions which we ask can be directed to Teddy's normal development before the complications of the separation of his mother and father are added.

Predivorce. Teddy was born weighing eight pounds, thirteen ounces. He was rather stocky in build with black curly hair, fair complexion but given to skin rashes, and with a sober, serious expression. In the infancy observations and tests he showed high sensory reactivity (minding bright light and loud noises), but with average drive and low activity level. His stability was high, he vocalized a great deal, and showed a drive toward persons rather than objects. He demonstrated excellent cognitive skills at twenty weeks and showed an ability to withdraw from excessive stimulation, to turn aside in rest and sleep after tiring. Dr. Heider therefore rated him as a low vulnerable child, with a rank of 1.

His mother showed a particular empathy and awareness of him from the beginning. For instance, she had vowed not to nurse him at the breast, but when he was brought in she relented and took him to her bosom. She said, "I didn't turn him down and now I haven't any desire to put him on formula since then." (SE, 1949) The infant would initiate an activity, such as rocking in the lap, and the mother would take it up and gratify his needs. (SE, 1949) She would handle him gently and with economy of movement. Teddy seemed to want body contact and would put his face up to the mother to rub up against her. The mother reported to the investigator, "He likes to be loved." Sylvia Brody rated this mother as one who was less free to enjoy physical or social contacts with infants. [1] However, this is probably because she appeared to be a person who held her emotions in check and did not feel free in interpersonal relations.

Teddy's father was described as a "hearty, well built, rather tall young man. In contrast to his wife he moves quickly and forcefully, speaks loudly, laughs readily and sort of exudes energy." (GH, 1949) He was in the armed forces at the time of Teddy's birth and, it will be recalled from the earlier report, never succeeded in anything but soldiering. "He tended to emphasize, in his conversation and

[1] *Patterns of Mothering,* p. 194.

in his play with the baby, the latter's strength, vigor and other masculine attributes." (GH, 1949) On the other hand, despite his rough play with the infant, he was quite obviously the weaker of the two parents, the more dependent, and, as it turned out, the least successful parent. This was not apparent to Teddy, however, while the father was at home. In fact, at the age of four Teddy would still defend his father as an idealized sort of man, though he may not have heard from him in a year.

Teddy as an infant of twenty weeks lived in a little apartment with his two parents, the center of their world. The mother had an infection and was incapacited for six weeks when Teddy was a month old and he was cared for by his paternal grandmother. In fact, the elder woman was to become quite a dominant person in Teddy's life, particularly when his mother went back to work as a nurse and the grandmother was called on to baby-sit with him. For most of the time between the age of nine months and four and a half years this grandmother provided Teddy's daytime care. The mother had certain ideas about discipline which she considered a balance between indulgence and neglect. On a questionnaire given at the time Teddy was twenty weeks, she defined indulging as "giving a baby things he doesn't need and has no use for," while neglecting is "not attending to his personal needs, not playing with him or teaching him things he should know at a particular age." The grandmother thought his mother too lenient, however, and did not spare the rod. The mother stated that she was a marvel, for she could "wind them around her finger and still be pretty strict." (GH, 1949) After a brief experiment as a policeman the father returned to service and on periodic returns home would try to discipline Teddy as a soldier. This, too, the mother resented, feeling it was too harsh.

It should be noted that not the mother, nor the father, but the grandmother attended to Teddy's toilet training. Teddy's mother would have trouble with him at the age of two. He would get angry if he wanted attention, such as being read to, or he wanted to be taken out or did not get his way. Her method of handling him was to "reason" with him to try to reach a compromise. She told the investigator if she spanked him he fought back; scolding bothered him and he would try to win her over. Sitting on a chair was what he seemed to mind most. (GH, 1953) The mother seemed to feel that the grandmother was better in handling Teddy, that all she had to do was say something and he did it. She readily acknowledged that her relationship with him "was not what it should be since she had been away from him so much." (GH, 1953)

Teddy developed normally and precociously. He was weaned to a cup at fourteen months, was toilet trained for both day and night by two years; he talked clearly and distinctly by two years as well. He had repeated throat infections from two through five, which did not clear up until he had his tonsils and adenoids removed just before entering school. He also had some feeding difficulties, vomiting before an illness. Thin and gangling before six, he suddenly gained weight and in the space of a year was over seventy pounds, the normal weight of a ten-year-old boy. (As we shall note the rapid gaining of weight may have also had something to do with the divorce.) He was a child who played and entertained himself alone, liking books and records more than active outdoor games. He was precocious in his reading, and taught himself to read, so to speak. The psychologist observed when he was examined at five that he could clearly designate the words on signs and could correctly identify figures into the fifties. (AM, 1954)

His mother and father were during Teddy's childhood growing further apart emotionally. When the father was called back into service, the mother took Teddy with her and they went to camp with him. After six months of this she decided this "was no life" and returned to Capital City. The father returned, too, when Teddy was four, but decided to reenlist and make the army a career. She told him that if he went she would not go with him, but would support herself with nursing. She took an apartment with another nurse and had Teddy with her. "Teddy would sleep with her at this time for any little excuse." In 1953 a second child was conceived, and as the time for its birth approached, she had no notion of whether the father would be there for its birth. The father evidently wanted her to quit her nursing and come with him; she did not want to, fearing the insecurity of an army life. The grandmother entered the argument, having had so much to do with Teddy's rearing to date, and, as the breach widened to separation, the grandmother made a bid to win Teddy from the mother.

The second child, a girl, Laura, was born in August of that year, and the parents were divorced a year later. The mother, desiring to keep the boy from his grandmother, took him without anyone's knowledge for three months to another state and in the divorce action got his custody, with the father having visiting privileges.

The grandmother did not give up easily, however, and during Teddy's kindergarten would visit the school, call him out of class, and try to win him over from the mother. It is reported by the mother that the grandmother tried to get Teddy to decide between the two of them, saying that it was up to him whom he would stay with. Teddy was quite upset emotionally at this period, and developed several tics on his face, and a general emotional excite-ment. The following spring the mother remarried. Teddy went to one school for the first two grades, and then settled in the home in which they presently live near a school where he could finish the elementary grades.

The visiting privileges did not work out too easily, either. The Christmas of 1959 Teddy and his sister were taken to his grand-parents' home by his stepfather. His father came out to the car saying he wanted to talk to the stepfather. Then he lit into him with his fists, roughing him up in front of the children. He accused him of interfering with the children. When the mother went over to pick them up the next day, she could not get them and had to call the police to get them back. The mother felt the whole episode was due to resentment at the father's having to pay the seventy dollars child support for Teddy and Laura, and she vowed she would not go through it again. (GH, 1960)

Now, perhaps we can return to the questions and ask the ones which are particularly relevant to Teddy's development before the divorce. In answer to the question about God-concept, it might be stated that Teddy learned about God from his religious mother, who taught him to pray, and also from his dutiful grandmother who cared for him in his mother's absence. However, it should be noted that Teddy had a strong male identification by age five and no doubt projected a male image of "father" upon God. It was quite obvious that he identified with his soldier father at this period, for he wore an Eisenhower jacket, engineer boots, and fatigues to the psychological testing, and he also acted out in MLT session that the wild Indians would be decisively defeated by the superior forces of the armed soldiers. With the father absent so much in the army, he tended to idealize him in the preoedipal period. At the time of the oedipal crisis, he literally took the father's place with the mother, as a substitute, sleeping with her and in a way assuming the male role in the family. The absent father, however, was projected upon God as unemotional like grandmother or mother, and as the one who perfectly loved the little boy. Perhaps some of this had some basis in reality, when he experienced the father's magnanimous outgoingness on his infrequent visits. The father's separation from the mother baffled the boy—in fact, we shall note in the puberty material it still baffles him—and the new father was taken as an opposite to the ideal father, not romantic or transcendent, but ordinary and close at hand. The God whom he came to worship was a projection of the preoedipal father, above the distraction and emotional stress of ordinary relationships, but tranquil and giving peace and inner security. This God is very meaningful to him at present in adolescence, and, as Absolute, represents for Teddy what human relationships have never revealed—some power which does not disappoint nor disappear from the scene. As the psalmist wrote, "When your father and mother forsake you, then the Lord will take you up." Teddy's God today is more than any father; in fact, he is the only child in the intensive group who did not choose the word "father" as descriptive of God.

Now as regards the question of Teddy's attitude toward authority, one must also look to the predivorce period. Teddy had a number of disciplinarians in the preschool period, in particular his mother and his grandmother. They applied different means of helping him gain control, ranging from outright force to the gentle arts of persuasion. He responded to his grandmother's authoritarian mode of gaining control over his body, in particular in toilet training; but he responded empathically toward his mother, particularly at the very early age. His mother used reason with him, and though he fought back she allowed him close body contact with her, and in gentle loving ways ensured that he would learn control. At the oedipal stage, in fact, with father absent, she let him substitute for father, and in a sense Teddy learned the social role by playing it in father's absence. He won the struggle, in fact, until his father left for good, and his mother remarried. Then he had to learn to take a secondary place.

It should be noted that at the preschool period, Dr. Murphy found him to be a very "skillful child who handles objects and people in a differentiated way." His good motor, cognitive, and emotional mastery, she said, serve the dual purpose of adapting him to social limits and implementing his own purpose as far as possible. (LBM, 1954) However, she noted some resignation in him as well at age five and emotionally some "toning down," as though already he was paying a high price in terms of boyish fun for his mature adaptation. (LBM, 1954) As we shall observe at adolescence as well, he is an able problem-solver at the time he starts to school, but by the time of the divorce he has learned to submit himself to adults and to their solutions to interpersonal difficulties and to quell his anger and his sexual curiosities. In a sense the divorce emphasized his cognitive maturity skills, but it also made him resign himself to the adults in his sphere. The choice between grandmother and mother was too much for him to make; his mother came to his rescue and made the decision for him to stay with her. Her authority, therefore, became uppermost in his mind in the realm of the moral and the interpersonal.

Postdivorce. These questions will need further exploration, however. Let us pick up Teddy's story at latency (a period in which materials are largely lacking because of extensive absence from town) and investigate his further development, looking particularly at the question of his attitude toward evil and his inwardness.

We have already described Teddy's "adult-like stance" and his lack of boyish dash and energy. Part of this was because of his bulk and his slowness. But part of it also was a mode of coping with his environment. Margaret Mead, his observer at the preschool party, described his approach to play. "It was an intellectual exercise as he might have used a mathematical symbol and that it had nothing to do with success or failure or frustration, but was merely trying some sort of virtuosity, some sort of playing with a possible position." (MM, 1954) On the Rorschach he was interpreted as a good coper. "He seems to be tempted to fall into passive attitudes, but his intellectual mastery pulls him out of that and he stays victorious most of the time. . . . He seems to attack frontally, and look more exactly (instead of looking away), to redefine unacceptable things in a way as to render them acceptable." (PP, 1955)

The CAT given at the time of the divorce, or shortly before, shows a modified stoicism. There are geographic responses—islands on the Rorschach, a metaphor of his family, now separated. There are the beginning uses of isolation, intellectualization, and some repression. (AM, 1962) In his memories for this period there is not much happiness. He says on an autobiography written for his sixth-grade teacher, "The divorce of my mother and father. The date to me is shrouded in mystery. I neither hear nor care much about this black period in my life." The memory is both mysterious—how could Dad have left me?—and dark in terms of the feelings experienced. He was given a bike when his mother remarried and brought him back from his relatives, but he did not remember that his stepfather bought it for him. Repression appears to be operating to screen off the painful memory of the divorce and remarriage.

The effect of the birth of his sibling should be mentioned as a crisis, not nearly of the major sort represented by the divorce, but one which involved Teddy and his mother just as much emotionally. The mother did not explain the biological facts to Teddy at the time, feeling that he did not notice her change in shape or would not be curious. He wanted to accompany his mother to the hospital to pick the baby out, and as far as its sex was concerned he knew that they would have to take "what Jesus gave them." (GH, 1958) The mother tried to get Teddy to accept the new sibling by getting him to help pick out the name for her. Nothing directly is known of his sibling rivalry following the birth of the baby, except that on the CAT, when Teddy was five and a half he did feel his mother was not filling her role with him because she was occupied with having other children. When the child is fearful on Card 6, he does not now call his mother, but tolerates the anxiety himself in solitude and talks the fear out. (WK, 1954) He is afraid at night, on Card 9 again, but does not feel his parents can be relied on to fulfill his passive dependent needs. His hostility toward the mother for paying more attention to Laura than to him is shown when he declines two invitations to talk about her, saying "I don't remember." (WK, 1954)

The material is very limited during the latency years, but one can surmise from the above tests that he developed tendencies which were normal modes of coping into what become life attitudes. For example, the psychiatrist noted in his examination of Teddy at age five that "he is always able to find his bearings in a situation. He frequently does this by comparing himself with others or by imitating others." (PT, 1954) This capacity for empathy and for finding his social role was also noted by the psychologist, who stated that Teddy noticed immediately "a subtle change from a quite permissive situation to one in which the examiner mildly but firmly set the pace." (AM, 1954) In the new situation in which Teddy found himself, he tried desperately to find his social role, that of boy-who-stays-with-mother-who-remarries-another-man. He found it in a sense by representing his "absent father" to his mother. This gratified his own passive dependent needs and also assuaged some of his mother's guilt for uprooting the boy from his father and putting him through the emotional trauma of a divorce. This is shown particularly in the prayer time which has extended clear into puberty. Teddy no longer crawls into bed with mother, but he must have his mother "tuck him in" as she did when he was a child and hear him read prayers which he did for as long as he can remember. This does ally his prayer time closely to the preoedipal situation, but also gives him support through the new trials which he faces at puberty, particularly the erupting of the old conflicts about the expression of sexuality and hostility.

Now how does Teddy look at puberty, and what in particular does this cross-sectional view tell us about his tendencies to isolation and to find meaning in his suffering? Perhaps the best way to discover him is through his projective tests. On the intelligence tests and in interview one is struck with the tremendous range of his knowledge and his social awareness. It is not until one reflects on the lack of color in his voice or the depressive quality about his attitude, that one is prepared for what the projective tests show. He is first of all detached and indirect, with no human figures and no color. The detachment inhibits his human concepts, says the psychologist

(PH, 1962), and makes him evasive and denying, particularly on Card 4. He sees museum pieces and shows enjoyment in retiring to his own room or backyard where he is safe. Sexual symbols are silly, in fact, any work of the imagination is silly to the adult ("these are his silly inner ears"—Card 1). He does show some fear of what the sexual drive will produce. He states that he feels under observation when he gets to the point of marriage, for fear others will perceive him as a child of divorce and wonder if it is in his heredity?

On the Godin Religious Projective one gets some personal themes, ranging over the divorce-marriage spectrum. On Card 4 he sees a family which is evicted by a landlord. They are thrown out and have to find a new house. The boy Teddy's age has no part in this but depends on the girl in the picture and the man. On Card 7, which shows a woman's face in the attitude of prayer or meditation, Teddy sees this as a time of sorrow, when her "trouble seems insurmountable, and he has exhausted every solution. In the last moment of desperation she turns to God for help. A friend comes along and forgives her (Teddy) and they join forces against a troublesome object (the new father?)." The women in the cards are in sorrow, they have bad days, and everything goes wrong. The men appear as saviors, as those who right the wrong, with God in the background on the side of the right. (CWS, 1963)

The psychiatrist's examination brings out most perceptively the operation of depression in Teddy's life. He says, "It seems that this depression is not only related to his life situation, representing mourning about his parents' divorce, but is also a feeling which gets used defensively against many other feelings which are not acceptable." (PT, 1961) He mentions anger, particularly against the mother for getting the divorce and the stepfather for taking the mother and the little sister who rivals him. As Dr. Mayman points out, intellectual pursuits—particularly pure mathematics—and music represent for him in adolescence a means of detaching himself from emotions, particularly the feelings surrounding his family. (MM, 1962) On the other hand, Dr. Toussieng thought that, though his thinking is impressive, he is quite laborious, and that the depression may be keeping him from being as creative as he might be if he were not so blocked on emotional subjects.

He is halting, obsessive, and considerably slowed down. In speaking of the divorce with the psychiatrist, in fact, Teddy broke down and tears came to his eyes.

Now let us look at the question regarding Teddy's religious orientation in the light of the developmental material. It was noted that he was always a highly sensitive boy, developing empathy with his mother and able to enter a role with adults in which he could understand their feelings. The divorce trauma coming as it did at the crucial age of six brought all his sensitivities to an acute point and enabled him to feel deeply the hurt his mother and father experienced, and the pull and tug he felt from each of them toward their side. He suffered and developed an acute sensitivity for suffering. For example, when his sister Laura started to school, he wept for his mother's loneliness now that the house was empty during the day. When Laura's spaniel died, she buried it with little feeling; it was Teddy whose feelings were hurt. And on mentioning the divorce, though it is now more than half a life away for him, he still gets tears in his eyes thinking of it.

The hurt of the world is felt by him, too. He told the psychiatrist why he chooses a comedy to see at the movies, "I always feel with all the stuff that's wrong with the world, I might as well have something to laugh about." (PT, 1961) And he told me, in speaking of some sorrow, "Unfortunately, there are too many things to be sorrowful about in this world." He finds that tragedy in life is not put here to make us miserable but to make us good. He sees in his Christian world view no devil, but a good God who transforms the bad that men do and the misfortune that happens to some in natural events into some character-building exercise. He cites Job as an example and, of course, Christ. He feels he has had to suffer some "little crucifixions," but that though he is hurt he will be made a better person because of it all. There does not seem to be any masochistic courting of suffering, but a willing bearing with courage of what life has dealt him. He has a restitutive and corrective theology, which finds pain and suffering a way through evil and sin to the right side. Feeling that God supports him and is *there* as he experiences the depths is enough. God has replaced the absent father in a very real sense at this point.

On the other hand he has developed this ability to turn aside and to survey the situation in a mode of coping with emotional stress that provides him a sense of integrity and personal identity. I called it the feeling he has that his "self is a citadel" (CWS, 1963), and Teddy agreed with this. He is aloof in interpersonal relations and is reserved to the point at which he remains uninvolved, looking at parties as "kid stuff" and the fun things as rather beneath his serious view of life. Yet he retires to his room or uses prayer as a means of gaining strength and removing the arrows from his sensitive skin which interpersonal forays bring. There are openings to God and to persons from the citadel—so he realized he must go back out into the world. However, there was a tendency to stay tied to mother's apron strings, feeling that he should not desert her as his father did. And there was some tendency to restrict his ambitions to service station operator or teacher—note the discrepancy in goals—because he felt he should not cause his mother the suffering of another separation, nor himself. He has tended to grow out of this in the past two years and now clearly sees the vocation of accountant as within his grasp. He has also cultivated the openings to music (playing in the band and a community orchestra) and to the social group (being on the student council and going now to parties with boys and girls).

Teddy began with a strong sense of autonomy, and even at the time of the divorce we noted his battling with his mother and his active coping with the stress he was experiencing. He has weathered this crisis and is in the second phase of his life, as he designates it. At age twelve he wrote, "I suppose I am a person trying to do better in my life. I only hope I can partially succeed." (School Record) Given the opportunity for advanced schooling and the freedom to develop, Teddy can be seen to make it. His religious faith has been an integral part of his coming to grips with life. I would predict that it will continue to be in the days ahead.

Teddy is a formerly low vulnerable child for whom the divorce and remarriage of his mother rendered him more highly vulnerable. The coping devices he established in childhood appear to be still operating in adolescence. Is the crisis of adolescence as difficult for this young man as the crisis he experienced at six? In what way is he like Terry in his religious devotion? In what way is he like Roddy in his secular pursuit? How is he unlike both in his intrinsic orientation toward religion? Does the reader see religious similarities between him and Helen?

The fact that his pastor was so little aware of him and the fact that he had developed his religious side independently of formal religious teaching should alert the minister and church school teacher alike. He is similar to Roddy in that he has potentialities for religious development that need guidance and direction that is not being offered him. The church is present as an institution but is not personally present to this youth's coping struggles nor to his problems of faith. How could a religious guide serve Teddy at this time? What does the reader think are the directions in which he might be pointed?

14

Conclusion

What have we discovered about youth? What are our final conclusions with respect to their capacities and their present stance in today's world? It has been evident, as other studies have shown, that youth by and large are a conformist group today. Many youth are conforming rather easily to the tastes and values of their contemporaries and trading their souls for the pottage of acceptance, easy friendship, and an anonymous protective coloration within the crowd. Many are drifting, with a lack of sensitivity to the problems which their generation face and with an easy role playing of the cool and uncommitted. Many are hiding their feelings and their real search for identity and integrity. That they are undergoing crisis is not admitted; that they desire meaning and purpose is denied. As Goodman says, they may be fatalistic and resigned to their lot before they have realized the challenge or the possibilities within their time. The conformist youth may not measure up to the challenge of their environment but may accept without undergoing crisis the beliefs of their parents. Or they may shade into the attitudes and values of their adolescent group without much questioning or forethought at the time.

Many of this group have that particular "conformist" orientation, but there are those within it who are actively coping with the challenge of their environment and bringing their full resources to bear, to do something to change themselves and it to become more harmonious, and to work with others in making a better society. We have discovered, particularly with the smaller group of six, that youth are vulnerable, they are open to stress. But they grow at the point of their hurt, they reach out for help, as well as finding resources (the grace of God) to undergird them and support them in their search. We have discovered that youth cope by bringing all their powers to bear upon a problem. When, in the face of mystery, they are unable to solve the problem, they may rest back upon the Ultimate mystery. Not in a resigned or in a fatalistic way, they may discover the resources of their family, their community, of nature, and of God coming to meet them and aiding them in their constructive and reconstructive efforts. They illustrate that man is not just a vulnerable animal, but a coping animal who finally, within his limits, must discover his ultimate loyalties.

The challenge of the present day is for youth not to conform but to cope with the revolutionary age before them. They face a world in which earth's natural resources, including water, will be depleted, in which there will be imbalances of food, shelter, drugs, etc. in parts of the earth in which the population will continue to escalate, in which there will be political conflict and racial revolution. However, they also face a period in which knowledge and technical skills will continue to expand. The National Education Association reports that the first doubling of knowledge occurred in 1750, the second in 1900, the third in 1950, and the fourth only ten years later. Within their day, the fifth and the sixth doubling of knowledge will occur. [1] What to do with these facts, how to understand them, how to bring them into some meaningful frame of orientation and value is their challenge. They will live in large cities, they will work shorter hours and have more leisure opportunity. They will engage in space travel and in ventures of which we do not yet know. Yet, in the present generation it was

[1] *Time* (January 29, 1965).

a man from a small town, John Glenn, who made the first space exploit. It was a man from a southern Negro parsonage, Martin Luther King, who led his people in the struggle for civil rights. And it was a man from a rich man's home who did not have to face economic struggle but rather the struggles of war, of illness, and personal tragedy to become the nation's leader, John F. Kennedy. Within this group there may be several who will rise above the anonymous crowd to leadership to cope with the challenge of this day. They have the capacities and they can rise to the challenge.

When we examine specific findings about adolescent religion, we discover that by early adolescence youth have learned their church's doctrines to varying degrees. Beliefs about God are generally more confused than beliefs about Christ; beliefs about heaven and hell are more nebulous than beliefs about right and wrong. The majority have faced the conflict between science and religion by the first year of high school, but only a minority have tried to cope with the problem of good and evil. Whether they have or not depends somewhat on their vulnerability to pain and tragedy. Traditionalism and conformity to parental beliefs are commonplace in this group of young adolescents leading to extrinsic belief (holding the idea for purpose of safety or security). Quest for meaning and struggle for self-identity merge, however, in some mid-adolescents, and their struggle is reflected in what beliefs they express.

The young adolescent is often not highly verbal and expresses himself more directly in action. His attendance pattern at church and church school tells us more about his acceptance or rejection of the adults' religion. Confirmation practices among Catholic families precede the questioning stage (ages seven to ten) and appear to lock the child in a dependent attitude toward the church. Protestant membership when allied with "early conversion practices" can similarly commit the child to an unexamined faith from which he may later recede. Our study concludes that confirmation in church membership may better be phased to the adolescent's identity crisis. Some youth at ages fifteen/sixteen may not want to join the established church when confronted with creeds he cannot believe or rituals which he cannot practice. However, he may be able to find his identity more clearly defined when he encounters the tremendous possibilities and flexible structure of growing discipleship within the family of God. The study definitely points to holding membership classes later than have been held, preferably in the ninth and tenth grades.

Youth's boredom with poorly taught church school classes and their impatience with poorly organized youth fellowships were readily apparent. The need for their participation in a meaningful church group with adult supervision guiding but not managing was also quite apparent. Prayer, it was observed, is poorly taught to youth and therefore neglected by early teens. Only a few, in particular the active Protestants and the devout Catholics, found religious worship and ritual meaningful at all. The liturgical revival needs to take adolescents into account, or else the next generation will empty the churches since the services are meaningless to them.

Vulnerability, or openness to stress, was discovered to be an important predisposition to religious experience in youth. It appears not to be a fixed variable as William James concluded. That is to say, vulnerability is not directly linked to constitution or temperament, although in childhood the individual's constitution (his intelligence, sensory thresholds, body build, etc.) are important factors. Neither is vulnerability entirely dependent upon environmental variables. We did note, however, that socioeconomic factors, the sex of the child, his place in the family, the nature of his school and church experiences all play an increasingly important place in his life as he approaches puberty. The longitudinal biographies make plain that the trauma and tranquility of the child's development from birth to puberty all precondition him to the adolescent life-tasks. His growth plan, the challenge of his environment are now met in particular, idiosyncratic ways as he becomes an adolescent. It is a crisis—yes—but not the only crisis he has confronted. The physiological aspects of it are not deeply felt until the demands of his peer group are perceived and the conflict of them felt internally against the demands and training of his parents.

All this calls forth coping responses from the adolescent. As Lois Murphy and her associates of the Normal Development Project have demonstrated, the youth may cope with these stresses in external, problem-solving ways or in internal, adaptive ways. Both modes of coping are used by the adolescent in the religious realm. The symbols, myths, and rituals previously taught him are "recollected" as he tries to solve the tasks of adolescence—identity, heterosexual relations, vocation, life's meanings. His motives and attitudes may not change drastically from childhood, but they may be muted or transformed in his struggle to bring himself into some kind of alliance with his exploding world. Dependence upon his mother, guilt over disobedience of the father must be outgrown; and the larger loyalties of group, church, school, nation, and God may be appealed to. *Who he is* is not decided overnight, but he is able to merge old identities and fuse new ones as he copes actively with his stronger drives and meets the greater challenges of his environment. Defenses are remobilized. But for him to become whole he must cope creatively with the adult and peer challenges with more of himself. Openness to the novel, to the creative and recreative forces of life, to mystery—the very stuff of religion— enable the adolescent to become who he truly is.

"When I was a child, I spoke . . . thought . . . reasoned like a child; when I became a man, I gave up childish ways" Paul wrote (I Cor. 13:11 RSV) . "Do not be conformed to this world but be transformed by the renewal of your mind, that you may prove what is the will of God." (Rom. 12:2 RSV.) Although the age when those words were first written and today's revolutionary age are drastically different, the growth process and the dynamic of faith are essentially the same. Youth may drift in conformity to the tradition of their elders or to the tastes and whims of their peers or they may creatively cope with today's challenges and discover a faith that transforms and renews them.

One final word to the teachers and parents of youth. The interview method, while adopted for research purposes, brought to my awareness a marvelous communication medium. We have all counseled with troubled adolescents, but how many have set aside an hour to listen to one youth or to a group of them when they were not demanding attention? The adult can learn a lot from youth when he approaches them nondefensively, i.e., without a program to push or a lesson to "get across." He may actually discover the youth responding to him earnestly across the room. Communication takes time to develop, and it takes more time to nurture. But the gulf between the generations can be bridged with such effort and by such openness. Curriculum and program can be planned later. The first priority is open conversation between growing youth and their parents and teachers!

Appendix

Investigators in the Division of Developmental Studies whose initials appear within the text of the biographies are identified below:

LBM   Lois B. Murphy, Ph.D., Chief Investigator and Director, Division of Developmental Studies
ME   Mary Engel, Ph.D.
MF   Mildred Faris, P.S.W.
RG   Riley Gardner, Ph.D.
SG   Sylvia Ginsparg, Ph.D.
VG   Vilma Gupta, Ph.D.
GH   Grace Heider, Ph.D.
ML   Mary Leitch, M.D.
BM   Baljeet Malhotra, M.A.
MM   Martin Mayman, Ph.D.
WM   Wilma Miller
JM   Joseph Morgan, M.A.
AM   Alice Moriarty, Ph.D.
JP   Julie Palmquist
PP   Paul Pulver, Ph.D.

RS   Ralph Sherfey
MS   Marie Smith
CWS   Charles W. Stewart, Ph.D.
PT   Povl Toussieng, M.D.
LW   Lila Weissenberg, Ph.D.
BW   Beatrice Wright, Ph.D.

Others of the Menninger Foundation staff who acted as panels of judges and reactors are:

Gardner Murphy, Ph.D., Director, Research Department
Seward Hiltner, Ph.D.
Paul Pruyser, Ph.D.
Phillip Woolcott, M.D.

Appreciation is particularly acknowledged to the Menninger Foundation, Topeka, Kansas, for the use of their excellent facilities, and for the permission of the Department of Developmental Studies for the use of original observational and test records at successive stages, analyses of these, and case summaries.

C.W.S.

Glossary

Adolescence—The age span between puberty and adulthood (12-21), in which youth learn social roles.

Autonomy—The capacity to handle one's life without undue dependency.

CAT—Children's Apperception Test. A children's form of the TAT with childish characters in the pictures—used for assessing personality.

Confirmation—The religious process whereby an adolescent becomes a member of an adult society.

Conformity—The tendency to pattern one's behavior after others, in particular, one's peers.

Coping—The organism's capacity to master situations; or, the ego-strength manifested in meeting external or internal stress.

Ectomorph—(from *ectoderm*) Sheldon's typology, meaning one with skin and nervous systems predominant in the body structure.

Endomorph—(from *endoderm*) Sheldon's typology meaning one with stomach and visceral organs predominant in the body structure.

Extrinisic religious experience—Religious experience engaged in for reasons other than itself; that is, for safety, status, comfort, talismanic favor.

Godin Religious Projectives—A set of pictures developed by André Godin, with sacred and secular themes and used originally in assessing religious attitudes of Catholic adolescent girls.

Id, superego, and ego—The Freudian division of personality into drives, conscience, and executive function.

Identity crisis—Erikson's term for the adolescent's struggle to make his own feelings about himself conform with the estimate others have of him.

Infancy—The period from birth to the period when the child can communicate through speech.

Inner-directed— (Riesman) One who is directed by conscience and whose values have been formed by parents and other authorities.

Instinctual anxiety—A feeling of dread or threat, the object of which is unknown.

Intrinsic religious experience—Religious experience in and for itself directed toward what one holds to be ultimate.

Introjection—A defense mechanism in which the ego takes in something from another person to protect itself from anxiety.

I.Q.—Intelligence quotient. A normative score which points to the individual's capacity to use verbal and manual skills.

Latency—The "juvenile" period from the beginning of school age until the beginning of pubertal changes (six to twelve) .

Likert Scale—A five-point scale ranging from very satisfactory to least satisfactory, used generally to measure individual attitudes toward a subject.

Male competence—The capacity to fulfill the masculine role successfully.

Mesomorph— (from *mesoderm*) Sheldon's typology, meaning one with muscle systems predominant in the body structure.

Miniature Life Toy Session—A method developed by Lois Murphy in which a child is given sets of toys in order to assess his life style, in particular, the relationship to his parents.

Narcissism—The tendency to center one's thoughts and feelings upon oneself, from the Greek legend in which Narcissus looked so long at his reflection in a pool that he turned into the flower.

Noetic states—those dreams, visions, and prayer states which one refers to as religious in origin.

Oedipus conflict—Feelings of incestuous desire for the parent of the opposite sex and hateful rivalry with the parent of the same sex.

Orestes complex—The boy's desire to be mothered beyond infancy and the resulting failure to develop male identity.

Outer-directed—One who is directed by peers and taste-setters within the society.

Puberty—The physiological and resulting psychological changes through which youth go marking their sexual maturity.

Projection—A defense mechanism by which one protects himself by placing his difficulties or problems upon another.

Q Sort Data—(Stephenson's Method) A means of sorting statements into a designated number of piles and forcing a normal frequency curve so as to get shades of agreement and disagreement.

Religion—The attitudes, feelings, and values surrounding what one holds ultimate, and the ethical and liturgical practices which ensue.

Sublimation—A means of channeling one's drives into socially acceptable behavior.

TAT—Thematic Apperception Test—A picture test (developed by Henry Murray and associates) in which the subject fantasies a story and thus reveals something about his personality.

Vulnerability—The organism's openness to stress, both external and internal, which may predispose to some functional breakdown.

WISC—Wechsler Intelligence Scale: Children's level—A standard intelligence test scaled for the child's age.

Selected Bibliography

I. Personality—General

1. Allport, Gordon. *Personality, a Psychological Interpretation*. New York: Henry Holt & Company, 1937.
2. Erikson, Erik. *Identity and the Life Cycle*. New York: International Universities Press, 1959.
3. Hall, C. S., and Lindzey, G. *Theories of Personality*. New York: John Wiley & Sons, 1965.
4. Menninger, Karl. *The Vital Balance*. New York: Viking Press, 1963.
5. Murphy, Gardner. *Personality; A Biosocial Approach to Origins and Structure*. New York: Harper & Brothers, 1947.
6. Sullivan, Harry Stack. *The Interpersonal Theory of Psychiatry*. New York: W. W. Norton & Co., 1953.
7. White, Robert W. *The Study of Lives*. New York: Atherton Press, 1963.

II. Personality—Longitudinal Study of

1. Allport, Gordon. *The Use of Personal Documents in Psychological Science*. New York: Social Science Research Council, 1942.

2. Gesell, Arnold, *et al. Youth: The Years from Ten to Sixteen.* New York: Harper & Row, 1956.

3. MacFarlane, Jean W., *et al. A Developmental Study of the Behavior Problems of Normal Children Between 21 Months and 14 Years.* Berkeley: University of California Press, 1962.

4. Murphy, Lois B., *et al. The Widening World of Childhood.* New York: Basic Books, 1962.

5. Piaget, Jean. *The Origins of Intelligence in Children.* New York: International Universities Press, 1956.

6. White, Robert W. *Lives in Progress.* New York: Holt, Rinehart & Winston, 1952.

III. Personality—Sociological and Anthropological Studies of

1. Erikson, Erik. *Childhood and Society.* Rev. ed. New York: W. W. Norton & Company, 1964.

2. Kluckholn, Clyde, and Murray, Henry A., eds. *Personality in Nature, Society and Culture.* Rev. ed. New York: Alfred A. Knopf, 1953.

3. Mead, Margaret. *Coming of Age in Samoa.* New York: The Modern Library, 1953.

4. ———. *Growing Up in New Guinea.* New York: New American Library [1930].

5. Riesman, David. *The Lonely Crowd.* New Haven: Yale University Press, 1950.

6. Seeley, J. R., *et al. Crestwood Heights.* New York: Basic Books, 1956.

IV. Childhood

1. Brody, Sylvia. *Patterns of Mothering* (Contains infancy reports of these children). New York: International Universities Press, 1956.

2. Escalona, Sibylle, and Heider, Grace. *Prediction and Outcome* (Contains infancy and childhood reports of these children). New York: Basic Books, 1959.

3. Freud, Anna. *Normality and Pathology in Childhood.* New York: International Universities Press, 1965.

4. Gesell, Arnold. *The First Five Years of Life.* New York: Harper & Row, 1940.

5. Josselyn, Irene. *The Happy Child.* New York: Random House, 1955.

6. Murphy, Lois B., *et al. The Widening World of Childhood* (Contains childhood reports of these children). New York: Basic Books, 1962.

7. ———. *Personality in Young Children:* Vol. I, *Methods for the Study of Personality;* Vol. II, *Colin—A Normal Child.* New York: Basic Books, 1956.

8. Spitz, René. *The First Year of Life.* New York: International Universities Press, 1965.

9. Stone, L. Joseph, and Church, Joseph. *Childhood and Adolescence.* New York: Random House, 1957.

V. Adolescence

1. Ausubel, David. *Theory and Problems of Adolescent Development.* New York: Grune & Stratton, 1954.

2. Blos, Peter. *On Adolescence: A Psychoanalytic Interpretation.* New York: Free Press of Glencoe, 1962.

3. Cole, Luella. *The Psychology of Adolescent Development.* New York: Holt, Rinehart & Winston, 1959.

4. Deutsch, Helene. *The Psychology of Women.* 2 vols. New York: Grune & Stratton, 1944-45.

5. Erikson, Erik, ed. *Youth: Change and Challenge.* New York: Basic Books, 1963.

6. Frank, Mary, and Frank, Lawrence. *Your Adolescent at Home and in School.* New York: New American Library, 1959.

7. Freud, Anna. *The Ego and the Mechanisms of Defense.* New York: International Universities Press, 1964.

8. Friedenberg, Edgar. *The Vanishing Adolescent.* Boston: Beacon Press, 1959.

9. Gallagher, James R., and Harris, Herbert I. *Emotional Problems of Adolescents.* Rev. ed.; New York: Oxford University Press, 1964.

10. Gesell, Arnold, *et al. Youth: The Years from Ten to Sixteen.* New York: Harper & Row, 1956.

11. Goodman, Paul. *Growing Up Absurd.* New York: Random House, 1960.

12. Hollingshead, August. *Elmtown's Youth.* New York: John Wiley & Sons, 1949.

13. Muuss, Rolf. *Theories of Adolescence.* New York: Random House, 1962.

14. Piaget, Jean. *The Growth of Logical Thinking from Childhood to Adolescence.* New York: Basic Books, 1958.

VI. Religious Studies

1. Allport, Gordon. *The Individual and His Religion.* New York: The Macmillan Company, 1950.
2. ———. *Letters from Jenny.* New York: Harcourt, Brace & World, 1965.
3. Godin, André. *From Religious Experience to a Religious Attitude.* Chicago: Loyola University Press, 1965.
4. James, William. *The Varieties of Religious Experience.* Paperback ed.; New York: Collier Books, 1961.
5. Johnson, Paul E. *Personality and Religion.* Nashville: Abingdon Press, 1957.
6. Lenski, Gerhard. *The Religious Factor.* New York: Doubleday & Company, 1961.
7. Ross, Murray. *The Religious Beliefs of Youth.* New York: Association Press, 1950.
8. Snyder, Ross. *The Ministry of Meaning.* Vols. 1, 3, 4. Geneva: Youth Departments of World Council of Churches, 1965.
9. Strommen, Merton. *Profiles of Church Youth.* St. Louis: Concordia Publishing House, 1963.

VII. Selected Articles

1. Becker, Russell. "The Proper Age for the Declaration of Faith," *Religious Education,* LX (July-August, 1965), 292-94.
2. Christiansen, Carl, "Religious Conversion in Adolescence," *Pastoral Psychology,* XVI (September, 1965), 17-28.
3. Cobb, Edith. "Childhood Religion," *Daedulus,* LXXXVI (Spring, 1956), 582-600.
4. Colm, Hanna. "Religious Symbolism in Childhood Analysis," *American Journal of Psychoanalysis,* XII (1953), 39-56.
5. Dittes, James. "Justification by Faith and the Experimental Psychologist," *Religion in Life,* XXVIII (1959), 567-76.
6. Elkind, David, and Elkind, Sally. "Varieties of Religious Experience in the Young Adolescent," *Journal for the Scientific Study of Religion,* II (Fall, 1962), 102-12.
7. Fichter, Joseph. "Religion and Socialization Among Children," *Review of Religious Research,* IV (Fall, 1962), 24-33.
8. Ginsparg, Sylvia, *et al.* "Young Teenagers' Responses to the Assassination of President Kennedy," *Children and the Death of a President.* Martha Wolfenstein and G. W. Kliman, eds. Garden City: Doubleday & Company, 1965.

9. Godin, André. "Faith and the Psychological Development of Children," *Lumen Vita,* XIII (1958) , 297-310.

10. Heider, Grace. "Vulnerabilities, Sources of Strength and Capacities to Cope in the Normal Child." Copenhagen, Denmark: 14th International Congress of Applied Psychology, 1961.

11. Heider, Grace. *Vulnerability in Infants and Young Children: A Pilot Study,* Genetic Psychology Monographs (1966) 73, 1-216.

12. Jacobson, Edith. "Adolescent Moods and the Remodeling of Psychic Structures in Adolescence," *Psychoanalytic Study of the Child,* XVI (1961) , 170-82.

13. Moriarty, Alice. *Coping Patterns of Preschool Children in Response to Intelligence Test Demands,* Genetic Psychology Monographs (1961) , 64, 3-127.

14. Murphy, Lois. "Coping Devices and Defense Mechanisms in Relation to Autonomous Ego Functions," *Bulletin of the Menniger Clinic,* XXIV (May, 1960) , 144-53.

15. Salzman, Leon. "The Psychology of Religious and Ideological Conversion," *Psychiatry,* XVI (1953) , 177-87.

16. Stewart, Charles W. "Confirmation and the Identity Crisis," *Religious Education,* LX (July-August, 1965) , 290-91.

17. ———. "The Religious Experiences of Two Adolescent Girls," *Pastoral Psychology,* XVII (Sept., 1966) , 49-55.

18. Strunk, Orlo. "Relationships Between Self Reports and Socialization of Children," *Psychological Reports,* LVIII (1960) , 583-87.

Index

311